Hilary Mantel

CONTEMPORARY CRITICAL PERSPECTIVES

Series Editors: Jeannette Baxter, Peter Childs, Sebastian Groes, and Sean Matthews

Guides in the *Contemporary Critical Perspectives* series provide companions to reading and studying major contemporary authors. They include new critical essays combining textual readings, cultural analysis, and discussion of key critical and theoretical issues in a clear, accessible style. Each guide also includes a preface by a major contemporary writer, a new interview with the author, discussion of film and TV adaptation, and guidance on further reading.

Titles in the series include:

Ali Smith edited by Monica Germana and Emily Horton
Andrea Levy edited by Jeannette Baxter and David James
Ian McEwan (2nd Edition) edited by Sebastian Groes
J. G. Ballard edited by Jeannette Baxter
Julian Barnes edited by Sebastian Groes and Peter Childs
Kazuo Ishiguro edited by Sean Matthews and Sebastian Groes
Salman Rushdie edited by Robert Eaglestone and Martin McQuillan
Sarah Waters edited by Kaye Mitchell

Forthcoming titles:

David Mitchell edited by Wendy Knepper and Courtney Hopf
Don DeLillo edited by Katherine Da Cunha Lewin and Kiron Ward
John Burnside edited by Ben Davies

Hilary Mantel

Contemporary Critical Perspectives

EDITED BY
EILEEN POLLARD
AND
GINETTE CARPENTER

BLOOMSBURY ACADEMIC
LONDON • NEW YORK • OXFORD • NEW DELHI • SYDNEY

BLOOMSBURY ACADEMIC
Bloomsbury Publishing Plc
50 Bedford Square, London, WC1B 3DP, UK
1385 Broadway, New York, NY 10018, USA

BLOOMSBURY, BLOOMSBURY ACADEMIC and the Diana logo are trademarks of Bloomsbury Publishing Plc

First published in Great Britain 2018
Paperback edition first published 2020

Cover design: Eleanor Rose and Toby Way
Cover image © Angelo Hornak/Corbis via Getty Images

A catalogue record for this book is available from the British Library.

Library of Congress Cataloging-in-Publication Data:
Names: Pollard, Eileen editor. | Carpenter, Ginette editor.
Title: Hilary Mantel: contemporary critical perspectives /
edited by Eileen Pollard and Ginette Carpenter.
Description: London; New York: Bloomsbury Academic, 2018. |
Series: Contemporary critical perspectives | Includes index.
Identifiers: LCCN 2018003558 | ISBN 9781474296502 (hardback) |
ISBN 9781474296526 (epdf)
Subjects: LCSH: Mantel, Hilary, 1952–Criticism and interpretation.
Classification: LCC PR6063.A438 Z75 2018 | DDC 823/.914–dc23
LC record available at https://lccn.loc.gov/2018003558

ISBN: HB: 978-1-4742-9650-2
PB: 978-1-3501-5482-7
ePDF: 978-1-4742-9652-6
eBook: 978-1-4742-9651-9

Series: Contemporary Critical Perspectives

Typeset by Integra Software Services Pvt. Ltd.

To find out more about our authors and books visit www.bloomsbury.com and sign up for our newsletters.

This book is dedicated to

Shafqat Nasir and in memoriam Ben and Jeff Carpenter

Contents

Foreword

Mark Lawson

Because she came to major public recognition and bestsellerdom only when *Wolf Hall*, her tenth novel, after a writing career of a quarter of a century, won the Man Booker Prize in 2009, there has been a temptation to see Hilary Mantel as a literary late-developer. A counter chronological statistic, though, is that, when she won the David Cohen Prize for lifetime literary achievement in 2013, Mantel, at 60, became the joint youngest winner of that award; only VS Naipaul had been so junior, while Muriel Spark (one of Mantel's biggest literary inspirations) was almost two decades older at the time of her selection. The significance of these height marks on the wall of cultural honour is that there appears to have been – at either side of the end of the first decade of the twenty-first century – a sudden broad consensus about what many readers, critics and scholars had long felt: that Mantel is among the most consistently inventive and interesting writers in contemporary literature. And, by the time that Naipaul, Spark and others won the Cohen, they were publishing work that seemed minor in comparison with their masterpieces. But, strikingly, Mantel's latest books at that time were generally thought to be among her best: the Thomas Cromwell novels, *Wolf Hall* and *Bring Up the Bodies*, and the memoir *Giving Up the Ghost*. I agree with that assessment, although it is important to stress that part of what swung the David Cohen Prize judges (I know as chair of the panel) was a desire to show readers that Mantel had not just found her feet as a writer, but had been confidently on them for the three decades since *Every Day Is Mother's Day* in 1985.

Apart from the fact that both won the Man Booker Prize, one reason that the two Thomas Cromwell novels dominate general perception of Mantel is that they gave her a brand: Tudor political drama. This was the first time in her career that the writer had proved so compliant to the busy sheep-dogs of critical and bookselling penning-in. Although her geographical inheritance – born in Derbyshire, raised in Cheshire, long resident in Norfolk – has informed some settings, she has never stayed in one location across enough books to be identified as a regional writer, which is one of the most popular grounds for filing a writer. Another easy publicity tag – autobiographical content – is also elusive in Mantel. The times she spent in Saudi Arabia and Africa (a consequence of professional postings with her husband, Gerald McEwen, a geologist) retrospectively became invaluable field-trips for *Eight Months on Ghazzah Street* (1988) and *A Change of Climate* (1994). Yet Mantel rarely seems to use personal experience with the visibility of a Philip Roth or JM Coetzee: there is no ex-pat novelist character married to a geologist. What seems to me Mantel's most powerful use of memory occurs in an extremely oblique manner. The story of the wives of King Henry VIII is a tragedy of fertility, in which how a woman bred or bled could prove a death sentence. The jeopardy is not remotely as great for modern women with reproductive problems, but my perception – which Mantel, in one of our interviews, gracefully accepted as possible – is that her long suffering with the fertility-threatening gynaecological condition endometriosis, described in the memoir *Giving Up the Ghost* (2003), might give her a particular emotional insight into the psychology of historical characters whose menstruation became a life-and-death-cycle.

The form of content most likely to build a fan-base – generic repetition – has also been almost wholly avoided by Mantel. In interviews over the years before the Man Booker double, the author had herself acknowledged that she might have been denied higher profile and sales by a desire to follow even a success with something dissimilar. Certainly, those who know her only as a chronicler of the Tudor era would be startled by the dark comedy of *Fludd* (1989) and *Beyond Black* (2005), and the contemporary marital tragedy of *A Change of Climate*. Recently arrived readers would perhaps be less surprised by the post-monarchic historical epic, *A Place of Greater Safety* (1992), which re-examines biographical cases – the French revolutionaries Danton, Robespierre and Desmoulins – in much the way that she later does with Cromwell. And, if Mantel were to be categorized, it would most easily be as an historical novelist, although of a non-conventional kind. Of the eleven novels from *Every Day Is Mother's Day* to *Bring Up the Bodies*, only one – the Mother's Day sequel, *Vacant Possession* (1986) – is predominantly set in what was the present day at its time of publication. Apart from the obvious period pieces from seventeenth-century England and eighteenth-century France, or eighteenth-century London (*The Giant, O'Brien*, 1998), *Fludd* takes place in the 1950s, *An Experiment in Love* (1995) in the 1970s, and events in the far past are central to the theoretically contemporary *A Change of Climate* and *Beyond Black*.

Regardless of its notional time-zone, in any Mantel literary vehicle, the rearview mirror is a crucial device. The opening line of *A Place of Greater Safety* – 'Now that the dust has settled, we can begin to look at our situation' (5) – might be taken as the writer's literary creed, whether the dust is decades or centuries old. In this context, perhaps the most interesting aspect of the media fuss over the publication and broadcast by BBC Radio 4 in 2014 of Mantel's short story 'The Assassination of Margaret Thatcher' was that its perceived crime of political lèse-majesté came a year after Baroness Thatcher's death and almost a quarter of a century after the end of her premiership. Whereas playwrights and songwriters in the 1980s had freely fantasized about violent ends for Mrs Thatcher while she was still in office, Mantel's literary interest was sparked when the politician had moved beyond statutes to statues, and become as distant a historical figure to a school or university student as Henry VIII. Some of those expressing horror at Mantel's temerity in fantasizing about the death of a public figure who was already dead were motivated by finding in the story's radio performance another weapon to turn against the BBC (which had been criticized by the right wing for anti-Thatcherism both during and after the politician's reign). Others, though, seemed surprised at such material coming from Mantel because it clashed with their idea of the sort of writer they thought she was.

As a result of *Wolf Hall* and *Bring Up the Bodies* being written in a literary form – the royal historical novel – that is associated with conservatism, there seemed to be a feeling that her anti-Thatcher story was politically and tonally unexpected. There was a similar reaction in some parts of the media and the reading public in a previous spat that followed Mantel's speech (and a related piece in *London Review of Books*) that was interpreted as criticizing the dress-sense of Catherine, Duchess of Cambridge, a supposed 'attack' that brought broadcast criticism of Mantel from both the then prime minister, David Cameron, and the leader of the opposition, Ed Miliband. However, this sense that Mantel was in some way letting down her hair or her self in declining to curtsey to the Baroness and the Duchess could only have come from those who had not read the Cromwell novels very closely, and had not read the writer's other books at all. In their sympathetic and even heroic reassessment of Cromwell, traditionally a villain or a blank, the first two books in the projected Tudor trilogy are politically radical and their complex and intricate use of viewpoint – which Mantel has strikingly described as a camera just behind Cromwell's shoulder at all times – make the books a stylistic experiment as well. Readers of the French revolution novel or *The Giant, O'Brien* – the protagonist of which is a super-tall Irishman who is brought to London for gawping at by the medical and social establishments – would also be aware that a recurrent subject of Mantel's has been the psychology of power and the dynamics of courts, official and unofficial. So, to long-time readers, the late Margaret Thatcher and the former Kate Middleton were logical subjects for Mantel inspection.

Among the things that the writer loses in *Giving Up the Ghost* is belief in the Holy Ghost, and Catholicism is an important presence, even when present as an absence, in her work. When Hilary Thompson was baptized into the Roman Catholic Church in 1952, the English Catholic Novel was a recognized and powerful literary form, of which the leading practitioners were Graham Greene, Evelyn Waugh and Muriel Spark, soon joined by Anthony Burgess. Mantel has sometimes shown clear influence of these writers: the sleaze and theological intrigue of *Fludd* are frequently Greeneian, and *An Experiment In Love* has the feel of an updated homage to Spark's *The Girls of Slender Means*, which also concerns female students in London. But, while the Greene-Spark-Waugh-Burgess model of the Catholic writer – for whom the faith provides storylines and moral framework – remains recognizable today, in the work of David Lodge, Piers Paul Read and Frank Cottrell Boyce, the genre now mainly exists in a strain of post-Catholic (or even anti-Catholic) writing by those who have turned from the Church. This fictional denomination is significantly different from that of an Anglican or agnostic author, and the most notable exponents at the moment are the screenwriter Jimmy McGovern (*Cracker, The Street, The Accused*), whose plots often dramatize moral dilemmas, and, among English novelists, Mantel. Both early and later books of hers are implicitly or explicitly written against the faith in which she was raised. *Fludd* and *Beyond Black* satirize aspects of belief systems: Northern English Catholicism and spiritualist contact with the dead (which is incidentally, a sin for Catholics), respectively. And an intriguing sub-text of *Wolf Hall* and *Bring Up the Bodies* is that they are pro-Reformation books written by an author who was once a Catholic. Mantel told me in an interview that she was struck by how touchy some Spanish and Italian critics and readers were about her enthusiastic dramatization of the Protestant revolution.

Perhaps most vital in her appeal to readers is that another strand running through Mantel's work is her ability to shape and pace strong narratives. The Tudor monarchy and the French Revolution are famously among the most compelling stories in history, but Mantel's invented tales – *Fludd, A Change of Climate, Eight Months on Ghazzah Street, Beyond Black* – are also adept at suspense and surprise. Her control of exposition, tension, twist and revelation reflects the movie critic (for the *Spectator*) that she was and the playwright she would become: adapting, with Mike Poulton, the first two Cromwell novels for the RSC, West End and Broadway. But whether she is seen as a quasi-theatrical, post-Catholic, disguised-autobiographical or multi-historical writer, Hilary Mantel is undoubtedly a major and original one. A reading of the range of her work kills the idea that she was a literary late-developer, but makes clear that she will be a long-laster.

Mark Lawson, January 2017

Series editors' preface

The readership for contemporary fiction has never been greater. The explosion of reading groups and literary blogs, of university courses and school curricula, and even the apparent rude health of the literary marketplace indicate an ever-growing appetite for new work, for writing which responds to the complex, changing and challenging times in which we live. At the same time, readers seem ever more eager to engage in conversations about their reading, to devour the review pages, to pack the sessions at literary festivals and author events. Reading is an increasingly social activity, as we seek to share and refine our experience of the book, to clarify and extend our understanding.

It is this tremendous enthusiasm for contemporary fiction to which the Contemporary Critical Perspectives series responds. Our ambition is to offer readers of current fiction a comprehensive critical account of each author's work, presenting original, specially commissioned analyses of all aspects of their career, from a variety of different angles and approaches, as well as directions towards further reading and research.

Our brief to the contributors is to be scholarly, to draw on the latest thinking about narrative, or philosophy, or psychology, indeed whatever seemed to them most significant in drawing out the meanings and force of the texts in question, but also to focus closely on the words on the page, the stories and scenarios and forms which all of us meet first when we open a book. We insisted that these essays be accessible to that mythical beast, the Common Reader, who might just as readily be spotted at the Lowdham Book Festival as in a college seminar. In this way, we hope to have presented critical assessments of our writers in such a way as to contribute something to both of those environments, and also to have done something to bring together the most important qualities of each of them.

Jeannette Baxter, Peter Childs, Sebastian Groes and Sean Matthews

Acknowledgements

We wish to thank David Avital and Clara Herberg at Bloomsbury for all their help, support and patience throughout this project.

We also wish to thank colleagues in our respective departments. Thank you to all the staff and students of the University of Chester, English Department, and most especially to Sarah Heaton, Deborah Wynne, Claire Copeland, Jen Davis, Alex Tankard and Ashley Chantler for your help and guidance. Thanks also to Rob Warner (Plymouth Marjon University) for all your encouragement and support and to Kaye Mitchell (University of Manchester) for your generous help at the start of this journey. At Manchester Metropolitan University, thanks to all colleagues in the English Department, most especially Berthold Schoene, Emma Liggins and Eleanor Byrne for their unwavering faith in this project. Thank you to the staff of Gladstone's Library, Hawarden, in particular Louisa Yates, and to the International Anthony Burgess Foundation for hosting the symposium that ultimately led to this collection of essays.

Thank you to all our friends, family and loved ones, and for all the support, kindness and love they have shown us both through the harsh difficulties of life that have happened alongside this project. Most especial love, gratitude and thanks to our very special partners, Shafqat Nasir and Dave Norman.

Thank you to our contributors for all their hard work throughout and thank you to Mark Lawson for his excellent foreword. Finally, thank you to Hilary Mantel for your incredibly kind and generous support of this volume from its inception and throughout as well as heartfelt and sincere thanks for the gift of your work: its fierce intelligence, beauty and depth are what makes a volume like this possible.

Contributors

Lucy Arnold is a Teaching Fellow in Contemporary Literature and Drama at the University of Leeds. Her research focuses on narratives of haunting and speculative fiction in contemporary women's writing.

Victoria Bennett was awarded a University of Kent 50th Anniversary scholarship for her doctoral work entitled *Hilary Mantel's Provisionality*. From 2015 she taught twentieth-century and contemporary literature there while completing her doctoral thesis.

Kathryn Bird is an Associate Tutor at Edge Hill University, with primary research interests in contemporary literature, biopolitics, animal studies and medical humanities. She has published articles and book chapters on liminality in contemporary fiction, animality in neo-Victorian fiction, the depiction of animals in ghost stories, and on anatomical dissection and the construction of human life.

Renate Brosch is Professor of English Literature at the Universität Stuttgart. She has published books on Henry James (2000) and on short story theory (*Short Story: Textsorte und Leseerfahrung. Trier*: WVT 2007). More recent research concerns cognitive narratology and reader response (*Anglistik: Focus on Reception and Reader Response* 2013). She is currently editing a special volume of *Poetics Today*: 'Ekphrasis in the Digital Age' (39.2, 2018).

Eleanor Byrne is Senior Lecturer in English at Manchester Metropolitan University where she teaches and researches in contemporary literature and film with a specialism in postcolonial theory, globalization, memory and trauma as well as children's literature. She is currently co-organizer of the BA/Leverhulme network 'Troubling Globalisation' and recent publications include articles on the work of Jamaica Kincaid, Caryl Phillips and Hanya Yanagihara.

Ginette Carpenter is Senior Lecturer in English at Manchester Metropolitan University. Her research interests are broadly focused upon discourses of gender, reading, space and history as articulated in contemporary women's writing and film. She has published work on Jeanette Winterson, Elizabeth Jane Howard, and women and the gothic.

Wolfgang Funk is Assistant Professor of English Literature and Culture at Johannes Gutenberg-Universität Mainz. He is the author of *The Literature of Reconstruction: Authentic Fiction in the New Millennium* (Bloomsbury, 2015) and an introduction to *Gender Studies* (in German; utb, 2017). He is the co-editor of *Fiktionen von Wirklichkeit: Authentizität zwischen Materialität und Konstruktion* (transcript, 2011) and *The Aesthetics of Authenticity: Medial Constructions of the Real* (transcript, 2012).

Mark Lawson is a journalist, broadcaster and author. He specializes in culture and the arts, presenting the BBC Radio 4 flagship arts programme *Front Row* for many years, for which he interviewed Hilary Mantel in 2013. He is also a *Guardian* columnist and presents *Mark Lawson Talks To* ... on BBC Four.

Siobhan O'Connor is currently completing PhD at Manchester Metropolitan University. Her project investigates the relationship between contemporary historical novels about the Tudor court and emerging ideas of Englishness.

Eileen Pollard is Lecturer in English at the University of Chester. Her interview with Hilary Mantel was published in *Textual Practice* in 2015. She is co-editor (with Berthold Schoene) of *Accelerated Times: British Literature in Transition, 1980–2000.*

Hilary Mantel: A Chronology

1952 Born Hilary Mary Thompson in Glossop, Derbyshire

1957 Attends St Charles's Roman Catholic primary school in Hadfield, Derbyshire

1963 Family moves to Romiley, Cheshire, attending the Harrytown Convent and taking on the surname of her de facto stepfather, Jack Mantel

1964 Loses her religious faith, which has a profound effect thereafter

1970 Attends London School of Economics to study law, then subsequently transfers to the University of Sheffield

1972 Marries Gerald McEwen, a geologist from Ashton-under-Lyne, Tameside

1973 Graduates with Bachelor of Jurisprudence

1972 Works as a social worker at a geriatric hospital

1974 Starts writing *A Place of Greater Safety*

1977 Moves to Botswana with Gerald for his work

1979 Very late diagnosis of endometriosis resulting in the need for a hysterectomy; manuscript of *A Place of Greater Safety* rejected the same year

1982 Following divorce and a couple of years apart, remarries Gerald and moves with him to Saudi Arabia again for his work the following year

1985 Publishes first novel *Every Day Is Mother's Day*

1986 Publishes sequel *Vacant Possession*

1987 Wins Shiva Naipaul Memorial Prize, starts work as film critic for the *Spectator* (continues in this role until 1991) and becomes a reviewer for a number of newspapers and magazines, in the UK and the United States, including *London Review of Books*

1988 Publishes *Eight Months on Ghazzah Street*, and returns to the UK

1989 Publishes *Fludd*

1990 Wins Southern Arts Literature Prize, Cheltenham Prize and Winifred Holtby Memorial Prize, all for her fourth novel, *Fludd*

1992 Publishes *A Place of Greater Safety* and wins the Sunday Express Book of the Year Award for this novel

1994 Publishes *A Change of Climate*

1995 Publishes *An Experiment in Love*

1996 Wins Hawthornden Prize for *An Experiment in Love*

1998 Publishes *The Giant, O'Brien*, Mantel then adapted this book into a play for BBC Radio 4 starring Alex Norton (as John Hunter) and Frances Tomelty

2003 Publishes both her memoir *Giving Up the Ghost* and debut collection of short stories *Learning to Talk*, winning MIND Book of the Year for *Giving Up the Ghost*

2005 Publishes *Beyond Black*; receives Honorary DLett from University of Sheffield

2006 *Beyond Black* shortlisted for Commonwealth Writers Prize and Orange Prize for Fiction

2008 Receives Honorary Fellowships from Royal Holloway, University of London and Bedford College

2009 Publishes *Wolf Hall* and wins Man Booker Prize and National Book Critics Circle Award for *Wolf Hall*, her tenth novel

2009 Receives Honorary DLitt from Sheffield Hallam University

2010 Wins Walter Scott Prize and Specsavers National Book Award, 'UK Author of the Year' for *Wolf Hall*, also shortlisted for Orange Prize for Fiction for *Wolf Hall*

2011 James Runcie presents *Hilary Mantel: A Culture Show Special* on the BBC, including an interview with the author; she receives Honorary DLitts from the University of Exeter and Kingston University, and a Fellowship from Kings College London

2012 Publishes *Bring Up the Bodies* and wins Man Booker Prize, Specsavers National Book Award, 'UK Author of the Year', Costa Book Awards (Novel) and Costa Book Awards (Book of the Year) all for her sequel *Bring Up the Bodies*

2013 Wins David Cohen Prize (considered to be the 'British Nobel') and South Bank Sky Arts Award for *Bring Up the Bodies*, also receives Honorary DLitts from Universities of Cambridge, Queens Belfast, London and Bath Spa; Mantel's 'Royal Bodies' talk at the British Library (later published in the *London Review of Books*) causes a media storm, she is criticized by, among others, the then prime minister David Cameron for her comments on the Duchess of Cambridge, Cameron later admitted to not having read the article

2014 Made a Dame of the British Empire (DBE), publishes second collection of short stories, *The Assassination of Margaret Thatcher*, which causes another controversy in the media for the title story, with Lord Bell calling for Mantel to be investigated by the police; Sky Arts commissioned portrait by Nick Lord hung in the British Library; *Wolf Hall* and *Bring Up the Bodies* performed as plays by the RSC in Stratford, London and then New York (2015); receives Honorary DLitts from Universities of Derby, London School of Economics and an Honorary Doctorate from the Open University.

2015 Receives Honorary DLitts from Universities of Oxford and Oxford Brookes; BBC Two broadcast six-part dramatization of *Wolf Hall*; the plays win Olivier Awards for Best Actor in a Supporting Role (Nathaniel Parker) and Best Costume Design (Christopher Oram) and a Tony Award for Best Costume Design of a Play (Christopher Oram)

2016 Wins the British Academy President's Medal and Kenyon Review Award for Literary Achievement; receives Fellowship of the British Psychoanalytical Society

2017 Announced as BBC Reith Lecturer, delivering a series of five lectures on historical fiction in Manchester, London, Antwerp, Exeter and Stratford-on-Avon, under the overall title of 'Resurrection: The Art and Craft'; receives Honorary Professorship from University of Exeter

'What Cannot Be Fixed, Measured, Confined': The Mobile Texts of Hilary Mantel

Eileen Pollard and Ginette Carpenter

'I don't know, you wait twenty years for a Booker prize, two come along at once!' was Hilary Mantel's laconic response to winning for the second time. A respected, if critically neglected, British author, she had in fact been writing and publishing for over twenty years when she won the Booker prize in 2009 for her tenth novel, *Wolf Hall*. She then made literary history by winning for a second time in 2012 with the sequel, *Bring Up the Bodies*, an unprecedented achievement that catapulted her into the realms of global stardom. The Tudor novels have since been adapted for the stage by Mike Poulton and have been performed to much critical acclaim in Stratford, London and Broadway. Similarly, the 2015 BBC dramatization has aired in both the UK and the United States to glowing reviews. Yet, despite Mantel's renown and popularity at home and abroad, there remains surprisingly little critical material interpreting the rich and varied content of her work. As a result, this collection of essays aims to introduce students, scholars and general readers of Mantel's writing to the diversity of her texts in order to showcase the extraordinary range and reach of this contemporary British author, currently at the peak of her writing life. The essays will explore the recurring themes of ambiguity, ghosts, trauma, childhood and memory that both trace and, in many ways, define Mantel's *oeuvre*. The collection will also examine the challenge to conventional evocations of the past that underpins Mantel's historical novels, from *A Place of Greater Safety* (1992) through to *Wolf Hall* and *Bring Up the Bodies*, as well as the complex experimentation with perspective and tense that really sets apart her later work on Thomas Cromwell. The main objective of this book is to provide a wide range of readers with a guide to Mantel's historical fiction, autobiographical writing and short stories, as well as some of her more experimental early novels, that will help explain those most ambiguous elements of her corpus while demonstrating her fearlessness and breadth as a writer.

'We chase the dead': The Reith Lectures and ghosts past and present in the body Mantel (Eileen Pollard)

Hours before the Manchester Arena bombing, I attended the recording of Hilary Mantel's first Reith Lecture in the city, which prophetically addressed our human struggle to understand history and the past. Mantel's lecture on chasing the ghosts of the past helps us understand the pull of ancient history as well as very recent 'pastness'. The truth of her argument, that documentary evidence alone cannot provide the answer you *crave*, became clear when, within hours of her delivering the lecture in Manchester, a bomb exploded elsewhere in the city. Speaking in a place from her own past, Mantel's reasoning that History is merely a method for organizing the past and that if we wish to glimpse its true shape we must listen and look in particular ways, appeared later strikingly prescient.

Mantel acknowledged our difficulty in understanding the past but argued we can develop techniques to see and hear it. This observation was heightened by Mantel's standing in a place from *her* past, Manchester, while speaking of another nearby one, Hadfield, Derbyshire, her birthplace. She began by summoning a ghost – 'Saint Augustine says, the dead are invisible, they are not absent' – and ended with the word 'home', revealing the route into history, the trick, the root, being those ghosts of or at home (2017a: 2). Returning to the evening in my mind there is a lingering uncanniness because of the explosion just hours later. There was 'something' electric in the air as Mantel kindled these ghosts, urged us to chase them. She has often written of forerunners and disjointed time in her novels. In *Fludd* (1989), housekeeper Miss Dempsey tells Father Angwin she hears footsteps overhead in the presbytery, he replies: '"I often think it is myself." "But you are here." "At this moment, yes. Perhaps it is a forerunner. Someone who is to come"' (1990: 26). From a writer preoccupied with ghosts, the whole lecture was spoken as if by a revenant.

Yet there was a second string to this vibration, which was an at-the-time knowledge of the situated-ness of the ghosts Mantel was raising from the streets of Hadfield. She channelled this séance through her limited, glance-from-the-corner-of- an-eye, knowledge of her Great Grandmother. There is one surviving photograph of Catherine O'Shea, and while Mantel gropes for other facts about her harsh and different life, she knows where this picture was taken. It is Waterside, a strange place, even for Hadfield. Catherine stands on the step of a house that faces the street but backs straight into the mill enclosure: 'In time the houses were knocked down, but the facades had to stand, because they were part of the mill wall. The windows and doorways were infilled by blocks of stone ... When I was a child these houses struck me as sinister: an image of deception and loss' (2017a: 3). This wall remained in Waterside for many years, yet peculiarly, the villagers, fearing its great height, the height of a house, thought it might fall on passers-by so cut its height in half. Changed again, but still eerily present.

Mantel's point is that 'history' has no access to thoughts, and even, at times, to facts. Her emphasis remains on the erasures, the silences, lack of evidence where evidence is expected. It is the 'No Entry' sign, signified by the wall with its stopped windows and doors, which lights the fire of our need to know, our hunger for the answer. Duplicitously, it also facilitates our feverish substitution of knowledge for The Story, The Fiction, so solid, so complete, that perhaps it is not a substitute at all. In a way, what Mantel says is that the fiction is more a reflection (or mirror image) of the truth, but that importantly it is not *inferior* to The Evidence, which is as much a refraction as the fiction: 'It's the record of what's left on the record [...] It is no more "the past" than a birth certificate is a birth, or a script is a performance, or a map is a journey' (2017a: 4). The example she gives is again personal: imagine, she suggests, the loss of a loved one. The moment they die they become fiction, and at the funeral such fiction will be invoked and there will be as many fictions as there are mourners. History is just the 'organising method' and its imperfection is why we cannot leave the past alone, it is the wall again, not houses anymore, but inscribed with a trace of them.

When we see CCTV images of terror suspects or fifty-year-old police photographs of notorious murderers, what we *have* is the what, but what we *want* is the why. In our collective imagination, 'we chase the dead, shouting, "Come back!" We may suspect that the voices we hear are an echo of our own, and the movement we see is our own shadow' (2017a: 2). What we learn from Mantel is that this recognition applies to ghosts of the very recent past just as it does to the lived moments of personal loss and ancient history.

'If you explain too much, you explain away': Hilary Mantel's un-anchorings (Ginette Carpenter)

In an article written to mark the twentieth anniversary of Princess Diana's death, Hilary Mantel claims that the icon's untimely demise 'released subterranean doubts and fears' (2017c). This description can be similarly applied to Mantel's own work in its refusal to adhere to limits, its insistent transgressions. Mantel's texts are not safe spaces, they are not places of comfort, they do not assuage dis-ease or salve consciences. It seems to me, that in this sense at least, Mantel has much in common with Angela Carter who in 1983 famously claimed to be 'in the demythologising business' and that she was 'interested in myths … because they are extraordinary lies designed to make people unfree' (1983: 69). Mantel is similarly preoccupied with deconstructing ideologies of containment, at undermining and disrupting the stories we are told and that we tell ourselves to feel safe. Mantel does this in a very different way to Carter but a line can be traced from the former's desire to put 'new wine in old bottles' (71) to Mantel's preoccupations with 'politics, power, transformation, evolution and revolution' (Arias and Mantel 1998: 277): both are motivated by the need to tell things differently. However, like Carter, Mantel is hyper-aware of the double-edge of storytelling: that it can be mobilized to anchor and fix, as much as to subvert and reposition. Mantel's fictional strategies are thus akin to a skilled pathologist, slicing incisively to expose the skull beneath the skin. Despite its seeming eclecticism, her work is united by this desire to penetrate beyond conventional limits or boundaries and is characterized by a repeated puncturing of that which might be deemed 'normal', obvious or common sense.

Mantel's concern with destabilizing the cultural truisms of both present and past means that her work recalibrates accepted narratives. Her extensive journalism – primarily for the *Guardian* and *London Review of Books* (*LRB*) – is similarly intrusive and troubling as she refuses to peddle in platitudes. Mantel's twentieth anniversary analysis of Diana's legacy is characteristically uncompromising as she dissects the princess's posthumous construction in the cultural imaginary: 'For some people, being dead is only a relative condition; they wreak more than the living do. After their first rigor, they reshape themselves, taking on a flexibility in public discourse' (2017c). For Mantel, Diana is a mobile signifier who has come to *mean* more dead than alive. (2013). The article is a carefully nuanced reading of the – self-engendered and imposed – myths that constructed the princess's persona during her life and that have continued to gain momentum with her death. Mantel observes that Diana was in some ways the victim of fairytales, of those tenacious and damaging stories told to proscribe and prescribe the lives of young women while simultaneously occluding the realities of finding one's prince: 'Fairytales do not describe the day after the wedding, when the young wife lost in the corridors of the palace sees her reflection splinter, and turns in panicked circles looking for a mirror that recognises her' (2017c). There is a schism between the misguided fantasist 'who believed she was basking with dolphins when she was foundering among sharks' and the public persona of the people's princess, an endlessly plastic 'phenomenon', 'self-renewing as the seasons, always desired and never possessed' (2017c). Mantel is far too astute to fail to recognize her own complicity in these processes and archly comments that 'we gossip about her as if she had just left the room' (2017c), none immune from the desire to bend a Barbie princess into the shape that best fits the story being told.

The responses to this article were depressingly predicable as the media, in oblivious affirmation of the very discourses that she is interrogating, criticized Mantel for her 'attacks' on Diana (Byrne 2017; *Daily Express* 2017), failing to recognize the rescue that is being undertaken. However, a previous piece for *LRB* – 'Royal Bodies' (2013), initially given as a lecture at the British Museum – sparked much greater controversy in response to Mantel's discussion of the pregnant Kate Windsor as 'precision-made, machine-made … capable of going from perfect bride to perfect mother, with no messy deviation' (2013). She notes her transition from 'a shop-window mannequin, with no personality of her own' to a woman whose 'only point and purpose is procreation' and laments her 'becoming a jointed doll on which certain rags are hung' (2013). This characterization of princess as nothing more than inanimate object to be dressed and positioned according to monarchical whim caused outrage from not only the usual media sources but also the then prime minister David Cameron and the leader of the opposition Ed Milliband (Murphy 2013).[1] Mantel begins this piece with reference to Marie Antoinette as clothes horse – 'a woman eaten alive by her frocks' – and also discusses the forced public performances of the Queen and Diana before turning to a more sustained examination of the nation's continuing fascination with Anne Boleyn. Clearly this is not a criticism of the women who are born to marry into royalty but rather of the gaze – both royal and public – that holds them frozen and immobile in some cruel, exaggerated and anachronistic pastiche of stereotypical femininity.

This paralysing gaze, so parodied by the fishbowl lives of the monarchy, is, of course, the dogged surveillance of patriarchy. Mantel's anatomization of public fascination with royal women – the obsessive, reductive scrutiny of their appearance and fertility – is part of what John Mullan calls her 'continuing attention to … the torments of femininity' (2015). This is a unifying theme of many of her texts and is explicitly played-out in *An Experiment in Love* (2010a) which articulates the experience of a generation of young women slowly being released from patriarchy's panoptic blinkers and emerging disoriented and myopic into the dawn of second wave feminist advance. The novel is narrated from a temporal distance as a much older Carmel reflects upon her first months at university in London in 1970, having been born and schooled in Lancashire. As in many of her novels, this echoes one of Mantel's own journeys as she moved from Hadfield in Derbyshire to study economics at LSE (Mantel 2004: 155–160). The narration moves back and forth between Carmel's recollections of her upbringing and schooling and her experiences at her hall of residence in Bloomsbury. The link between the three is Karina, a daughter of Eastern European refugees from Nazism, who lives on Carmel's street and attends the same school, Catholic grammar and then university. The novel is a dissection of female friendships and alliances and, in typical Mantelian style, refuses to embrace a polemic of sisterhood as easy redress to patriarchal oppression. The narrative evokes young women as complicated, contradictory and conflicted, capable of great acts of kindness and great acts of (self) sabotage. Carmel's uprootings – from home, the North, Catholicism, the working class – mirror the slow, contemporaneous recalibration of the carefully policed privileges of class and gender. As Mary Eagleton argues: 'The women are interested also in understanding their place in a wider movement of social change, and they are highly aware of living at a particular historical juncture' (2014: 104). Yet processes of empowerment are complex and Carmel and her contemporaries oscillate between embracing new-found liberations and struggling with the myths they have internalized. As is so often the case in Mantel's work, these themes are worked through via the medium of embodiment. Thus, although her gaining a place at university makes Carmel feel 'holy, lucky. Selected' she recognizes that this is at odds with her ongoing sense of uneasiness in her new environs, so removed from the more restrictive mores of her family and education. Her anxiety physically manifests via 'an insistent migraine pain behind my left eye ... which left me shaking sometimes, uncertain in the traffic, unsure of the parameters of my own body' (43).

As the novel continues this disassociation is reinforced by Carmel's problematic relationship with food, explained away by her as the need to adhere to a tight budget but gradually recognized by the reader as something more serious and damaging. Her eventual collapse, towards the denouement of the novel, is described in terms of 'drowning' (235) – 'sailed along the Aldwych ... paddled the shadows of Drury Lane' (233–234) and 'swum into Tonbridge Hall' (234) – as the waters of familial expectation, cultural displacement and financial shame finally close over her head. As Carmel shrinks, tries to disappear, so Karina swells and takes up more space, stuffing herself with the cheap, bland carbohydrates (188) that her similarly small budget allows. Karina's amorphous shapelessness seems to echo her plainness, her lack of distinction, but the close of the novel reveals her steady expansion to be due to a disguised pregnancy and her assumed ordinariness a cloak to conceal layers of bitterness and malevolence. Mullan characterises Karina as 'a monster from Dickens or Victorian gothic' (2015) but to cast her as monster oversimplifies the subtleties of Mantel's work. Karina's implied murderous revenge is borne of the slights of childhood that maintain into her experiences at university – not fitting-in, being shunned and ignored. She is also Carmel's distorted other, grotesquely mirroring the protagonist's own insecurities. These in turn reflect wider cultural discourses that teach that female bodies are 'an encumbrance, a necessary evil' (69) and 'the dangerous, disruptive, upsetting knowledge of our … female nature' (165). The underlying monstrosity here is the abjecting of women's bodies alongside the false promise of intellectual advance: 'When men decided women could be educated … they educated them on the male plan … the products of the system would always be inferior to the original model' (164). Mantel expertly demonstrates how young women like Carmel and Karina are caught in a suspended moment as a revolution swirls around them but fails to carry them in its wake and, in multiple ways, they struggle to come up for air. Thus, the gutting of Tonbridge Hall by fire (an image that resonates extremely uncomfortably as I write this in the summer following the Grenfell Tower tragedy) symbolizes not only the fragility of forced friendships but also the choking suffocation of their dreams of escape from the binds of conventional femininity. The surviving of Lynette by her fox fur – by 'something limp and slaughtered' (245) – implies that it is still the performance of the feminine, the story, that matters more than women's self-realization.

Mantel is extremely cognizant of the fact that these performances, *stories*, get appropriated, nailed down and normalized. These processes of ideological anchoring fix people, places and things in confining roles that refuse difference and inhibit growth. Thus, Mantel's fictions repeatedly demonstrate the need to question the stories with which we are regaled as well as those we tell ourselves. Nowhere is this more evident than *The Giant, O' Brien* (2010b) where the grand narratives of science and enlightenment rationalism are juxtaposed with the transformative possibilities of fiction, the soulless, corpse-strewn existence of John Hunter with the world-enriching tales of the Giant. The novel astutely addresses the paradoxes of storytelling whereby it can be mobilized to both reinforce and interrogate dominant discourses. Charles O' Brien is a consummate weaver of tales, a spinner of fantastic yarns, but his storytelling sessions are repeatedly interrupted by his listeners (see for example, 41–51; 143–147) as they attempt to second guess the narrative and he himself begins to worry about the cohesion of his work: 'The fine workmanship of the flask: how did she see it in the dark?' (54). Stories in *The Giant, O'Brien* are porous things, flexing and bending to accommodate audience and location; the 'truth' of the tale is relative. At the close of this novel, as the Giant lies dying, he begins to question the structures and conventions of language itself: 'Where meaning evaporates into air like ether' (190). Language too is just another fiction, another construction to pin down meaning, to fix interpretation, to stop the world inexorably spinning away. It is this recognition of the impossibility of fixing anything that characterizes all of Mantel's writing. She is a writer of ghost stories in the sense that the 'ghosts' that haunt us are not supernatural beings from another realm but that which is hidden, ignored or erased and thus interrupts a cohesive sense both of self and the phenomenal world. Her questioning of Diana's mythic status refutes fairytale and replaces it with a more disturbing story of princess as mobile site for public appropriation and consumption. In insisting upon complexity and refusing overarching explanation in order to explore 'subterranean doubts and fears' (2017c), Mantel's work demands a questioning of our own complicity in the structures that bind us and, as such, haunts long beyond its reading.

'There are no endings [...] They are all beginnings': Overview of chapters

Coming so soon after her Reith Lectures of 2017, this book offers a timely guide to any reader of Hilary Mantel, whether they be student, scholar or someone merely wishing to know more about one of Britain's most accomplished authors. The Reith Lectures spawned Mantel's inclusion in all episodes of the Summer 2017 series of BBC Radio 4 impressions show *Dead Ringers* demonstrating, by virtue of her value as a figure of parody, a level of fame unprecedented by any other contemporary writer.[2] This volume aims to begin to redress the limited critical attention paid to the oeuvre of a writer with such a broad cultural reach and affect. As such, this text is a wide-ranging, exciting and challenging selection of the cutting-edge work being done on Mantel's writing now; it carries an infectious enthusiasm that convinces the reader that such discussions offer emerging criticism well worth reading. In addition to summaries at the start of each new essay, the volume gives a detailed chronology of Mantel's writing life at the outset and an interview with the author herself at the end. It provides undergraduates and postgraduates studying Mantel's work on existing courses, as well as those planned or emerging in the near future, a wide range of critical material for reflection and scholarship. It is also designed to give general readers and fans of Mantel's writing, as well as those of the hugely successful RSC adaptation and BBC dramatization of the Tudor books, a point of reference for understanding what has produced Mantel's unique and elusive form and style. It precedes the publication of the much anticipated final volume of the Tudor trilogy, *The Mirror and the Light*, forthcoming 2019. The chronology, chapter summaries and author interview, coupled with a variety of theoretical ideas and the number of Mantel's texts explored, means that the collection offers a point of entry for every level of reader, from the beginner to the expert.

The chapters begin with Eleanor Byrne's analysis of 'social work gothic' in *Every Day Is Mother's Day* and *Vacant Possession*, illustrating how Mantel's early state-of-the-nation novels use the conventions of trauma to highlight the hidden crises in 1980s social care. Byrne argues that the novels' representation of the repeated occlusion and burying of past crimes results in a cycle of haunting that eerily prefigures the exposure of endemic child sexual abuse in more recent times. Siobhan O'Connor's chapter opens by precisely tracing some of the source material for Mantel's *Wolf Hall* and thus the complex interweaving of memory, nationalism and symbol in this first novel of Thomas Cromwell's rise. O'Connor continues by reading Mantel's mobilization of the spaces of hall and theatre as representative of both Cromwell's memory systems and his reworking of the past, marking the historical transition from Christian cosmopolitanism towards a more modern individualism. Eileen Pollard examines the figure of the ellipsis in Mantel's two volumes of short stories to date, in order to demonstrate that they are more *sequences* than straightforward collections. Pollard argues that it is the gaps in the stories that provide the link between them and that Mantel's interweaving of fiction and autobiography destabilizes and augments the indeterminacy of both. The effects, both alienating and immersive, of Mantel's unusual focalization of *Wolf Hall* are analysed in Renate Brosch's chapter to illustrate how Mantel convincingly constructs her character's complex subjectivity. Brosch's detailed and careful readings of the novel's narrative devices demonstrate the instability of identity and the relevance of challenging accepted conceptions of history to ultimately reveal that we should trust neither Cromwell nor Mantel. In her chapter Victoria Bennet explores the unsettling relationship between language, writing and self in Mantel's memoir *Giving Up the Ghost* and her hospital diary *Ink in the Blood* to illustrate the theme of 'openness' in Mantel's writing in general. Bennett argues that the lack of closure to Mantel's work creates what she terms a 'provisonality' which invites spectral, bodily and textual invasion. Wolfgang Funk is concerned with the effects of what he labels 'spectral realism' in Mantel's representations of ghosts and the supernatural. Funk discusses the literary ghost and its appearance in a range of Mantel's fictions before turning to detailed readings of *Wolf Hall* and *Bring Up the Bodies*, concluding that ultimately this ghostliness is the product of the 'unfinished business' in the past and the future. Ginette Carpenter deploys the conceit of walking as a lens through which to read Mantel's practice as historical novelist to argue that *A Place of Greater Safety* challenges conventional conceptions of history as static. Carpenter contends that this spatial un-fixing is mirrored in Mantel's disruptive representations of embodiment and disembodiment in both her wider writing and the specifics of this epic novel. Lucy Arnold's chapter explores Mantel's excessive intertextuality and use of self-quotation in *Wolf Hall* and *Fludd* to illustrate the way in which Mantel's texts haunt each other and resist interpretive containment. Arnold argues that Mantel's repeated emphasis upon textiles symbolizes this textual interweaving as well as the structural fashioning of her work to encourage proliferating spectral interventions. And finally, Kathryn Bird reveals the fraught relationship between domestic space and homeland security in Mantel's novel of mediumship and trauma, *Beyond Black*. Bird reads the novel through the prisms of female gothic, haunting and hospitality to illustrate Mantel's evocation of the porous boundaries between public and private, inside and outside, concluding that in *Beyond Black* homes and suburbia are far from safe spaces. It seems only right though to give the final word in this introduction to Mantel herself, so here are the last words of her last published novel to date: 'There are no endings. If you think so you are deceived as to their nature. They are all beginnings. Here is one' (2012: 407).

Notes

1 For an account of the media backlash, see Brown 2013.
2 What is more the *content* of the parody demonstrates the impressionist's understanding of Mantel's central argument in her 2017 Reith Lectures; that the past is uncertain, and you cannot trust it.

Bibliography

Arias, R. and H. Mantel (1998), 'An Interview with Hilary Mantel', *Atlantis* 2 (2): 277–289.

Brown, M. (2013), 'Kate Speech, Hate Speech and Hilary Mantel's Dissection of Royal Bodies', *The Guardian*, 19 February. Available online: https://www.theguardian.com/uk/2013/feb/19/kate-hilary-mantel-duchess-cambridge (accessed 30 August 2017).

Byrne, P. (2017), 'Hilary Mantel Launches Attack on Diana and the "Princess Myth" and Even Questions Her Compassion', *The Daily Mirror*, 27 August. Available online: http://www.mirror.co.uk/news/uk-news/hilary-mantel-launches-attack-diana-11067211 (accessed 30 August 2017).

Carter, Angela. (1983), 'Notes from the Frontline', in Micheline Wandor (ed.), *On Gender and Writing*, 69–77, London: Pandora.

Eagleton, M. (2014), 'The Anxious Lives of Clever Girls: The University Novels of Margaret Drabble, A. S. Byatt, and Hilary Mantel', *Tulsa Studies in Women's Literature* 33 (2): 103–121.

Jamieson, T. and N. Fountain (2017), *Dead Ringers* (BBC). Available online: http://www.bbc.co.uk/programmes/b08xcwz4 (accessed 22 August 2017).

Mantel, H. (1990), *Fludd*, London: Penguin.

Mantel, H. (2004), *Giving Up the Ghost: A Memoir*, London: Harper Perennial.

Mantel, H. (2008a), 'Author, Author', *The Guardian*, 24 May. Available online: https://www.theguardian.com/books/2008/may/24/1 (accessed 30 August 2017).

Mantel, H. (2008b), 'Ghost Writing', *The Guardian*, 28 July. Available online: https://www.theguardian.com/books/2007/jul/28/edinburghfestival2007.poetry (accessed 30 August 2017).

Mantel, H. (2010a), *An Experiment in Love*, London: Fourth Estate.

Mantel, H. (2010b), *The Giant, O'Brien*, London: Fourth Estate.

Mantel, H. (2012), *Bring Up the Bodies*, London: Fourth Estate.

Mantel, H. (2013), 'Royal Bodies', *London Review of Books* 35 (4): 3–7, 21 February 2013.

Mantel, H. (2017a), 'First Reith Lecture: The Day Is for the Living', BBC, 13 June 2017. Available online: http://downloads.bbc.co.uk/radio4/reith2017/reith_2017_hilary_mantel_lecture%201.pdf (accessed 22 August 2017).

Mantel, H. (2017b) 'Second Reith Lecture: Silence Grips the Town' (BBC). Available online: http://downloads.bbc.co.uk/radio4/reith2017/reith_2017_hilary_mantel_lecture%203.pdf (accessed 23 August 2017).

Mantel, H. (2017c), 'The Princess Myth: Hilary Mantel on Diana', *The Guardian*, 26 August. Available online: https://www.theguardian.com/books/2017/aug/26/the-princess-myth-hilary-mantel-on-diana (accessed 27 August 2017).

Mullan, J. (2015), 'The Strange and Brilliant Fiction of Hilary Mantel', *The Guardian*, 17 January. Available online:https://www.theguardian.com/books/2015/jan/17/-sp-hilary-mantel-profile-adaptation-wolf-hall (accessed 30 August 2017).

Murphy, V. (2013), 'Lay off Kate: David Cameron and Ed Miliband Defend Duchess of Cambridge after Hilary Mantel Jibes', *The Daily Mirror*, 19 February. Available online: http://www.mirror.co.uk/news/uk-news/kate-middleton-david-cameron-ed-1717821 (accessed 30 August 2017).

The Daily Express (unattributed). (2017), '"It's a Myth" Hilary Mantel Attacks "Mystical Realm" Surrounding Princess Diana', 29 August. Available online: http://www.express.co.uk/news/royal/846088/princess-diana-death-anniversary-latest-prince-william-prince-harry-royal-news (accessed 30 August 2017).

1

Mantel's Social Work Gothic: Trauma and State Care in *Every Day Is Mother's Day* and *Vacant Possession*

Eleanor Byrne

This chapter offers a reading of the gothic vision of Hilary Mantel's first two published novels, *Every Day Is Mother's Day* (1985) and *Vacant Possession* (1986), arguing that they deploy gothic themes of the haunted house and the world of spirits and mediums in order to produce work that offers a critical view of the 'State of the Nation' in British culture and society. It argues that these black comedies – which focus on the central characters of a socially isolated mother Evelyn and her daughter Muriel, who has an undisclosed intellectual disability – seek to explore a series of social crises in Britain in the 1980s, brought about by the dismantling of social welfare and care structures, through the prism of one social worker's interaction with a troubled family and their real or imagined ghosts. It explores the ways in which Mantel deploys tropes associated with the experience of trauma, such as hauntings and repression, to reflect on the unburying of past crimes and unspeakable acts of cruelty to children.

*****

In 1974, after graduating, Hilary Mantel began her first job as a social work assistant for the National Health Service in Stockport on a small wage and with the idea that she would 'learn on the job'. Reflecting on this experience in a 2009 article in the *London Review of Books*, she recalls how she spent her days 'in a ferment of anger and indignation' at the conditions in the geriatric hospital she worked in and recounts her demoralizing attempts to intervene in the lives of abandoned and isolated TB patients by visiting their extended families to persuade them to visit their relatives. Her community visits led to first-hand encounters with devastating experiences of extreme poverty, desperation, mental illness, neglect and a climate of violence. Mantel goes seeking family support for those already in care but on one occasion ends up bringing that family member into care as well. An old lady, Mrs B, the sister of an inpatient, who answers the door, crying and distressed with a house infested with fleas and rats, can clearly not be expected to offer support to her ill brother. Instead Mantel's superiors arrange for her to be given an emergency psychiatric bed, and the next time she meets Mrs B she is in the dining room of the day hospital and has had a perm and electroconvulsive treatment (ECT). Mantel's horror at the results of her own intervention is palpable: 'Impossible to say if it was human company or an electric current through the head that had jolted her back into personhood. Depression doesn't usually lift so fast. It was already a liberal axiom that ECT was barbarous. And I proceeded by liberal axioms. Mrs. B's case worried me for years' (2009: 2). Mantel is demoralized by how little she achieves, by the unintended violent consequences of her actions, by the scale of social crisis in the post-industrial north.

As Mantel notes, public discourse around social workers in Britain is complex and ugly, representations are riven by contradictions that swing back and forth between busy-body and 'gormless uncaring drain on the public purse' (2009: 4). These views are periodically punctuated by tragic and shocking scandals as individual cases of abuse and neglect reach the public via scandalized media framings. In Mantel's day the death of seven-year-old Maria Colwell at the hands of her mother's partner had been fresh in people's minds, for Mantel writing in 2009 it was the case of Baby P. After each case, Mantel ruefully notes, there is a period of societal examination, a restructuring and altering of procedures, but the phrase 'it must never happen again' is 'an empty piety [...] like saying "God have mercy on us" and expecting the immediate result' (2009: 5). For Mantel in the 1970s, the social workers she met held what she saw as naïve views of the people they were supposed to help. Although liberal in her views about mental health treatment, as a girl from a northern working-class background she detested what she saw as misguided middle-class views in the profession. Notably, she felt that the working class were characterized, by her colleagues, as culturally different, chaotic, unlike other people, to the extent that neglect and abuse were tolerated and children were put at risk.

It is with this quickly abandoned career in mind that this chapter proposes to consider Hilary Mantel's first two published novels, *Every Day Is Mother's Day* set in the mid-1970s and its sequel, *Vacant Possession*, set ten years later.[1] It will read both novels through the prism of her social work experiences as they trace the tragicomic relationships that form between a young, newly qualified social worker, Isabel, and her recalcitrant and threatening clients, Evelyn and her daughter Muriel. In *Every Day Is Mother's Day*, Evelyn, a widow and medium, lives alone in a stifling haunted house with her silent daughter Muriel. Isabel first comes into Evelyn and Muriel's lives as a bright but naïve young woman making a house call to follow up on Muriel's absence from her day centre visits. After a short and unsuccessful interview with Muriel and her mother, Isabel leaves the house disturbed and certain that Muriel is heavily pregnant and that her mother is concealing this. Muriel's pregnancy, achieved despite almost never leaving the house, causes a crisis in this enclosed world and subsequently, after a secret home birth, Evelyn convinces Muriel that her baby is a 'changeling child' who must be drowned so that a real baby can be swapped into their care. The narrative works itself up to a crescendo, with the murder of the baby at the close of the novel, and Evelyn falling to her death on the stairs of the house, helped by Muriel's vengeful involvement, as Isabel and social services attempt to intervene in the lives of the two women.

Vacant Possession reads as a revenge plot; set in 1984, it picks up the story ten years later after Muriel is released from a secure psychiatric unit as part of the closure of secure asylums under the Conservative government's Mental Health Act of 1983. Living a half-life in rented rooms, as far away from the eyes of social services as she can get, Muriel seeks to take revenge upon all those who were involved in her persecution. To this end, she finds and murders the man who assaulted her sexually and is father of her child. In a convoluted plot twist, it transpires he is Isabel's disgraced father. Muriel then lures Isabel into another dangerous house where she has been lodging with another ex-asylum resident: a pyromaniac who appears to be burning down churches. Muriel's objective is to seek out a newborn baby to replace her lost child, hoping to repeat the earlier drowning and 'baby swap' from the first book in order to retrieve a 'changeling child' to be her companion.

This chapter examines the ways in which domestic spaces are mobilized in Mantel's writing, not as sites of private refuge or retreat, but as dangerously inhabited by the traces of dark family histories and secrets that act as vectors to wider social ills, pervading the environments of her characters' lives like a bad smell coming up the stairs. In these texts both pregnancy and mothering are traumatic and traumatizing, haunted by abuse or paedophilia, and the resulting children, in particular Muriel, unwanted or un-nurtured, bear marks of monstrosity and trauma. Muriel's pregnancy in *Every Day Is Mother's Day* is not a sign of new life but rather a visitation from beyond the grave and it remains inexplicable: whatever actions have made it possible remain unknowable and incommunicable by mother or daughter. Despite the claustrophobic domestic atmosphere of both these novels, a wider set of social observations form the central preoccupations of the world that Mantel creates. Through a depiction of domestic and embodied female sexual trauma Mantel also offers a trenchant critique of British society in the late 1970s and early 1980s, examining the concept of state care in her exploration of social work and healthcare interventions in the domestic sphere of Muriel's family. *Vacant Possession* as a 'State of the Nation' novel deploys black humour to satirize the political enactment of 'Care in the Community' legislation and to depict the nation as a haunted house inhabited by aberrant and traumatized maternal presences, ones that witness but cannot coherently speak of abuses of women and children but which must nonetheless be attended to. Read together these two novels – the first bleak and airless, tormented by multiple hauntings, the second suddenly active and vengeful – explore a set of social concerns and crises that emerge under Thatcherism in 1980s Britain. In particular, the dismantling of aspects of the welfare state affects a range of social services: the housing of single mothers, shifting orthodoxies in social work and the slow privatization of state assets. Furthermore, they gesture towards the embedded and repressed knowledge of sexual violence at the heart of British culture, in that they presciently anticipate, if do not fully realize, the unearthing of child abuse and neglect as a key trauma at the heart of the state; trauma that emerged into the British public realm in the late 1980s and early 1990s. In such a reading, Muriel, appears as a figure for sexual trauma, whose identity as mentally disabled acts as a metaphor for her inability to speak or represent her abuse in the early novel and the legacy of which propels her need to return to the scene of the crime in the sequel and take her revenge.

The first novel opens with a failed séance as an elderly neighbour visits Muriel's mother Evelyn, who works privately in her front room as a medium, to speak to her dead husband, only to be told he is roasting in Hell. For those readers familiar with Alison, the medium in Mantel's later novel *Beyond Black* (2005), there is a partially recognizable figure here, a medium who practises her art for a paying public, but is far from being a charlatan. Evelyn, having found a route to the 'unseen', now cannot close the open gap between physical and spiritual worlds enabling malevolent spirits to pass freely into her house and take up residence in various rooms. In *Unclaimed Experience* (1996), a key text in the field of trauma studies, Cathy Caruth suggests that certain traumatic experiences are impossible to experience at the time they occur and may also defeat easy access in the present; thus, trauma is always partially experienced after the event itself. One such index of this 'belated' experience, well used by Mantel, is of course the ghost. It is now a truism for all journalistic articles on Mantel to recount, as *The New Yorker* did in 2005, that her own childhood was one 'assailed by ghosts', and as she does later herself in her memoir *Giving Up the Ghost* (2010). Evelyn's opening séance suggests immediately that the concerns of the text are with unsettling the border between what can be spoken or seen and what remains hidden or repressed. As Esther Peeren suggests, the continuing power of the medium is to 'draw attention to the disavowed, un-sensed spheres of reality and the marginalised subjects occupying them' (2013: 205).

After Evelyn's frank admission to her customer that her husband is burning in Hell, her striking claim to a truly 'other' knowledge is as yet unproven. The narrative then segues into a series of letters and reports on Muriel and her mother between members of social services. The letters conjure the pressures of a stretched social service provision, alternating between cheery social worker memos, 'dumping' Muriel's case on yet another colleague, and Home Visit notes, where difficult conversations, and inconclusive observations, mean little concrete action appears to have been taken in response to Muriel's neglect. They reveal a trail of lost opportunities, indicating that Muriel has barely attended school, has had no formal assessment of any condition she may have and has stopped attending her day centre. These mundane scripts of the state appear flimsy in the face of a mother who can speak to the dead and whose house is potentially haunted. Tongue in cheek, they deploy the blackest of comedy as they recount home visits by different social workers where the discourse of social work management clashes with the defensive wall of words Evelyn keeps around her: 'Explained to her that Muriel had been placed on the waiting list for five-day care at the Centre and that in the event of her decease a place would be found for her in a residential institution or hostel. Mrs Axon stated "Do you mean Holloway?" and when queried stated "She has murderous inclinations"' (Mantel 2013: 22). The social workers are unable to apprehend the kinds of cruelty or dimensions of domestic horror that they seek to engage with. Always belated, they come too late to address the present moment, caught in the interminable backlog of a creaking social services system. The objects of their attention, Muriel and her mother Evelyn, exist in another dimension, barely visible, almost entirely interior to the two women concerned, one that might be the most 'abject' possible, if we use Julia Kristeva's influential use of the term to signify a kind of collapse of the borders between self and other (1982). Muriel and her mother appear as a merged subjectivity, locked onto the secrets and repressions of their complex and suffering relationship, one that appears to have slipped outside of social constraints and norms.

Mantel maintains the Axon's domestic environment as one always teetering on the fantastic, offering a modern-day version of Henry James's masterful exercise in unsettling haunting, *The Turn of the Screw* ([1898] 2008).

That text famously walks a tightrope of undecidability where the governess cannot decide if her infant charges are evil or innocent. Mantel replaces the governess role with the social worker, a modern-day 'carer' allowed access to the private, domestic sphere of the family armed with liberal guilt and a mundane set of guidelines. The reader too becomes a strangely concerned onlooker, reading intensely for signs of what appears to be taking place in the house, exploring the border between existing and believable events and those without rational explanation, haunting and uncanny. In those passages most deeply interior to Evelyn's role as a medium, talking with ghosts is also a form of talking to herself, monitoring the screams and shouts that have caused her to believe they have moved into her house. She can hear and sense them, and sometimes Muriel can too, but they also leave little notes, ghostly versions of more benign domestic messages about running out of milk exchanged between housemates or family members:

> On the floor of the hall lay a crumpled piece of paper. Evelyn's gorge rose. Low stinking entities, she said to herself. Once she had been able to smell them, but her senses were becoming blunter with age. Increasingly they were choosing this method of communication, this, their tricks, the sharp raps on the wall from different rooms of the house.[...] She picked it up and straightened it out. The wavering great letters were familiar by now, fly-track thin: GO NOT TO THE KITCHIN TODAY. (Mantel 2013: 20)

Some of the incidents that haunt Evelyn are later explained as actions Muriel has taken, but some are not. Other uninvolved witnesses see faces at different windows of the house and Evelyn herself is covered in bruises which she believes come from attacks by the ghosts. After her death they are blamed on Muriel, who it is assumed has terrorized her mother, yet our privileged access to the domestic life they lead at other points in the novel would suggest that the power dynamic is definitely the other way around. Despite Evelyn's attempts to restrict Muriel's movements to the house, Muriel defeats house arrest on a number of occasions and enables Isabel's first visit to the house by answering the door to the social worker's insistent knocking.

It is into this demonic/domestic space that Mantel unleashes her unsuspecting social worker, Isabel Field, setting the tone for the darkly humourous pleasures of the text. Isabel blunders into the Axon house as innocent passers-by do in haunted mansions or murderous hotels, served up as the ideal victim to a landscape of desires that are perverse and murderous, inhabited by characters drenched in gothic perfumes. Following her first short interview with Muriel and Evelyn, after pursuing them for weeks, Isabel flees the house, unsettled by Muriel's silent brooding presence, her suspicions that Muriel may be pregnant and Evelyn's ravings. She later reflects on her own sense of impotence with her lover, a married teacher, Colin: 'I shouldn't talk about it – oh, but I must, I must. Spit it out. Get the foul taste out of my mouth [...] You handled it badly, said the voice inside her. You were brusque and unprofessional; and then you let the situation completely defeat you' (69). Isabel's experience in the Axon house suggests that the central tenet of social care provision has already become profoundly unsettled: 'We're not supposed to worry. Only to display professional concern. It's different. You mustn't identify with your client or let her life touch yours. It's unprofessional to get involved' (70). Mantel brutally upends this social work maxim, by making Muriel's life touch Isabel's in every possible way. Isabel is already traumatized, as her vague apprehension of Muriel's pregnancy acts as a flickering of unconscious knowledge of sexual abuse, which the text will go on to reveal connects her very personally indeed to Muriel. Even as Isabel attempts to impose order on the demonic chaos of the Axon household, it is her own abusive father who has already gained access to Muriel. Isabel's father is her awful secret, kept at home as far as possible, with a long line of sexual assaults and depraved acts hidden from public view. Isabel's harbouring of her father is mirrored by Evelyn's domestic past, and the latter's veiling of her husband Clifford's crimes. Social worker and client alike both witness but do not fully verbalize or report sexual crimes against women and children.

The slow unravelling of lives at the Axon household is interspersed with sections following the more ordinary helplessness and futility of Colin's domestic life and his short affair with Isabel. This is a different or adjacent kind of domestic hell, mundane, disappointed, powerless, where Colin takes himself out of the house for secret rendezvous with Isabel at a creative writing group. Mantel's cold satire of the fantasies of prisoners of suburban lives seeking self-expression through art is wickedly dismissive of the joys of fiction. The workshop meetings become little more than a veil for the affair Colin conducts with Isabel, and fatally cause her to lose her case notes on Muriel, which have been left in the back of a car. The documents fall into the hands of Colin's colleague Frank, who, to Colin's abject horror, decides to write them up as a novel, effecting a darkly funny mise-en-abyme: 'Finders keepers. It's about two dotty women. It's a gift. Grist to the mill' (159). Colin must try to retrieve the files so that Isabel's case notes on Muriel are not turned into an amusing satire by and for the complacent middle class. Mantel's horror of this literary crime is encapsulated in her portrayal of a lavish dinner party scene where Frank outlines his plan, 'You can't imagine the lives some people lead. I might turn it into a sort of allegory, you see, about the state of our society' (Mantel 2013: 159). This metafictional gesture queries the politics of the 'State of the Nation' novel as a hollow social form, written by and serving a condescending and contemptuous middle-class audience.

As Muriel's pregnancy progresses, Evelyn's memories of her own pregnancy begin to resurface, leading her back to reflect on her own early marriage as an orphan at the age of seventeen and to relive the life she led with her now-dead husband. The remains of his life with her have been moved out of the house to the 'lean-to' in the back garden, whose paving stones Muriel fittingly mistakes for gravestones, as, indeed, all sorts of dead things are buried here. His possessions are unearthed by Muriel as she explores the house, unable to voice her own traumas but acting like a blind seeker, tripping over the relics of the traumatic past, bringing objects back into the house and with them the histories that are attached. The lean-to is a gothic space, full of her father's past, symbolically pressing against the back of the house, where domestic secrets and horrors are hidden. It is a kind of graveyard, not for actual bodies, but for the physical trappings of the man who had terrorized this house and left Evelyn inhabited by ghosts.

Mantel's central motif, one that she will go on to deploy effectively in her later work *Beyond Black*, where it reaches its apotheosis, is to link the hauntings that plague Evelyn with repressed trauma. In Evelyn's case it is her late husband Clifford's use of the garden shed for years of child abuse soon after Muriel was born. Although Evelyn is also his victim, it is something she has tacitly colluded with for fear of her own life and that of her daughter. It is a trauma for which neither resistance nor escape was possible and has overwhelmed Evelyn's own systems of self-defence and she is unhinged and disturbed by it. The text delays revealing this trauma until quite late on in the narrative, as the dead husband enacts a slow ghoulish return to the domestic interior. Muriel, almost mute throughout the novel, digs up the filthy piles of archived papers, magazines, clothes and rotten material until she finds a 'sign', a signifier of all that has been buried here:

> She held up the coat and shook it out. It was thick and heavy, its dark wool mildewed but intact. Muriel wrinkled her nose at its ancient and complex smells. At first she wondered whether it had been left there by one of the corpses under the stones outside the door of the lean-to. Then her eye caught some writing. Writing in a coat? [...] Evidently corpses wrote in their clothes; evidently they had a strong sense of private property. She spelled it out for herself. CLIFFORD F. AXON. (81)

When Muriel brings the coat into the house and hangs it by the front door Evelyn is terrified: 'She raised her eyes to the dark shape that swung gently above Muriel's head. Its folds were dense in the half-light. Clifford had come back and hung his coat on the hallstand' (86). The return of her long-dead husband is a haunting too far and although the simple explanation is that Muriel has brought the coat in from the lean-to, retrieved it from the filth of the decaying archive of Evelyn's past, it is suffused with a wretched and barely hidden history of paedophilia in which Evelyn has been complicit. Evelyn approaches this history fearfully, circling her own life story, recalling fragments and partial histories, until late in the novel she recalls a fuller scene:

> After Muriel, Clifford had not wanted to risk repetition. He said that he would amuse himself. He would go down to the shed and she must turn a blind eye. A blind eye to whatever he kept in there and whatever comings and goings there were. And that was what she had always done until one day she had seen the child from next door heading down the path. (174)

Up until this point, marvellously unsympathetic Evelyn has been a troubled or deranged persecutor of her daughter, here she appears for the first time as a more comprehendible monster, a fellow victim produced by a life terrorized by her husband: '"What are children to you" Clifford had sneered. His own eyes not blind, but pale and rimless, turning now to all the wastage on the table, the messy spillings of her fear' (174). Her remembering of this era of her life is also of a kind of death of the self, and a burial, that has produced the medium that Mantel portrays, who has crossed the line between living and dead: 'Years passed like this, the nameable fears giving way to the unnameable, the familiar dread of evening muffled under a pall of fog, of blackness of earth; all the days lived as if underground, and Muriel, she thought, if I could have mourned myself, if I could have drawn breath, I might have pitied you' (174).

This image of being buried alive tips Evelyn herself into being a quasi-spectral figure, whose full claim to subjecthood has been compromised. This fear of becoming a ghost has already been rehearsed in her depiction of Muriel as ghostlike and her sense of the baby as a phantom pregnancy, not 'imagined' by Muriel, but an impregnation somehow done from beyond the grave by her husband: 'She looked down at the baby and saw Clifford again, sitting behind its eyes; behind the glassy layers the years peeling away' (189). This ghostly fathering seals the baby's fate; both mother and daughter look at the newborn unable to grasp at a maternal relation to it. Thus Evelyn begins to weave a story of the child being a changeling, coaxing Muriel to drop it in the river in exchange for a real child that they could actually love: 'You have to find some water, a river or something. Float it along. And sometimes they pick it up and give you your own back' (Mantel 2013: 189). Evelyn dispossesses Muriel of her newly born baby even as it lies in a cardboard box next to her crying.

The novel's conclusion allows Muriel to enact swift retribution for this infanticide through her own role in the matricide that quickly follows, as she decisively pushes her mother down the stairs. But ultimately there is no justice for Muriel who is taken away to be incarcerated for her own good.

Unworthy Colin, split from Isabel, buys the now empty house at a knock-down price and sets up home with his wife there. It is unsurprising that Mantel feels compelled to return to this story in her sequel, for she ends with a rather superficial painting over of the walls of this haunted house, and Colin's impending sense of doom as the demonic presences in the fabric of its bricks and mortar appear to be infiltrating his children. As his unsuspecting wife Sylvia says, 'the devil's got into that child since we moved house' (211). In other words, she has created the perfect unhappy ending.

It is perhaps hard to believe after her colossal success with the Cromwell series that Mantel developed a reputation mid-career for being unclassifiable, and writing a different book each time. As Anna Murphy comments in her introduction to an interview with Mantel, 'skipping seemingly effortlessly from place to place, era to era, in her books, be it England in the 1970, Botswana in the 1950s or Saudi Arabia in the 1980s' (2017). Cromwell is figured as the stopping point where Mantel found her genre. But *Vacant Possession*, the sequel to *Every Day Is Mother's Day*, uncannily echoes that later pattern as it stays with the same characters and subject matter, compulsively wanting to follow the next part of their lives and is suggestive of Mantel's inability to let the story end. Repetition is key to trauma, whether of the acting out or working through kind, and this sense of repetition is what Mantel will do with her later historical novels. One of the uncanny effects of her sequel *Vacant Possession* is the way it makes the first novel historical by moving forward ten years. It suggests Mantel's overriding interest in how the past inhabits the present, making it hard to let go of any story, unburying things, repeating, not letting anything lie. As Adam Phillips notes, 'revenge is nothing if not a riveting way of keeping memories alive. It is conservative in that it seeks to recover a supposed status quo ante' (2013: 20). Whereas the first novel trembles with hidden traumas, the second acts as a postmodern revenge tragedy, which explores, just as Renaissance tragedies did, the unstable relation of private revenge to questions of state sanctioned forms of justice. Muriel, a victim of state neglect, maternal torture and sexual assault – and having already murdered her mother – takes matters into her own hands to avenge the murder of her baby and her rape by its father.

Muriel acts as the engine for this revenge plot. She recasts herself as a changeling, following her mother's darkly deceptive storying that caused her baby's death, and decides that she is in need of the company of her own kind. Her belief that she can exchange a new human baby for the original changeling, by repeating the act of drowning, propels her back into the lives of the neighbours and social workers from her earlier life. Through wearing multiple disguises, she effects a terrifying infiltration of the domestic spaces of those involved who now live literally in what used to be her house. The narrative again propels itself ferociously towards the demise of a second baby that she abducts, until, by a series of chance events, the remains of the first child are posted to Muriel in a cardboard box. This effects the exchange that she had desired and saves the life of the new child. Mantel's return to Muriel suggests a dissatisfaction with the destiny she had ascribed to the opaque and mute anti-heroine of the first novel. Muriel has been produced as a 'case' for Isabel, a trauma for Evelyn and a victim for an unscrupulous would-be fiction writer. Her release from state care transforms her into an active agent of change and retribution in the sequel.

In *Vacant Possession*, orphaned and still haunted by the loss of her child, with her family home sold from under her and with ten years of time to reflect on her fate, Muriel appears standing outside her old home, scrutinizing the situation, ready to unbury the past one more time. Arguably, Mantel seems to have had a change of heart, whereby Muriel's previous 'blankness' is now not a sign of learning difficulties but the very incarnation of the changeling. She moves between multiple 'socially invisible' identities in the novel, calling herself Lizzie Blank and infiltrating different aspects of the characters' lives as she plays the role of both a cleaner and care-worker, with wigs and voices to fit each character. This invisibility, which appears to be due to the extremely low social status of her jobs as much as her wilful disguising of herself, ensures her success. She passes through the minds of her employers with only the briefest amount of interest and no real recognition. Her first victim, Isabel's father – Philip Field, the father of her lost baby – is recovering from a stroke in hospital when she enters his room as an old woman: 'an orderly, a downcast and shrunken personage' (Mantel 2006: 100). But as he looks at her

> a change seemed to come over her. Her bony shoulders straightened. She grew by an inch or two, and her melancholy manner fell away. The years fell away too; it was 1974, she was a girl alone, on a go in the park, and a lonely old gentleman was hanging around by the swings. (100)

Muriel enacts a transformation where the passage of time simply falls away, and the original trauma can be seen again. Nonetheless, in the intervening years she has acquired a gutsy vulgarity, and a clear agenda for retribution: 'Muriel grinned at him. "Hello, old cock" she said' (Mantel 2006: 100). She enacts revenge for the child she once was, her performance of social marginality enabling her to infiltrate the same state mechanisms that once incarcerated her.

As Mantel's State of the Nation novel, *Vacant Possession*, documents the dismantling of residential social care in the early 1980s with the emptying of long-term mental health accommodation and the advent of 'care in the community'. It also takes Margaret Thatcher's calculated advocacy of Victorian values for a walk, satirizing the chronic anachronism of a historically backward looking and haunted political present. Colin's daughter, now grown up, is pregnant after a short affair with Isabel's husband, bringing their lives back together after years of separation. Colin goes to plead with him to pay for an abortion: 'This is 1984. Victorian Values [...] It isn't the scot-free seventies, you can't expect to go littering the countryside with your blow by blows and expect the state to pick up the tab. You've got to feel the guilt Mr. Ryan, you've got to put your hand in your pocket' (164). Thatcherism's neo-liberal attack on the state turns society into individuals, and as individuals everyone must be made to pay. Muriel is the avenging angel, who becomes a vigilante who will ensure that they do.

The phasing out of residential care also affects Colin, whose mother, Mrs Sidney, is released from state care after she appears to have miraculously recovered from a semiconscious state due to Muriel infiltrating the ward in her geriatric hospital. Mrs Sidney comes back to consciousness as Princess May of Teck, the young Queen Mary. It is as if the resurgence of Victorian values has managed to open cracks in time allowing historical figures to step through into the present. Her recovery from her previous catatonic state, as a member of royalty, forces the family to take her back from the nursing home and from the rows of ancient ladies who sit propped on the wards. Mantel shows little mercy for the old women, as Colin, his wife and sister walk through the ward: 'their beaky heads swivelled, like a row of birds on a telegraph wire' (p. 153). Muriel's act of revenge here is to somehow reignite the spirit of Colin's long-gone mother and return her to the house, setting the stage for Muriel to pursue further acts of retribution. Colin's mother is now a revenant, a ghost of past crimes haunting the present. Ultimately, she too is unceremoniously seen off by Muriel, forced to take handfuls of her pills.

But taking revenge is also a complex unbalanced equation, as Deborah Willis notes:

> It is not a symmetrical payback but exceeds the original wrong [...] Since revenge requires excess to contain the emotional legacy of trauma it is hardly surprising that it creates the conditions for potentially endless cycles of retaliatory killings. Grief keeps reasserting itself hence the tendency for revenge to become obsessive; when the self has not come to terms with its losses, revenges satisfactions prove temporary. (2002: 33)

Willis proposes an image of the revenger as trying to 'return' the trauma to the perpetrator, translated into an object as one would an unwanted parcel, so that one no longer owns it. This 'return to sender' logic is one that structures Muriel's behaviour, her main preoccupation, disguised as the daily cleaner, is to try to convince Colin's daughter to give up the baby she is carrying; the baby that she can then exchange for her lost child.

Muriel's frenzied acts of revenge are mercifully stopped when she already has the newborn in her arms, when a different 'misdirected' parcel finally arrives for her. She turns to find the box with the baby replaced by a different package: 'And now for little Diddums. She turned from the foot of the stairs and gaped. Sweetie Pie had altered; altered out of all recognition. Displayed on the hall table, neat and sweet and perfectly articulated, was a skeleton; fine and tiny, and set together with a deft and knowing hand' (236). The skeleton of her lost baby has been retrieved from the riverbank by children and is posted unwittingly by them to her address for safekeeping. With remains to grieve over, Muriel's original loss is translated back into an object, an actual child she can mourn. Mantel appears to take pity on her murderous revenger and ends the narrative before we can find out what becomes of Muriel. She spares her the fate of most revengers, caught out by the excess of murderous logic in their actions, destroyed by their own desire for revenge. The furious motor of revenge is finally stilled as justice has been done, as far as it can be, by a series of chance events. A group of innocent children, each also neglected in their own way, have hauled the bones from the mud of the river, and have treasured the baby's skeleton, valued its meanings, possibly mixed its bones with that of other creatures, and turned it into a changeling, creating a place of consignation, bringing the feverish revenge of the ghosts to an end. Yet Mantel has also stayed true to Muriel's logic, the occult logic of the changeling, for the live baby has indeed been swapped as the folk tradition would have it.

While Muriel's own personal vendettas have ended, the two novels have traced the outline and partially exposed the many buried histories of abuse that have yet to fully emerge from 1980s Britain. Mantel's bitter satire of state provision in these works bleakly assesses the state of state care and child protection, and also gestures, perhaps with a prescient eye, to the future unveiling of widespread state-enabled child abuse that would rock multiple institutions in the coming decades. Sexual abuse, its traumas and its repression at the personal and state levels saturate the lives of the characters and the spaces that they occupy. Their partial exposure here, where remains are disinterred in order to be properly named and grieved, indicates the haunting work that will be necessary to overcome private and public denials, burials and institutionalized violences that still resist this traumatic knowing.

Note

1 Mantel had already written the manuscript of her first as yet unpublished novel, an historical account of the French revolution, *A Place of Greater Safety*, but this had yet to find a publisher.

Bibliography

Andrew, A. (2009), 'Baby P: Born into a Nightmare of Abuse, Violence and Despair, He Never Stood a Chance', *The Observer*, 16th August. Available online: https://www.theguardian.com/society/2009/aug/16/baby-p-family (accessed 23 November 2017).

Caruth, C. (1996), *Unclaimed Experience: Trauma, Narrative and History*, Baltimore: John Hopkins University Press.

James, H. [1849] (2008), *The Turn of the Screw*, Oxford: Oxford University Press.

Kristeva, J. (1982), *Powers of Horror: An Essay on Abjection*, New York: Columbia University Press.

Mantel, H. (2005) *Beyond Black*, London: Harper Perennial.

Mantel, H. (2006), *Vacant Possession*, London: Harper Perennial.

Mantel, H. (2009), 'Diary: On Being a Social Worker', *London Review of Books*, 31 (11): 34–35.

Mantel, H. (2010), *Giving Up the Ghost*, London: Fourth Estate.

Mantel, H. (2013), *Every Day Is Mother's Day*, London: Fourth Estate.

The New Yorker (unattributed) (2005), 'Devil's Work: Hilary Mantel's Ghosts', 25 July. Available online: https://www.newyorker.com/magazine/2005/07/25/devils-work (accessed 28 February 2017).

Murphy, A, (2010), 'Hilary Mantel Interview', *The Telegraph*, 1 March. Available online: http://www.telegraph.co.uk/culture/books/7345476/Hilary-Mantel-interview.html (accessed 26 February 2017).

Peeren, E. (2014), 'Other Senses: The Politics of Mediumship', in O. Jenzen, and Sally R. Munt (eds), *The Ashgate Research Companion to Paranormal Cultures*, 203–213, Farnham: Ashgate.

Phillips, A. (2013), 'A Symposium on Revenge', *The Threepenny Review*, 135: 18–21.

Willis, D. (2002), 'Revenge, Trauma, Theory and Titus Andronicus', *Shakespeare Quarterly* 53 (1): 21–25.

2

History, Nation and Self: *Wolf Hall* and the Machinery of Memory

Siobhan O'Connor

This chapter examines the treatment of historical revisionism in *Wolf Hall*, arguing that one of its key concerns is the way memory is transmuted into narratives of the past whose purposes are political: to shape the intended nation of the future. It approaches the novel through one of its sources, Frances Yates's *The Art of Memory* (1966) from which Mantel derives two important metaphors: Simonides and the collapsing hall and the memory theatre ('machine') of Giulio Camillo. It contends that Mantel's Cromwell is synonymous with both of these key figures of mnemonic art, while the structures of hall and theatre represent both his imagination and the emerging nation-state of an England which is founded on his reconfigurations of the past. 'Wolf Hall' is England at a moment of profound historical change in which the cosmopolitan communality of Christendom disintegrates into the individualism of modernity and the 'wolf' who can 'chase the dead' and 'rewrite their lives' controls the future (Mantel 2009: 649).

*****

A distinctive feature of Hilary Mantel's historical fiction is her connection of history with memory; her 'attempts to duplicate not the historian's chronology but the way memory works in leaps, loops and flashes' (2012b). In this way she establishes a meta-narrative, a text that talks to itself about how the stories of history are constructed and about the political power of those who shape them. Those who control the national memory are able 'to say what England is, her scope and boundaries' (Mantel 2009: 338). For this reason, memories are re-worked as convenient national stories that rationalize present structures. History is a political creation whose purpose is to justify the way things are.

A key context for *Wolf Hall* is the Henrician Reformation. Facilitated by the rise of print culture which systemized the preservation of what would now be called data, this was marked by its de-familiarization and re-memorizing of preceding times to consolidate the monarchic state's supremacy. Mantel has confirmed that a source for the novel was Frances Yates's 1966 study of classical and Renaissance memory systems, *The Art of Memory* and that this 'rich book' supplies two of the novel's key metaphors – Cicero's Method of Loci and the Memory Theatre of Giulio Camillo (significantly termed by Mantel's Cromwell as a 'machine') (Mantel 2016). Accordingly, I read *Wolf Hall* through the lens of Yates's work, exploring the use of these motifs to trace the morphing of experiential memory into historical narrative.

The re-structuring of sensory recollection into text began the social transformation of the mind described by Michel Foucault in *Discipline and Punish*, whereby a communal 'civilization of spectacle' evolved into one of individuals divided and ruled by the state (1977: 216). The Reformation practice of iconoclasm brought about the destruction of Catholic artefacts. Because these were associated with the communal life of the Church and were experienced visually, they embodied a public history that was collectively understood. This shared legacy was replaced by vernacular literature that made spirituality private and, in rejecting the pan-European language of Latin, asserted geographical identity. This enabled the modernizing English state to undermine the universal authority of Christendom. Mantel's consistent emphasis on the continental origin of these texts and their links to the roots of free trade and democracy highlights English opportunism (both early-modern and contemporary) in hijacking global movements for domestic political purposes. Tyndale, for example, is 'somewhere in Germany' (2009: 100) from where Cromwell's books arrive alongside 'Castile soap', 'packaged as something else' (37). Of the contemporary context, David Marquand complains, the 'British no longer know where they have come from or who they are' (2014: 6–7). In forgetting much of its past, including its affinity with the continent, key aspects of English identity have been lost. By exploring the ways in which heritage is invented, *Wolf Hall* is self-referentially aware of its own role as a historical novel in this continuing process. Integral to its historiographical perspective is the emphasis placed throughout the text upon Cromwell's connection with the culture of Renaissance Europe and in particular with Italy. As More remarks, 'Cromwell, you are an Italian through and through, and you have all their vices, all their passions' (2009: 567).

According to Mantel, the historical Cromwell was credited by his contemporaries with possession of a powerful memory and at points in *Wolf Hall* she associates this with super-human menace (2016). This is evident in accountancy metaphors such as Cromwell's claim to 'have a very large ledger. A huge filing system, in which are recorded (under their name, and also under their offence) the details of people who have cut across me' (2009: 481). Mantel has remarked that Cromwell 'had spent time in Italy, so I wondered if he learned some tricks' (2016). The 'tricks' I examine here represent different systems for remembering: the classical art of imaginative reconstruction as opposed to sixteenth-century compartmentalization which, according to Yates, 'represents a new Renaissance plan of the psyche' (1992: 173). The new-found command of memory was associated with a divine power which Mantel's Cromwell seeks. He is a master of surveillance and in his attempts to systematize memory seeks also to manage the past, aspiring to be like Foucault's panoptic ruler 'who looms over everything with a single gaze which no detail, however minute, can escape' (1977: 217).

Following the advent of the printing press, the sixteenth century saw a surge of attempts to create effective systems for the access, retention and utilization of memory. Possession of a single gaze over all that has ever been known over the whole of time was their common objective. As Lina Bolzoni observes, they aimed to gather in one place the entirety of human expression, to bring order to disordered recollection and then recombine established knowledge to create anew (2001). Command of time was the essence of power as indicated by the time symbol of Prudence, whose image is found within Camillo's Memory Theatre, and whose three components are '*memoria, intelligentia, providentia*' (memory, intelligence and providence) (Fraser 1992: 36). Renaissance practice often used animal symbols for human characteristics and in Prudence's case, intelligence is a lion, providence (or foresight) is a dog while memory is shown as a wolf (165). All three animals are important motifs within the novel and all are associated with Cromwell but his role as eponymous wolf is the primary concern here. In conflating Cromwell's identity with the wolf of *memoria,* Mantel merges it with the two inventors of memorial art – Simonides and Camillo.

Mantel uses interplay between the two memory systems and between the concepts of 'theatre' and 'machine' to highlight the practice of breaking down and ordering historical narrative for authoritarian purposes such as 'to make good use of the money that flows yearly to Rome' (220). Deconstruction was a principle of the Renaissance memory systems that attempted to harness and then mechanize creativity. I will suggest that Mantel's reinvention of Cromwell's interior world and his imaginative journey from classical to early modern art of memory explores the roots of contemporary England's problem with identity. The close association of early-modern memory systems with alchemy is reflected in their processes of assembly, analysis and recombination (190). Mantel has stated that alchemy is 'a recurring theme in my stories' and thus Cromwell can be seen in this sense as the alchemist who re-forms the English state (Mantel 2016).

The text as theatre

Wolf Hall's innovative narrative stance consists, to an unusual degree, of thought report and free indirect thought. For the most part, the reader is positioned within Cromwell's mind but while he is a member of the 'Cast of Characters', the novel is not exclusively preoccupied with him or his psychological state. Speech category techniques are combined with the present tense and are largely observational: Cromwell watches others, watches events unfold and the narrative method effectively dramatizes his interior commentary. This is Cromwell in the mode of '*intelligentia*', prudentially assessing present situations (Yates 1992: 35, 36). In order to convey an empathic sense of being present as history is made, there are occasional shifts to the first person plural pronoun as well as deployment of the subjunctive tense. This is the tense, indicated by the conjunction 'if' at the start of a clause that signals the conditional or speculative: along with the future tense, it emphasizes his unknowingness. An example of this comes when Cromwell and Cavendish attempt to settle the doomed Wolsey at Esher – 'If we can get partridges we can slice the breasts, and braise them at the table. Whatever we can do that way, we will: and so, if we can help it, my lord won't be poisoned' (Mantel 2009: 64). The feeling of being in the moment is further consolidated by the generic second person pronoun – 'Whichever way you look at it, it all begins in slaughter' (66). At some points the second person is also used in direct address to the reader – 'You must understand that he is not really dead' (Mantel 2009: 66). Cromwell's own feelings are mainly ambiguous because, despite his objective to steer subsequent narratives, he cannot know the future. The present tense gives the sense of life being lived and events being 'spun' as they occur, suggesting two things: the inevitable subjectivity of memorialization and the impossibility of translating individual experience into authentic literary form. Life, as it is lived, lacks the ironic perspective of the reader who has foreknowledge of the characters' fates. These narrative techniques evoke a theatrical sense of history being choreographed to favour particular perspectives. This is at the heart of Cromwell's complaint about More: 'And what I hate most of all is that Master More sits in the audience and sniggers when I trip over my lines, for he has written all the parts. And written them these many years' (563). In a novel which revises perceptions of this figure, Cromwell's theatrical metaphor signals narrative acknowledgement of historical bias.

When detached from Cromwell's perspective, the narrative voice takes on the mantle of Chorus. Examples of this can be found in the opening sections of 'An Occult History of Britain' and 'Alas, What Shall I Do for Love?' (65, 66). Contextualization of plot and character is the traditional choric function and so too is scene-setting. Both functions are evident in the passage below where reflection is followed by the imperative mood and adverbs to establish time, place and character:

> Time now to consider the compacts that hold the world together: the compact between ruler and ruled, and that between husband and wife [...] Imagine debating these matters with George, Lord Rochford. He is as witty a young man as any in England, polished and well read: but today what fascinates him is the flame-coloured satin that is pulled through his slashed velvet over-sleeve. (338)

The novel's theatricality is signalled in other ways. Its front matter contains both a 'Cast of Characters' and 'Family Trees' (ix–xiv). The former is a reminder of history's choreography while the latter represents official history and is generally used to lend authenticity to popular historical fiction. Elsewhere in the preliminaries, an extract from 'Vitruvius, *De Architectura*, on the theatre, c.27BC' authenticates Camillo (xvii). Below this is the list of players from 'Magnificence: an Interlude, John Skelton, c.1520'. Theatre is present tense storytelling with differences in every enactment – a reminder of the instability of historical narrative consolidated by many instances where the recent past is pragmatically revised. For example, Katherine of Aragon has 'half a lifetime waiting to be expunged, eased from the record' (30). Wolsey 'never lives in a single reality, but in a shifting, shadow-mesh of diplomatic possibilities' (27) and 'the recent past arranges itself only in patterns acknowledged by his superior mind, and agreeable to his eye' (28). By recalling the structural discipline of theatrical technique and linking it with her own novelistic method, Mantel acknowledges her form's participation in the alchemical recombination of history for the purposes of the present.

The combination of ancient and early-modern theatre in the preliminaries reflects textual inter-play of classical and early-modern thought, redolent of the cultural transitions of sixteenth-century Europe. The theatre is both public and private. It represents the collectiveness of the classical age described by Foucault as a 'civilization of spectacle' (1977: 216). On the other hand, Bonzoli explains that theatre was seen by Camillo as an 'artificial mind' that 'projects outside the soul those images with which, universally, man perceives the world' (2001: 159). Techniques of memory following Camillo's innovations became 'a matter of constructing an actual mental theatre in which one places the characters that are needed' and those 'who practise the art of memory have to function like directors or playwrights' (2001: 159). The novel, located mainly as it is, in Cromwell's thoughts, works accordingly as his artificial mind, externalizing the interior spectacle of a mental theatre which is set at key points, in a hall.

The falling roof of Christendom

Crucial to *Wolf Hall* is an embedded narrative that centres upon a hall. This room has multiple meanings related to space, time and memory; among them, invention of the Method of Loci. The story of how the art of memory came to be invented originates with Cicero and is reproduced, via Yates, by Mantel's choric narrator. At a nobleman's banquet, a poet called Simonides chants a poem in praise of his host but because he includes a passage praising the twins Castor and Pollux, his host will agree to pay only half the agreed fee. Later Simonides receives a message saying that two young men wish to see him outside. He duly leaves the banqueting hall but finds no one (Mantel 2009: 157, 158). As he turns back inside, he hears 'the cries of the dying as the roof of the hall collapsed. Of all the diners, he was the only one left alive.' The dead are 'broken and disfigured' to the extent that they cannot be recognized. In order to help relatives to retrieve their kin, Simonides is able to identify the dead of the collapsed hall by recalling location – 'linking the dead to their names, he worked from the seating plan in his head' (158). Mantel's version stresses the importance of correlating memory with the 'moment of historical change' which Michael Gardiner argues (2013: 66), the English emphasis on continuity tends to occlude: 'He [Simonides] remembered exactly where everyone was sitting, at the moment the roof fell in' (Mantel 2009: 158). The emphasis on relative positions denotes the importance of context.

The collapsing hall develops as extended metaphor through association of the falling roof with the subsidence of Christendom and elision of Cromwell's identity with that of Simonides. Following a supper at the house of the merchant Bonvisi with Thomas More, Chapuys and others associated with the old order of Christendom (an event whose 'whole purpose', Cromwell realizes, has been 'to warn him off' his impending alliance with the Boleyns) Simonides's story is re-enacted (196). In this case, Cromwell is in the role of Simonides while Richard Cromwell and Rafe Sadler take the parts of Castor and Pollux. Like Simonides's host Scopas, Bonvisi objects to Cromwell's divided allegiances. At the end of the evening, Cromwell 'looks around the room', remembering the positioning of guests at the table: 'That's where the Lord Chancellor sat. On his left, the hungry merchants' and imagines the placement of other key players in unfolding events: 'There is a place set for Lady Anne [...] There is a place for William Tyndale, and one for the Pope'. Mirroring, almost exactly, the words of the Simonides narrative, a servant tells him that 'two young gentlemen are outside, master, asking for you by name' (196). Cromwell reflects at this point that:

> He will remember it, the fatal placement: if it proves fatal. That soft hiss and whisper, of stone destroying itself; that distant sound of walls sliding, of plaster crumbling, of rubble crashing on to fragile human skulls? That is the sound of the roof of Christendom, falling on the people below. (196)

The overlapping identities of Simonides and Cromwell imply the latter's control of what is remembered and how. The hall at this point represents 'Christendom' and its place in the novel's title suggests reader participation in Cromwell's 'one last look' before the medieval world of European cohesion is brought down in favour of the state power he engineers. The imagined obliteration of the banqueters recalls what Bolzoni terms 'the art of forgetting'. These were techniques recommended by the teachers of memory for clearing the mind of unwanted images consisting of imagined scenarios 'characterized by a crescendo of destructive violence' and subsequently given material form by Protestant iconoclasm (2001: 143).

Recurring features of the art of forgetting, such as burning, are replicated in Mantel's depictions of a state judicial discipline which reduces people to 'thick sludgy ash' (Mantel 2009: 356). The reader's knowledge that Cromwell himself will eventually be destroyed by the power he augments lends dramatic irony. Unlike Simonides however, Cromwell understands that *memoria* bestows *providentia* and believes he can steer the future. The hall is what Yates terms 'his memory building' but it is also his inner theatre where he plots the future (1992: 18). An example of this occurs in the novel's sequel, *Bring Up the Bodies*, when following a meeting with Norfolk and Surrey, he 'closes his eyes. He sits, his breathing calm. In his mind, a picture appears. A lofty hall. Into which he commands a table' (Mantel 2012a: 194). Around this mental table, Cromwell assembles the figures he will destroy – the Courtneys and the Poles. He is again identified, this time by the seating arrangements, with the humble Simonides: in contrast to 'the weighty chair' occupied by each of the guests, Cromwell sits on 'a humble three-legged stool, down at the end of the table. He gazes up at his betters' (196). The 'magnificent hall' of *Wolf Hall* is more than Cromwell's memory and imagination; it represents his England recombined:

> He glances up at the beams. Up there are carved and painted the faces of the dead: More, Fisher, the cardinal, Katherine the queen. Below them, the flower of living England. Let us hope the roof doesn't fall in. (2012a: 196)

Cromwell's identity as memorial wolf is signalled by a predatory metaphor at Thomas More's trial – 'He thinks, I remembered you, Thomas More, but you didn't remember me. You never even saw me coming' – that exemplifies a language of hunting threaded through the text often associated specifically with wolves (2009: 640).

The Method of Loci

The Method of Loci is the system used by Simonides to identify the bodies in the hall and marks his invention of artificial memory. 'In Italy' Cromwell 'learned a memory system, so he can remember everything' (2009: 156). This system of memorization involves the placing of imaginary objects at various points within a fictional space, attaching words or images to them and then mentally travelling from one to the other. It is part of a larger pattern in the novel, of pictures as memory triggers and its classical function as rhetorical aide-memoire, affords insight into a pre-literate imagination where language and sensation were integrated into what Yates terms 'faculties of intense visual memorization which we have lost' (1992: 20). The notion of history/memory as a carefully plotted journey through imaginary space is evident in Cromwell's belief that the system helps him to 'remember everything: every stage of how he got here' (Mantel 2009: 156). Later on, however, he wonders 'Why is it that his life as a child doesn't seem to fit, one bit with the next?' (357). The instability of his recollection is illuminated in *Bring Up the Bodies* when Gardiner reveals the cause of the paternal beating with which *Wolf Hall* opens. Cromwell has forgotten that he stabbed a boy to death (2012a: 72).

The discrepancy between Cromwell's version of the system and that of Yates who draws directly upon the classical texts may explain the incoherence of his memories. Cromwell's process creates the images before identifying the loci – 'When you have made the images, you place them about the world in locations you choose, each one with its parcel of words, of figures, which they will yield you on demand' (2009: 216). According to Yates, place and order are primary (1992: 22). Cromwell's inconsistency lies in the instinct to disconnect image and space, seen, for example, in his rejection of experiential maps of England with 'battlements prettily inked, their chases and parks marked by lines of bushy trees, with drawings of harts and bristling boar' for ones simply showing 'where the bridges are, and to have a note of the distance between them' (Mantel 2009: 648, 649). The older, illustrated maps represent a sensory relationship with space which supersedes the literate. Furthermore, Cromwell's desire to fix in time, geographical relation and proportion, ignores progress and process, the fact that 'England is always remaking herself' and that, like the shifting surfaces of the loci, 'the histories that trail us; the faces of the dead fade into other faces, as a spine of hills into the mist' (629).

In foregrounding ephemeral images, Cromwell de-couples the present from the past. A clearly ordered set of loci is not only essential for understanding historical process as suggested above; it is important because the images are merely for functional short-term memorization. The time symbol of Prudence, found in Camillo's theatre, emphasizes the interdependence of intelligence, providence and memory – the importance of understanding 'every stage'. According to Yates, the loci 'remain when what is written on them has been effaced and are ready to be written on again' (1992: 23). Conversely, Cromwell promotes Tudor shortcuts to legacy, denying the historical plurality signified by the loci's palimpsest. In the classical system, pasts co-exist but in Cromwell's England, this continuity is lost through the abrupt re-branding of locales. Reformation effacement of Catholic iconography forced rapid cultural change and Mantel highlights the extension of this practice to the political sphere. For example, 'Gardiner's arms have been burned off the paintwork' of his boat (2009: 570), Katherine's 'old one, rebadged' (462) and the cardinal's arms are painted out to 'leave a space' (271). For Cromwell personally, it matters that after his death 'his name will be there. His arms will be carved over the doorways' because he desires legacy (583). He lives with one eye to posterity but denies this to others. Repeated references to the visual erasure of inconvenient pasts are a reminder of political 'edit' (649) but the novel also acknowledges persistence of the relationship between the invisible dead and their spaces. The deceased Wolsey remains integral to Cromwell's world – 'In these courts, Wolsey lingers; he built them' (270) and his legacy is incorporated into Cromwell's own coat of arms and therefore into his very identity (421). England is depicted as a multi-layered site of historical loss which is nevertheless haunted by an embedded past that is denied form. There are 'loose rattling bones under the paving of the Tower, those bones bricked into staircases and mulched into the Thames mud' (97). Cromwell senses its presence in the river's 'always moving water', 'the drowned men with bony hands swimming'. He knows that on 'the mud and shingle there are cast up belt buckles, fragments of glass, small warped coins with the kings' faces washed away' (271). For Cromwell, 'there cannot be new things in England. There can be old things freshly presented, or new things that pretend to be old' (118). Textiles are recycled – notably Wolsey's 'scarlet clothes' which 'will be cut up and become other garments' (265). This re-presentation recalling the alchemical art of recombination resonates with the historical Tudors' imperative to signal ancient royal descent. 'You can't know Albion [...] unless you can go back before Albion was thought of' says Wolsey (94). The palimpsest of the classical Method of Loci is a layering of pasts as articulated by *Wolf Hall*'s choric narrator: 'Beneath every history, another history' (66). Cromwell's dislocation of time reflects Escobedo's analysis of sixteenth-century English nationhood in which he identifies 'a perception of historical loss' (2004: 3).

The Method of Loci is spectacle and theatricality. Cromwell's reliance upon images for memory (which include saints – 'St Ursula a crossbow, St Jerome a scythe' [Mantel 2009: 216]) apparently contradicts his willingness to collude in 'picking up a chisel and gouging the sapphire eyes out of saints' (533). It is performative in its emphasis on plot: Cromwell keeps his images 'in strict order, in the gallery of his mind's eye' and upon *dramatis personae* – 'it is because he is used to making these images that his head is peopled with the cast of a thousand plays, ten thousand interludes'. In its requirement for visual impact – 'it is no use hoping to remember with the help of common objects, familiar faces. One needs startling juxtapositions, images that are more or less peculiar, ridiculous, even indecent' (216) – it reflects the early modern memorial practice, outlined by Bolzoni, of using stock figures, along with shocking signifiers, to represent psychological or behavioural traits. These would 'build a gallery of images in which the invisible takes shape and becomes usable in the theatrical play of representation and metamorphosis' (2001: 173). In this respect therefore, Cromwell's mental methods reflect iconic codes of the sixteenth century as well as the caricature of the masque. The danger of caricature is that it distorts cultural memory as shown by the Hampton Court Interlude that ridicules Wolsey (Mantel 2009: 266). The fact that the plot of *Bring Up the Bodies* pivots upon the Cromwell's intense memory of the interlude testifies to its perceptual influence as well as attributing to Cromwell, Simonides's positional command of memory.

The memory 'machine' of Giulio Camillo

In linking Cromwell with Camillo's innovations, Mantel explores the political power intrinsic to owning memory. Camillo was preeminent modernizer of memory and 'one of the most famous men of the sixteenth century' (Yates 1992: 135). According to Bolzoni, his planned theatre of memory would 'mean celebrating the entire potential of *imaginatio*; to build the images of memory would also mean recreating the world' (2001: 140). There are references throughout *Wolf Hall* to Camillo and his structure. For example, Cromwell 'thinks about Guido[*sic*] Camillo in Paris, pacing and fretting between the wooden walls of his memory machine' (Mantel 2009: 494) and claims to 'remember Calais, the alchemists, the memory machine' (614). He clearly understands that, to paraphrase Bolzoni, re-building national images of memory means recreating England.

Camillo's planned structure 'is a theatre on the ancient Vitruvian plan' quoted in the novel's preliminaries (472). According to Yates, it rises in seven grades divided by seven gangways. On each gangway are seven gates and on each gate are many images. The structure unites the classical and Renaissance memorial arts. It starts with the images on the doors but under the images are drawers or boxes containing masses of papers on which are speeches by Cicero on subjects related to the images. In ordering, categorizing and linking image to text, the Theatre dispenses with the ephemerality of classical remembrance by assigning knowledge to 'eternal places' (1992: 148). It encapsulates the transition from a sensory memory of 'loops and flashes' to cognitive order and literacy (149).

Cromwell explains to Henry that it is 'a system of human knowledge. Like a library, but as if – can you imagine a library in which each book contains another book, and a smaller book inside that? Yet it is more than that' (Mantel 2009: 472). Camillo imagined an aerial view of a 'vast forest' (Yates 1992: 147) but Cromwell's vision is oriented towards closure and constraint: it is 'the abyss of the divine', a 'device' of 'crannies and crevices' (Mantel 2009: 647). It reflects his clerical attachment to data and a mental landscape characterized by reductive language:

> Suppose within every book there is another book, and within every letter on every page another volume constantly unfolding; but these volumes take no space on the desk. Suppose knowledge could be reduced to a quintessence, held within a picture, a sign, held within a place which is no place. Suppose the human skull were to become capacious, spaces opening inside it, humming chambers like beehives. (482)

The layering of Cromwell's conceptualization corresponds with multiple images of enfolding within the novel and assimilates thematically with the choric narrative (66). Through Cromwell's mechanized version of the Theatre, Mantel ironically anticipates the power conferred by late-modern digital technology: 'these enfolded boxes of wood' will enable him 'to see all the forms and customs that will one day inhabit the earth' (615).

Significantly, Mantel diverges from Yates in the structure's name. In *Wolf Hall*, theatre is replaced with 'machine' – 'a thinking machine that marches forward as if it were alive' (615). The term is not anachronistic – the *Oxford English Dictionary* records its first use as being in the sixteenth-century 'originally denoting a structure'. In its atomizing bureaucracy, its compartmentalization, its affording of an omnipotent gaze, it relates to Foucault's concept of the all-seeing state 'panoptic machine' which gives exclusive access to 'the instantaneous view of a great multitude' and for which figures like Cromwell laid the foundations (1977: 217). Camillo's structure embodies the early-modern social change – a world 'turning on its axis' – that Cromwell senses and implements (Mantel 2009: 495). The direction of the Reformation was away from the collective experience of public spectacle towards the privacy of text. Camillo's inversion of the theatrical function where, instead of an audience watching a play, there is a solitary spectator on the stage gazing at the auditorium, precisely encapsulates this trajectory (Yates 1992: 141). Cromwell recognizes the creative possibilities of commanding knowledge but his vision is more instrumental than Camillo's. The former's interiorizing conceptualization of the structure as 'machine' seems more prescient than Camillo's panoramic vision of coming 'to the knowledge of things from their causes and not from their effects' (147). Cromwell's panoptic 'machine' reflects the reverse – Foucault's modern state which 'treats actions in terms of their results, introduces bodies into a machinery, forces into an economy' (1977: 210). Cromwell's analytical gaze over the past can conjure historical precedents and channel them into an economy of justification for Henry's snatched supremacy. According to Bolzoni, Camillo likened the inner human body 'rendered visible in a theatre of anatomy' to being able 'to dissect texts and penetrate their compactness' so that 'the mechanisms of their structures can be forced out and made visible' (2001: 59). Subsequently, his idea gave rise to 'rhetoric machines' in which 'the elements derived from the anatomy of the literary tradition' are 'revitalized simply by inserting them in a new organism' (66, 67). Cromwell's textual alchemy forges new from old to re-brand change as continuity. He reflects that if 'people don't like new ideas, let them have old ones. If they want precedents, he has precedents' (Mantel 2009: 588). Through memorial recombination 'he has already done much that no one else has even dreamed of' (611). Theatre and machine, Camillo's structure serves as metaphor for Cromwell's remix of history for the changing English state. The trauma of this recalibration is spatially signified on the day of More's trial by the Thames 'bubbling like some river in Hell' (or alchemist's pot) as he pits 'the living against the dead' (637).

A further point here is that, as shown, *Wolf Hall* itself anatomizes the elements of historical narrative and insert them into a new organism. Camillo's structure (as theatre and machine) can therefore be regarded as a reflexive metaphor for Mantel's own reinvention of the genre.

Wolf Cromwell: The time symbol of the Memory Theatre

Wolf Hall is more than the intended destination at the novel's conclusion – the next stage of history. The title is also linked to Prudence's symbolic use of animals for temporal dimensions (Yates 1992: 147). As demonstrated, the wolf's command of *memoria* enables navigation of present and future. Cromwell's identification with Simonides and Camillo suggests that he is ultimately synonymous with the wolf and that the hall, his memory building, is his domain.

This is not to dismiss the title's connection with the retrospective future which is signalled by its being the name of Jane Seymour's family home and by references to her liminal presence. Past and future are elided at the very end of the novel when Cromwell's planning of the King's summer progress comes to symbolize his directing of Henry's (and England's) destiny: he plans five days at Wolf Hall (Mantel 2009: 650). Cromwell hopes to shape the future by conquering the 'buried empire' of the past with laws 'like spells' that 'make things happen'. As wolf, he will 'chase' the dead but is aware of 'another landscape [...] where he fears his commissioners cannot reach' (575). His premonition of failure reinforces parallels with Camillo, as do allusions in the novel to a tale recounted by Yates, of Camillo diverting a lion (symbol in his Theatre of *intelligentsia*: the present) which seemingly affirmed his power (138). Cromwell in turn, reflects that 'it is a great thing, to be able to divert the wrath of the Lion of England' (340). The lion is both metaphor for Henry VIII and heraldic icon of the English State. It signifies Cromwell's political *intelligentsia* but also its limits: his abilities and Camillo's serve the purposes of kings.

Cromwell strategically effaces histories for political ends, so it is ironic that, regarding the personal, his natural memory reflects the indeterminacy he exploits. Following the deaths of his family, the dead become 'less individual forms and faces than a solid aggregated mass' (154). Parenthesized interrogative pronouns deployed within free indirect thought suggests uncertainty of recall: 'She was –what? – about twenty years old' (2009: 66). This example is also a wry in-joke alluding to historical conjecture about Boleyn's age which, as Antonia Fraser remarks, 'can never be known with absolute certainty (like so much about Anne Boleyn)' (1992: 115). He is well aware of 'how the innocent end; used by the sin-sodden and the cynical, pulped to their purpose and ground under their heels' (Mantel 2009: 498) and of course, re-assembled in his cultural memory machine. As he proceeds in his pulping work for Henry, bonds with his own past fade – 'He says to himself, I never think of Anselma now, she is just the woman in the tapestry, the woman in the weave'. Thoughts on the woman who resembles Sheba in the tapestry are prompted by reading the inscriptions in his wife's Book of Hours. In a revisionist act recalling both the wolf and the art of forgetting, he 'holds the pages down flat, and strikes out the name of her first husband'. His wolfishness is immediately confirmed when he tells Christophe that 'the wolves all died when the great forests were cut down. That howling you hear is only the Londoners' (499). Furthermore, an example of reflexive narrative – 'we rewrite their lives' – elides the historical novel with politicized national pseudo-memory; its imaginative space therefore suggesting that *Wolf Hall* is 'Wolf Hall'.

To conclude, I suggest that Cromwell is synonymous with Simonides, Camillo and the wolf in the symbol of Prudence while the hall is both memory building and spatial metaphor for the England he is attempting to re-shape. Both this imaginative space and that of the Memory Theatre represent the changing psyche of early-modern Europe, the emerging machinery of contemporary state power. The novel depicts an age shaped by a philosophical preoccupation with collection, classification and the imaginative potential of knowledge. On the one hand, Mantel's Cromwellian England exemplifies 'the world' that is 'turning on its axis', that is 'not what it was'. On the other, it is shown to be a place where both Tudor and contemporary narratives have decontextualized and de-democratized the past: where the story of global shifts has been nationally inflected to consolidate minority control. It is a domain where, in the words of Queen Katherine, Cromwell is 'the blacksmith'. who 'makes his own tools' (291) to re-shape a national memory and identity which can be seen still to resonate with today's British view of 'what England is' (338).

Bibliography

Bolzoni, L. (2001), *The Gallery of Memory: Literary and Iconographic Models in the Age of the Printing Press*, translated by Jeremy Parzen, Toronto: University of Toronto Press.

Escobedo, A. (2004), *Nationalism and Historical Loss in Renaissance England*, New York: Cornell University Press.

Fraser, A. (1992), *The Six Wives of Henry VIII*, London: Weidenfeld and Nicholson.

Foucault, M. (1977), *Discipline and Punish: The Birth of the Prison*, translated by Alan Sheridan, London: Penguin.

Gardiner, M. (2013), *The Constitution of English Literature: The State, the Nation and the Canon*, London: Bloomsbury Academic.

Mantel, H. (2009), *Wolf Hall*, London: Fourth Estate.

Mantel, H. (2012a), *Bring Up the Bodies*, London: Fourth Estate.

Mantel, H. (2012b), 'How I Came to Write Wolf Hall', *The Guardian*, 7 December. Available online: https://www.the guardian.com/books/2012/dec/07/bookclub-hilary-mantel-wolf-hall (accessed 15 May 2016).

Mantel, H. (2016), Personal communication, 17 May.

Marquand, D. (2014), *Mammon's Kingdom: An Essay on Britain, Now*, London: Penguin.

Yates, F. (1992), *The Art of Memory*, London: Random House.

3

Making History Otherwise: *Learning to Talk* and *The Assassination of Margaret Thatcher*

Eileen Pollard

This chapter will explore ambiguous representations of history in Hilary Mantel's two short story collections to date, *Learning to Talk* (2003) and *The Assassination of Margaret Thatcher* (2014). The chapter will consider the figure of the ellipsis, which is traced metaphorically and literally in the stories, as a pertinent means by which to read them, including the titular 'The Assassination of Margaret Thatcher' in Mantel's more recent collection. Despite the media furore that followed the publication of this book, this chapter will argue that it is *less* the fantasy of the shooting of the premier that disturbed, but rather the pervasive sense of ambiguity. The uncertainty of individual biographies in *Learning to Talk* develops into an unsettling national narrative in her 2014 collection. For example, as stated in the titular story concerning Thatcher, 'note the cold wind that blows through [the door] when you open it a crack. History could always have been otherwise' (2014: 239–240).

*****

The 'workings of cause and effect are veiled' (2003), so writes Sophie Ratcliffe of the short stories in *Learning to Talk*. And it is true that Hilary Mantel uses the short story to demonstrate the fragility of personal narratives, and she does so by privileging the unseen, the ambiguous and the elliptical. This chapter will illustrate that this emphasis on the indeterminate is further reflected by the form of her two collections to date. Separated by eleven years, both *Learning to Talk* (2003) and *The Assassination of Margaret Thatcher* (2014) blur the line between short story and memoir in complex and significant ways. While the two texts are 'arranged' differently, they share several distinctive formal characteristics in common: an embedded memoir, dedications to people made explicit reference to in one of the stories, Northern Ireland, ambiguity, grotesque characters, retrospection and the inclusion of verses from popular song – all of which contribute in different ways to a destabilizing of the idea of a 'personal' narrative.

In her *Times Literary Supplement* review of *Learning to Talk*, Ratcliffe also suggests that 'these fictional autobiographies are, above all, fictions about autobiography' (2003). Such a combination could perhaps be classified as 'auto fiction', but in Mantel's work the truth is acknowledged as plural the moment writing begins and there is no sense of a single, stable 'autobiography' ever grounding or tethering the text. In an extract from *Giving Up the Ghost*, deliberately republished at the end of *Learning to Talk*, Mantel paraphrases Wilde, implying that the truth is seldom pure and never simple: 'The story of my childhood is a complicated sentence that I am always trying to finish [...] It resists finishing [...] I am haunted by the ghosts of my own sense impressions, which re-emerge when I try to write, and shiver between the lines' (2006: 144). This sense of resistance as inherent within the process of life writing in particular suggests a postmodern lens on these short story collections might be more appropriate than an autobiographical one. Postmodernism famously problematized the relationship between writing and truth, in part by exposing autobiography as reliant upon the same mainstays as fictional narratives (Hutcheon 2002).

This chapter will illustrate the pertinence of these ideas for reading Mantel's short stories by considering the premise from which the first collection emerged, and by outlining the nature of the gap, or ellipsis, often at the 'centre' of the stories themselves. In his seminal critical exploration of the double, Nicholas Royle's *The Uncanny* describes the duplicitous nature of writing: 'Writing is the double, writing is a double writing, from the beginning' (2003: 188). Significantly this sense or imagery of duplicity traces the first collection of short stories as a project from its inception. *Learning to Talk* was published in July 2003 just two months after Mantel's memoir *Giving Up the Ghost*, which was much more widely reviewed and recognized. The collection is mysterious, duplicitous. Ratcliffe again has characterized the intertextual relationship in the following way: 'The memoir, [Mantel] argued, is an attempt to utter the self, while *Learning to Talk* "is done by the doubles, the triples, the variants of myself ... small sub-personalities delegated to try on unused lives"' (2003). Therefore, not only is the collection itself a double, a satellite to *Giving Up the Ghost*, like a moon orbiting the planet of the memoir, the narrators and protagonists are *themselves* inherently duplicitous too.

The argument here is that writing as a double writing can be observed in the déjà vu of the gaps and omissions in the two collections. Again, the memoir extract points the way, appearing retrospectively at the end of *Learning to Talk*: 'I know, too, that once a family has acquired a habit of secrecy, memories begin to distort, because its members confabulate to cover the gaps in the facts; you have to make some sort of sense of what's going on around you, so you cobble together a narrative as best you can' (2006: 145–146). It is the imagery and expression of these gaps that mark the joins in these short story narratives, initiated perhaps in the memoir but easily detectable in the structures of the first collection as well as the second. For example, in 'How Shall I Know You' from *The Assassination of Margaret Thatcher*, the biographer narrator's migraine threads the story with images of visual absence/disturbance, hallucination and eclipse, inscribing the ellipsis, lacuna, caesura: 'My migraine aura was now so severe that the world on the left had ceased to exist, except as an intermittent yellow flash' (2014: 160). Then, again, in 'The Heart Fails without Warning', the confusing gap between a mother's speech and her meaning is attributed to another biological fault line or fissure: 'Often what she said meant something else entirely, but they were used to it; early menopause, Morna said' (170). Tracing and analysing such ellipses in stories from both the collections is the method by which this chapter will demonstrate Mantel's use of the form to expose the inherent vulnerability of personal narratives.

However, any analysis of the missing 'centres' of individual stories also requires a consideration of the wider form of the collections themselves first. In Ratcliffe's review of *Learning to Talk*, tellingly interspersed with quotations from Mantel as if through interview,[1] provides some clues about how these short stories, all previously published as stand-alone tales, emerged as a collection:

> One recognizes that in both memoir and short-story collection [Mantel] is pacing over the same ground [...] The interest lies in the repetitions between the two works, and in the reasons behind this unusual act of self-plagiarism [...] *Learning to Talk* can be read as a literary notebook that reveals her mental efforts to look into and arrange the past. (2003)

The fact that the stories were published previously, that the connections between the stories and the memoir are made explicit by the inclusion of the extract, as well as the sense of effort that has gone into this arrangement –

taken together suggest that *Learning to Talk* is closer to being a short story *sequence* than a traditional collection. More often now referred to as short story cycles, such linked or connected stories published in one volume, were presented as 'a distinct genre [...] worthy of serious attention' (Boddy 1995) in *Modern American Short Story Sequences*, edited by J. Gerald Kennedy in 1995. This groundbreaking text considers how sequences can be read in terms of both the connections between stories and, significantly for Mantel's work, by paying 'attention to discontinuities' (Boddy 1995). Some of the essays in this volume also 'discuss the issues involved in the emergence of a sequence as a published book' (Boddy 1995), which is also important since Mantel had a clear vision of what she wished *Learning to Talk* to achieve as a book. Following on from (and referring back to) the memoir published just two months earlier, the two texts must have been composed simultaneously. They are therefore the second installment in a 'sequence' yet also offer a cycle in that the stories culminate with the extract, thus looping back to the memoir.

Also in 1995, Maggie Dunn and Ann Morris published their definition of a sequence or cycle, preferring instead the term composite novel: 'The composite novel is a literary work composed of shorter texts that – though individually complete and autonomous – are interrelated in a coherent whole according to one or more organizing principles' (xiii). For example, Dunn and Morris consider James Joyce's *Dubliners* a composite novel that is organized according to the principle of 'common setting'. They also identify two other organizing principles, potentially of interest for thinking through *Learning to Talk* as a sequence, cycle or composite novel. The first is the frequently used single, unifying protagonist 'upon whom a work's text-pieces focus or around whom they cohere [...] this may be a narrator protagonist' (15). Seemingly chiming with this principle, Ratcliffe again makes the following observation: 'While Hilary Mantel chooses a different speaker for each of her tales, all share [the same] accent, stemming, it seems from the same Northern village' (2003). The title story concerns the narrator's experiences of elocution lessons and examinations, and all the stories are unified by first person narrator protagonists and their accents and places of origin.

Take, for example, the opening lines or first few sentences of 'King Billy Is a Gentleman', 'Curved Is the Line of Beauty' and the title story concerning elocution 'Learning to Talk'. These are, respectively, 'I cannot get out of my mind, now, the village where I was born, just out of the curl of the city's tentacles' (1), 'When I was in my middle childhood my contemporaries started to disappear [...] some of them [...] were found buried on the moors. I was born on the edge of this burial ground' (45) and 'When I was a child I went to school in a Derbyshire mill village' (77). There is not only a sense of repetition to these openings, but also of reset, and for anyone familiar with the geography of Hadfield, Derbyshire, where Mantel was born, the 'common setting' becomes clear. For readers who know the area, *Learning to Talk* is both map and guide, for example: the references to Manchester, Hadfield is just twenty miles away, linked by the 'regular train service' (1) mentioned on the first page of the first story; the 'pink housing estate' (1) is Hattersley, built to rehouse those cleared from the slums in Gorton, Manchester. Infamously this estate was once home to Ian Brady and Myra Hindley and it is the murders committed by Brady and Hindley that are alluded to in 'Curved Is the Line of Beauty' and the 'burial ground' referred to is Saddleworth Moor. The 'calm steel-surfaced reservoirs' (5) and the 'school [...] situated handily, so as to increase the risk between two bends in the road' (46) are also instantly recognizable to locals from such descriptions. There are also numerous 'real' places laid down, almost like markers, or parts of a picture or puzzle: the Methodist Central Hall, Manchester, Derwent, Ladybower Dam, Ashopton, Bamford, Waterside, Glossop. Ratcliffe argues that this repetition of 'wet roofs and mill chimneys' is 'stage Northern' and, what is more, that it is 'intentional' (2003).[2] Yet all these places are grid references both for a *specific* geography and for a geography of a particular time. They offer points on a compass and illustrate that the text itself can be read like a map, while also helping to form an imagery of duplicity because they are after all merely fictional doubles of the 'real' thing.

This place or 'common setting' is also present in 'Comma' in the later collection *The Assassination of Margaret Thatcher*, and what is potentially even more unifying is the recurrence there of what Terry Castle has described as Mantel's 'knowing, if not cynical, first-person female narrators' (2014). However, this raises the question, is it narrator singular or plural? As well as the single protagonist as an organizing principle for cycles or sequences, Dunn and Morris also identify the more complex 'collective protagonist', which is 'often used to forge complex interconnective links in composite novels that cut a wide swath through historical time [...] As we define it, the collective protagonist is a "composite" – perhaps literally [...] or perhaps figuratively' (15). This definition fits more snuggly with Mantel's own earlier statement about *Learning to Talk*, that it is 'done', or arranged 'by the doubles, the triples, the variants of myself ... small sub-personalities delegated to try on unused lives' (Ratcliffe 2003). Moreover, the 'composite' or portmanteau character concept recurs throughout all Mantel's work, the short stories and the novels. For example, Fludd in Mantel's 1989 novel of the same name, is both 1950s curate and seventeenth-century alchemist, and alchemy itself is described in the 'Note' to that novel as having both a 'literal' and a 'figurative' meaning (1990, n.p.). Therefore the 'composite' is perhaps the most appropriate 'organising' principle to consider when reading Mantelian short stories, beginning with *Learning to Talk*, but recognizing that the same may apply to her second collection too. After all, in reading *The Assassination of Margaret Thatcher*, Castle also described 'Mantel's imaginative world [as] all of a piece' (2014).

As explained, *Learning to Talk* was published just two months after Mantel's memoir came out in May 2003. It is comprised of six stories, all previously published elsewhere between 1992 and 2001, as well as a short extract from *Giving Up the Ghost* that is accompanied by a very brief introduction by an unknown hand. In the opening story, 'King Billy Is a Gentleman' (a reference to a song about William of Orange) the narrator is Liam, a Catholic who grows up to become a lawyer. Liam describes the tensions in his village, especially in terms of religion, and those within his own family's household following the arrival of a new lodger. Their neighbours Bob and Myra, or more specifically Myra, cause a stink about Liam's mother's 'immoral way of life' (Mantel 2004: 6) after Liam's father leaves and the lodger takes his place. The difficulties extend to Liam's relations with the neighbour's children, Philip and Suzy, and the acrimony is even more deeply felt because the family are Protestant. In fact, it is Suzy who sings out the jaunt taken for the title: 'King Billy is a gentleman/He wears a watch and chain/The dirty Pope's a beggar/And he begs down our lane' (13). By the end of the story, Liam has qualified and moved away, but while on a visit home he learns that Philip killed himself some years ago: 'Philip had constructed, in Bobby's garden shed, a sugar and weedkiller bomb […] it had been popularized by events in Belfast' (19). This is significant because in this initial story Mantel signals her intention to address questions about Irish identity, sectarianism and The Troubles, which thread themselves all the way through this collection and indeed the later one too.

In the second story, 'Destroyed', this time the narrator is unnamed and female, and there is a stepfather whose name she is made to take: 'My surname was changed officially […] So the years began in which I pretended to be someone else's daughter' (34). She is given a puppy for her eighth birthday, Victor, but her stepfather cannot bear that the runt will be destroyed, so they adopt him too and call him Mike. The two dogs are wildly different, Victor is calm and placid, Mike[3] frenetic and impossible to train. Like many of the stories it is laced with the image of the double or composite: 'When somebody went out of the door I always wondered who or what they'd come back as, and whether they'd come back at all' (25). Interestingly, in light of the narrator's uncertainty, Victor turns vicious and Mike first goes blind, then, once the family have moved, goes missing. 'Curved Is the Line of Beauty' is also written from the perspective of a Catholic child, growing up on the edge of moorland, and is similarly nameless and female. This story too includes a visitor to the household, Jack, who usurps the narrator's father and on a trip in his car to see an African friend living in Birmingham, her mother sheepishly explains: '"When we are visiting Jacob, don't say 'Jack'. It's not suitable. I want you to say," and here she began to struggle with words "Daddy … Daddy Jack"' (58).

'Learning to Talk', the title story and therefore a potential key to the meaning of its arrangement, is again from the perspective of a woman who 'went to school in a Derbyshire mill village' and later, when she was eleven, moved to Cheshire. The story concerns the need to learn to 'talk proper' and to acquire the necessary shibboleths to get on in life. The nameless narrator attends elocution lessons in Cheshire with a Miss Webster who runs a shop selling wool and baby clothes, has a 'precariously genteel, Mancunian with icing' (80) accent, only one lung and a previous history as a northern repertory actress. It is a very funny story, which culminates with the narrator arriving for her final oral examination at the Manchester Methodist Central Hall only to be told by Miss Webster that her boots were 'not proper dress' (88) and would not do for the examiners. Miss Webster provides her own shoes, 'court shoes, of fake crocodile; they had ferocious points in front, and three-and-a-half-inch spike heels' (89), they are also two sizes too big. After the narrator's reading of the set piece from *Henry VIII*, where Queen Katharine remonstrates with the King, a performance 'most remarkable from the ankle down' (90), the narrator resolves to keep her mouth shut and become a writer.

'Third Floor Rising' describes the nameless, female, eighteen-year-old narrator's experience of working in a department store (where her mother is a supervisor) the summer before she goes to university. There is a clear and recognizable geography here too, this time for Mancunians; Affleck and Brown, near Oldham Street, mother and daughter walking arm in arm up to Piccadilly train station, past the NHS clinic for donating blood. The final story 'The Clean Slate' similarly concerns a nameless female narrator, this time, intriguingly, a novelist: 'I assume you've read my new novel, *The Clean Slate*' (126). This aspect links well with a story in *The Assassination of Margaret Thatcher*, 'How Shall I Know You', which similarly takes a writer as its protagonist, in this case one seeking to emulate more recognizable ones, 'come now, what would Anita Brookner do?' (Mantel 2014: 156). In 'The Clean Slate', the author is attempting to gather further information about her family's origins from her mother, Veronica, who (like the now uncannily familiar narrator) is reminiscent of other mothers in the volume: 'She likes to make mysteries and imply she has secret knowledge' (Mantel 2003: 124). However, it is this final story that articulates the significance of the 'ellipsis' most explicitly as a motif uniting Mantel's short stories. The narrator hails from a drowned village, therefore her 'origins' are buried, inaccessible, beyond what can be accounted for. More than this, as a child, the narrator always imagined the 'drowning' of the village as a sudden flood, that the villagers were driven out by the water in the middle of knitting, or shelling peas, 'folding away the morning paper with a phrase half read, an ellipsis that would last their lifetimes' (124). Bizarrely, these images of gaps or lacuna could themselves become an organizing principle, in much the same way that paralysis recurs again and again, just as much as the Dublin setting, in Joyce's *Dubliners*. Moreover, there is a link between the uncertainty of such gaps and the ambiguity inherent to such a composite narrator. These gaps are what brings together, or unites, these composite narrators, as they all lead such 'gaping' lives.

As stated previously Castle writes of *The Assassination of Margaret Thatcher*: 'Despite the phalanx of themes [...] one can't help feeling that Mantel's imaginative world is all of a piece' (2014). Perhaps then, taking the two collections together will reveal something of the organization of each. Castle makes many astute observations about Mantel's style, or rather the oscillation thereof, and the author herself has previously noted that she wants the reader unsure whether to laugh or scream. Castle also notes the significance of what she observes as a 'bleb moment' (2014) in each of the stories. The example she uses is 'Comma', a short story (also mapped onto the specific Derbyshire geography outlined earlier) about two little girls, Mary and Kitty, who become preoccupied by a house on the edge of their village. Mary has seen a child there, who only comes out after dark, who she claims has no feature and whose shape can only be described as like that of a comma. Castle notes that prior to the two girls finally seeing the child (the climax of the story) there is a description of some roses: 'From there we saw that in the beds of this garden the roses were already scorched into heavy brown blebs on the stalk' (Mantel 2014: 43). Castle is not familiar with the word[4] so is forced to interrupt the immersion of being near the Hathaway's house in order to look it up. A bleb is 'a small swelling on the skin; also on plants' or 'a bubble of air in water, glass, etc' (Onions 1978: 202).

Castle's argument is that the image is a forerunner, a moment of prescience, quite literally embedded in the undergrowth of the story. It signals and prefigures the ending when the girls see the child, who has no face, but only the 'negotiating position' (2014: 55) for a face. The meaning of the story is inscribed in this most casual of images, and Castle uses this analysis to illustrate that with each of the stories in the collection, there is such a 'bleb moment'. Not unlike James Runcie in his Culture Show interview with Mantel where he tells her that her fiction makes him feel 'unstable' (2011), Castle similarly describes the 'bleb' effect as 'an eerie ramification of terms' leaving the reader 'off-kilter' (2014). Likewise, a review of *Learning to Talk* in the *Financial Times* links her work together by positing that 'Mantel gets more adventurous, and better and better' (2006, n.p.), and there is a sense of development or even *continuum* in *The Assassination of Margaret Thatcher*. There are similar organizing principles in terms of narration/narrator place or geography, as well as the links to memoir. For example, just as *Learning to Talk* is tethered to *Giving Up the Ghost*, so too is *The Assassination of Margaret Thatcher* bookended by one story previously published as 'memoir' and another based upon a 'real life' reverie. Yet it is still the image of the ellipsis, 'or bubble of air', that really connects the two texts, albeit in a typically ambiguous way. As Castle writes:

> You know you're in the hands of a master storyteller when, as here, some curious yet minor verbal oddity, some seemingly rhetorical blip, turns out to be so cunningly related to a story's metaphorical unfolding. (2014)

When I interviewed Mantel about these 'blips', or ellipses, she suggested that the gap, or lacuna, did not always appear on the page, but that even so 'it went on in the reader's mind' (2015: 1043). This idea of readerly experience relates to Mantel's description of her childhood as 'synesthetic' (2006: 144), which is a neurological phenomenon where the stimulation of one sensory or cognitive pathway triggers the involuntary, automatic stimulation of another. It is a useful paradigm that articulates the breakdown between cause and effect reflected in every level of Mantel's writing, from theme and content right down to linguistic oddities. It is this combination of the elliptical or synesthetic that creates such a consistent emphasis on erasure, traces and gaps across the two collections, as can be seen initially from analysis of the centrality of these images in *Learning to Talk*.

Thus, in 'King Billy Is a Gentleman', it is the narrator's problematic and tense relationship with his protestant neighbour, Philip, that forms the uncrossable void that the story then orbits and skirts. For example, Liam describes the conversations with Philip as 'wary and elliptical' (Mantel 2006: 12) and later that he 'wiped [Philip] from [his] mind' (16).[5] Philip is then literally obliterated when his homemade bomb explodes in his face. Buried within these gaps and cracks is a ghostly vision of Ireland and the IRA, as Liam says 'we all have a buried nature, a secret violence' (11), and this violence that is just below the surface here concerns Irish nationalism. At the end of the story, Liam suggests that it was Ireland that 'got' Philip in the end, and employs a double meaning of the word 'provisional': 'and here I was still alive, one of life's Provisionals' (20), a reference to Ireland that incorporates the ellipsis, the ambiguous, the provisional.

This question of provisionality is approached differently in 'Destroyed'. Through this story about the adoption of two puppies, Mantel is able to explore the uncertain nature of both language and naming. As in the memoir, the duplicitous nature of words is emphasized: 'Until I was older I didn't know widow meant a husband had been there' (23). This sentence is very reminiscent of the child 'ilary's account in *Giving Up the Ghost* that the 'nature' of things remained elusive because of the apparently arbitrary (and changeable) relationship between words and things. In the memoir, interestingly, it is the similarities between a dog and a cow that are 'corrected', leading to the accusation that no adults would say plainly what was what not if they could help it (Mantel 2004: 46). This problematic is thrown into greater relief in 'Destroyed' with the introduction of the motif of 'substitution'. Two stories, or storylines, run parallel both reflecting and echoing one another. The substitution of one dog for another and also one *father* for another, ultimately resulting in the 'loss' of *both* in both sub-plots. The 'father' substitute, which reverberates through the collection like a primal scream, particularly disrupts this child narrator's relationship with meaning, as already quoted: 'When someone went out of the door I always wondered who or what they'd come back as and whether they'd come back at all' (Mantel 2006: 25). This trauma is marked most explicitly though through renaming, when after moving to a new town 'My name changed officially' (34). Retroactively tracing this doubling illustrates its importance here. Ironically (or not) despite the haunting sense of supplement in her life and household, the mother of this story rejects the notion of replacement utterly: 'Substitutions were constantly made, in our house. Though it was said that no one thing was like any other' (28).

The title story of the collection offers a moment of reset, as cited: 'When I was a child I went to school in a Derbyshire mill village, the same school where my mother and my grandmother had learned not very much' (77). It concerns a child's elocution lessons, but it is a story as much about getting-to-the-point-of-writing, or becoming a writer, as it is about learning to talk. After the disastrous final examination where the narrator reads Shakespeare wearing her tutor's incongruous shoes, there comes a rhetorical question:

> Surely it was not necessary to talk for a living? Wouldn't it be possible to keep your mouth shut, and perhaps write things down; perhaps write what Miss Webster would call bucks? (92)

Of course, that is not what the narrator would have called them before she learnt to talk 'proper'. The 'sparrow-like' Miss Webster with only one lung with a voice that is 'correspondingly unimpressive' (80). She is one of Mantel's 'grotesques'; Miss Webster is of this Mantellian short story world, but somehow not of ours. In terms of Mantel getting 'more adventurous [...] as she goes', this is true in terms of characters like Miss Webster, who, when compared with a later character, Kinsella from 'Kinsella in His Hole', she appears by contrast strikingly realistic. Mantel crafts quite a different tone in her short stories than that in her novels, it is another voice but one which remains the same across the short stories, both the collections and those published on their own. Remarkably they hold the same note. There are traces of the novels though, for example, in this elliptical description of the problematic and flawed accumulation of meaning during the elocution lessons:

> So if a short-winded child took a breath in the wrong place, or introduced through ignorance or boredom some nonsensical inflection, it would be taken up by the others, and become definitive, and hang around for years. (86)

Likewise, in *Wolf Hall* Cromwell says to More, a 'lie is no less a lie because it is a thousand years old' (566). The accidental inflection is an early example of Mantel's mistrust of the foundation of how a thing's meaning came to be established.

'Third Floor Rising' is both the most darkly humorous and the most haunting of the stories in this collection, again reminiscent of Runcie's comment that reading Mantel's work makes one feel 'unstable', or what Castle describes as Mantel's 'uncanny moments' (2014). Here, in 'Third Floor Rising' they explicitly concern ghosts though, which creates a link with the Mantel's historical fiction, or breathing life into the dead. The short story is set in a 1970s department store, as already explained our heroine is working there as a shop assistant the summer before she goes to university, and she find there is something odd about the racks of clothes:

> Sometimes, behind some packed rail draped in yellowing calico, behind some pile of boxes whose labels were faded to illegibility, I could sense a movement, a kind of shifting of feet, a murmur: 'Mrs Solomons?' I would call. 'Mrs Segal?' No answer: just the whispered exhalation of worsted and mohair [...] It is easy to imagine that hanging fabric is bulked out by flesh, or that stitch and seam rehearse, after hours, a human shape without bones. (105)

In her first Reith Lecture, Mantel said she had fulfilled the dream of engaging in conversation with the long-dead Cardinal Wolsey (Mantel 2017a). She has also spoken of the bodily cold she has felt following writing the moment of a character's death – in recent years that of a 'real', historic person. Further to that, she described *Beyond Black*, a novel about a medium, as nothing more than a vast preparatory project for the Tudor books (Pollard 2015: 1042). It seems that here, with the hanging fabric, there is an even earlier preparatory project in 'Third Floor Rising'. Elsewhere in this volume, Lucy Arnold has rightly equated fabric with text in Mantel's work, so again, like 'Learning to Talk', it looks as if this story is another statement about becoming a writer; the hollow fabric of the text signalling both possibility and haunting as perhaps the same thing. However, unlike in the Tudor books, where Mantel discombobulates the reader through voice, tense and perspective, here she lurches them from horror to absurdity using tone:

> You had to make categories for the garments that had no name, like the birfurcated items that head office had sent several seasons ago; made of hairy grey-blue tweed, they were some kind of flying suit perhaps, of a kind to be worn by Biggle's nanny [...] later I would aim secret kicks at the flying suits, and torture them by wrapping their legs more tightly around their necks and knotting them behind the hanger. (110–11)

The flying suits are in a made-up category; they catalyse a story through the image of Biggle's nanny and the personifications of them through secret kicks and torture. They provide the humorous counter-weight to the haunted fabric, though again it is the inanimate made animate that turns the screw, however funny. It is a dark, duplicitous laughter, as Royle says: 'Writing is the double [...] from the beginning' (2003: 188). There is a deftness to the story, perhaps due to this careful balancing, which does not speak of or to the grotesques who so often populate Mantel's stories, but rather is a forerunner to the ghostly reanimation of history in the Tudor novels.

In *The Assassination of Margaret Thatcher*, the short story that opens the collection was previously published as a memoir. Yet here, as if in disguise, it returns as fiction dressed in new clothes. As Castle has noted the collection is framed either side with women answering the door to a stranger and letting them in (2014). This link is not the only thread running through the book however, the final story, 'The Assassination of Margaret Thatcher', also has a connection to memoir, as it is based on a 'real' fantasy. Thus, the first story is a memory transformed into fiction and the last a fiction inspired by reverie: '[Mantel] was just standing by the big sash window in her bedroom when she spotted Mrs Thatcher "toddling" around the hospital gardens unguarded. As she explained at the time of publishing this short story in the *Guardian*: "Immediately your eye measures the distance," says Mantel, measuring each syllable, her finger and thumb forming a gun. "I thought, if I wasn't me, if I was someone else, she'd be dead"' (Barr 2014). There is also self-quotation at work in 'Sorry to Disturb' for those readers familiar with *Eight Months on Ghazzah Street*. It is not only the Saudi Arabian setting that marks a return, but the motifs of streets that move, the fourth flat in the narrator's block standing empty and doors being mysteriously removed from hinges by unknown hands within the flat itself. There is also a strong sense of being observed: 'For one was always observed: overlooked, without precisely being seen, recognised' (2014: 10). Although this is not a story that thematically considers ghosts, this characteristic of seeing without being seen defines the revenant in Derrida's *Specters of Marx*, which is based upon the ghost of Hamlet's father. The ghost is wearing a helmet with his 'beaver' up, so he can see but cannot be seen himself. Derrida argues that such a position is the ultimate insignia of power (1994: 2ff), which is reflected in the representation of power/sight in 'Sorry to Disturb'.

Another connection with the earlier collection is the reference to the wider text's dedication, which also appears in this first story. The female narrator is a writer who has submitted her work to an agent in London: 'Their office is where? Ijaz sniffed, and I pressed on, trying to make my case; though why did I think that an office in William IV Street was a guarantee of moral worth?' (2014: 22). The dedication of the collection is addressed to Mantel's own agent: 'To Bill Hamilton, the man in William IV Street: thirty years on, with gratitude' (Mantel 2014: n.p.). It is a clue, but to what remains unclear. There is an identical moment in *Learning to Talk* in 'Third Floor Rising'. The female narrator is describing life at home with her mother and family:

> In time the chip pan got banned, to save the paintwork and to make a class statement, but by then I was living up the road with my friend Anne Terese, and what the others got for rations was something I preferred not to think about. (Mantel 2006: 98)

The dedication reads: 'Once again with love to Anne Terese: and her daughter: and her daughter' (n.p.). It is almost as if Mantel is deliberately laying the reader a trap, she is *telling* you that the stories are autobiography, no? Such self-referencing is reminiscent of Jeanette Winterson's visceral riposte to critics of *Oranges Are Not the Only Fruit*: 'If a man, Paul Auster say, wrote a text with themselves as a main character [she was perhaps really thinking of Salman Rushdie here] then that was an experiment, it was postmodern, metafiction, poststructural – in short, it was marvelous. If a woman did it, it was autobiography' (Brooks, 2000). By contrast, Mantel merely makes the text look askance at you when you draw this simple conclusion, so that you cannot help feeling you have missed something. As Cusk says of Mantel's writing, it is as if something (the thing you are missing) is vibrating beneath the surface of the text all the time (1995: 39).

As explored, Castle has analysed what she calls the 'bleb moment' in the short story 'Comma'. It both describes and prefigures the disfigured child, the void at the heart of the story, making the text possible, but ultimately and inevitably, unreachable, unknowable. Castle argues that there is such a moment in every story. It is my argument that certainly in the case of *The Assassination of Margaret Thatcher* these moments all collectively build towards such a moment in the titular tale. In particular, I am thinking of the references to Ireland that reach back into even the earlier collection through 'King Billy Is a Gentleman' and 'Learning to Talk', where the 'nursery' of the narrator's vowels is named as Belfast (94).[6] Here, in 'The Assassination of Margaret Thatcher', a story that took Mantel over twenty years to write and finish, a story therefore started before *Learning to Talk* was published, all these moments culminate – like an over-determined end point.

There is a sense of synesthesia, like the migraine in 'How Shall I Know You', when the narrator buzzes the assassin into her building: 'On the entryphone there was the usual crackle, as if someone had set fire to the line, "Come up, Mr Duggan," I said. It was as well to be respectful to him' (2014: 213). The neurological phenomenon – the stimulation of one sensory or cognitive pathway leading to the involuntary, automatic stimulation of another – is thus embedded in the text. It is also the substitute again, like that of the stepfather of earlier stories, not what is expected but still what is *accepted*. The key to the story though is another ellipsis, a 'bleb moment', a void at the heart, and, as said, it does not have to be present on the page to be *present*:

> Who has not seen the door in the wall? It is the invalid child's consolation, the prisoner's last hope [...] It is a special door and obeys no laws that govern wood or iron [...] That the assassin was a flicker in its frame, you know. Beyond the fire door he melts, and this is how you've never seen him on the news [...] This is how, to your certain knowledge, Mrs Thatcher went on living till she died. But note the door [...] And note the cold wind that blows through it, when you open it a crack. History could always have been otherwise. (239–240)

This is Mantel's Frank Underwood moment, turning to you, telling you how it is – what you know, what you do not know.[7] The frame. It is perhaps a kind of auto-fiction we have witnessed with these short stories, or even a kind of auto-theory. In the second of her Reith Lectures, Mantel discusses the drowned village of Derwent, which serves as backdrop (and ellipsis) within her short story 'The Clean Slate'. In the story, the narrator seems angry to have been told 'AS A FACT' (2006: 131) that when the weather was hot people could still see the church spire emerging from the depths. The spire was blown up in the 1940s. However, in the lecture, Mantel was more sanguine, it was not a fact, she said, it was something else (Mantel 2017a).

As Castle has said of *The Assassination of Margaret Thatcher* and could be fittingly applied to all Mantel's short stories: 'Despite the phalanx of themes [...] one can't help feeling that [her] imaginative world is all of a piece' (2014). Moreover, there are organizing principles, especially in terms of the first person female narrators, which suggest that the collections are of-a-piece formally too, like cycles or sequences. There is also the sense of retrospect that haunts the stories and the connections to Ireland, thrown into relief by the explicit agenda of 'The Assassination of Margaret Thatcher'. Similarly, the dedications mark a departure from the novels, which certainly have dedications but not explicitly referenced in the text itself. Then there is the role or position of memoir, *Learning to Talk* orbiting *Giving Up the Ghost, The Assassination of Margaret Thatcher* with the memoir embedded. Overall, Mantel's short story world is a laboratory she enters to undertake very specific experiments, the novels exist in a different laboratory altogether, a longer term one, which might not even be a lab at all, but a crypt.

Notes

1 In the absence of critical material and since she is such an astute and ready interpreter of her own work, Mantel has become the 'go to' literary critic for incisive quotations on her own writing.

2 It is easy to read any representation of the north as a stereotype because it is not part of mainstream experience. It is perhaps easy for those who did not grow up in the north to misrecognize its representation here as stereotype, especially as it is repeated. The north is so marginalized that this is the only acceptable way that it can emerge; yet 'local' readers will recognize the specificity and authenticity of both this geography and the experience of it.

3 Mike operates like an id in the text, which is also how Mantel has described Christophe to Cromwell in *Wolf Hall*.

4 Another characteristic of Mantel's writing is the elasticity of her vocabulary and the range of her reference.

5 This idea is explored in *Fludd* too, where no one can hold the memory of Fludd's appearance or facial features in their mind the moment he has left the room.

6 Like 'King Billy Is a Gentleman', there is also a song in this 'final' story, this time a song from the football terraces (2014: 218).

7 Frank Underwood is the main character in *House of Cards*, both a UK and US television series inspired by the novels of Michael Dobbs. Underwood is known for turning to the camera, directly addressing his audience and thereby breaking the fourth wall.

Bibliography

Barr, D. (2014), 'Hilary Mantel on Margaret Thatcher: "I Can Still Feel That Boiling Detestation"', *The Guardian*, 19 September. Available online: https://www.theguardian.com/books/2014/sep/19/hilary-mantel-interview-short-story-assassination-margaret-thatcher (accessed 22 August 2017).

Boddy, K. (1995), 'Review of *Modern American Short Story Sequences*'. Available online: https://www.cambridge.org/core/services/aop-cambridge-core/content/view/S002187580002466X (accessed 22 August 2017).

Brace, M. (2003), 'Hilary Mantel: The Exorcist', *Independent*, 9 May.

Brooks, L. (2000), 'Power Surge', *The Guardian*, 2 September. Available online:https://www.theguardian.com/books/2000/sep/02/fiction.jeanettewinterson (accessed 22 August 2017).

Castle, T. (2014), 'Within Her Sights', *New York Times*, 2 October. Available online: https://www.nytimes.com/2014/10/05/books/review/the-assassination-of-margaret-thatcher-by-hilary-mantel.html?mcubz=3 (accessed 22 August 2017).

Cusk, R. (1995), 'All Her Flesh Was as Glass', *Times*, 2 March, 39.

Derrida, J. (1994), *Specters of Marx*, translated by P. Kamuf, New York and London: Routledge.

Dunn, M. and Morris, A. (1995), *The Composite Novel: The Short Story Cycle in Transition*, New York: Twayne Publishers.
Gerald Kennedy, J. (1995), *Modern American Short Story Sequences*, Cambridge: Cambridge University Press.
Hutcheon, L. (2002), *The Politics of Postmodernism*, 2nd edn, London: Routledge.
Mantel, H. (1990), *Fludd*, London: Penguin.
Mantel, H. (2004), *Giving Up the Ghost*, London: Harper Perennial.
Mantel, H. (2006), *Learning to Talk: Short Stories*, London: Harper Perennial.
Mantel, H. (2009a), *Wolf Hall*, London: Fourth Estate.
Mantel, H. (2009b), 'Someone to Disturb', *London Review of Books* 31 (1): 13–17.
Mantel, H. (2014), *The Assassination of Margaret Thatcher: Stories*, London: Fourth Estate.
Mantel, H. (2016), 'Kinsella in His Hole', *London Review of Books* 38 (10): 7–10.
Mantel, H. (2017a), 'First Reith Lecture: The Day Is for the Living' (BBC). Available online: http://www.bbc.co.uk/programmes/b08tcbrp (accessed 22nd August 2017).
Mantel, H. (2017b), 'Second Reith Lecture: The Iron Maiden' (BBC). Available online: http://www.bbc.co.uk/programmes/b08v08m5 (accessed 22 August 2017).
Onions, C. T., ed. (1978), *The Shorter Oxford English Dictionary*, Oxford: Clarendon Press.
Pollard, E. J. (2015), '"Mind What Gap?": An Interview with Hilary Mantel', *Textual Practice* 29 (6): 1035–1044.
Ratcliffe, S. (2003) 'Learning to Talk: Hilary Mantel's Fictions of Past and Present Selves', *Times Literary Supplement*, 25 July. Available online: https://www.the-tls.co.uk/articles/public/learning-to-talk-hilary-mantel/(accessed 22 August 2017)
Royle, N. (2003), *The Uncanny*, Manchester: Manchester University Press.
Runcie, J. dir. (2011), *Hilary Mantel: A Culture Show Special* (BBC).

4

Reading Minds – *Wolf Hall*'s Revision of the Poetics of Subjectivity

Renate Brosch

This chapter will account as precisely as possible for the extraordinary appeal of the first novel in Mantel's Tudor trilogy, *Wolf Hall*, arguing that this results, at least in part, from its complicated narrative perspective. It examines the way tense, deixis and focalization work, to discern how form translates into function, or how the poetics of representation informs its meanings. The novel's narrative perspective maintains a strict intra- and homodiegetic focalization, so that everything is seen through Cromwell's eyes; Cromwell's perception therefore guarantees textual coherence and defines the vision of the world represented, since it sets the limits of what is possible within this world. *Wolf Hall* thus employs history as this character's individual perception, creating for the reader an illusion of empathic proximity to the focalizer. However, while this strict focalization resembles interior monologue, Mantel's use of the third person 'he' is unusually difficult and confusing as the third person narrative is easily confused with references to other male characters. This chapter claims that in offering this compelling indeterminacy at the centre of its construction of character, *Wolf Hall* not only rejects the notion of received history, but also educates its readers that any identity is unstable, a process rather than an entity.

*****

The historical novel *Wolf Hall* (2009) deals with the time of Henry VIII, a favourite period of historical fictions for generations of British readers, movie goers and TV viewers. In these fictions – most prominently Robert Bolt's play *A Man for All Seasons* – Thomas Cromwell typically features as a Machiavellian arch villain, who manipulates and tortures, a backstairs manoeuverer who engineered Henry's break with Rome to increase his own power.[1] Even in the scholarly *Oxford Dictionary of National Biography* he is 'tyrannical' and 'unprincipled' in his policy and displays a combination of 'cruelty' and 'abject submissiveness' in his behaviour at court (1986: 200). Thomas Cromwell was widely hated in his lifetime and makes an unlikely hero now. Yet that is what he becomes in Mantel's fictional revision of history, in which Cromwell is a thoroughly likable central character and the traditional saintly icon Thomas More a pedantic, ruthless inquisitor.

In this chapter, I want to account as precisely as possible for the construction of the main character's subjectivity in *Wolf Hall*, which to my mind is the key to the novel's achievement. As Blakey Vermeule has so convincingly argued, character is still, in spite of what teachers of literature might claim, our most intrinsic reason for reading novels. Novels cater to our predilection for spontaneous commonsense psychology; they exploit our obsession with other human beings (Vermeule 2010: 2). *Wolf Hall* satisfies this basic desire for affective affinity with a protagonist and – at the same time – interrogates our values regarding fictional subjectivity. The novel presents Cromwell as an unusual combination of historical and contemporary qualities, using a peculiar mixture of styles and registers to render this central character simultaneously appealing and attractive, but ultimately puzzling, thus encouraging readers to engage with their own imaginative constructions of what they would value in this ambiguous personality and by extension in fictional heroes in general. Although *Wolf Hall* seems at first glance to be the success story of Cromwell as a proto-capitalist reformer, the novel ultimately invites its readers to question the very characteristics that determine his superiority and success. For this purpose, *Wolf Hall* combines the narrative techniques of high modernism with those of contemporary popular fictions; it presents its story entirely from the perspective of the protagonist, with the result that its both fanciful and plausible accounts of the past are legitimized by their subjectivity. My reading depends on a fine-tuned narratological analysis not as an end in itself, but as a means of demonstrating how the novel manipulates the readers' desire for affective engagement, enabling them to finally realize that they have been complicit in constructing a morally questionable Cromwell as a hero. Thus the formal analysis is meant to lead to more philosophical and political conclusions about this particular novelistic understanding of the subject in history and its relevance for the present. This relevance, I will argue, lies *less* in a reinterpretation of history but rather in a reconceptualization of identity and subjectivity as necessarily social and intersubjective.

Wolf Hall and its sequel *Bring Up the Bodies* are part of a planned trilogy about Cromwell, the third volume of which has not yet been published. In these, as well as in a prior historical novel about the French revolution (*A Place of Greater Safety* 1992), Mantel has proved an elegant and moral 'anatomizer of malevolence and cruelty' (Laing 2009: n.p.). These novels belong to a period of resurgence of historical fictions since the 1990s (Wilson 2015: 145). Since then, the genre, which was eschewed as trivial by the modernists, has shifted from the periphery to the mainstream of literary production. As Ann Rigney points out, what defines the historical novel is precisely the interplay between invented story elements and historical ones, 'they [...] are not "free-standing fictions" [...], they also call upon prior historical knowledge, echoing and/or disputing other discourses about the past' (2001: 19). Mantel's novels surpass recent mainstream production in this genre with their unusual mixture of painstakingly researched historical facts and a strange and ghostly sense of 'pastness'. *Wolf Hall* especially has appealed to readers and critics because here the dialectic of historiography and fictionality is rendered vivid and vital.

Following on from Hayden White's groundbreaking argument that even serious history writing employs literary elements such as narrativity and metaphor (1973; 1978), postmodern theories, such as Linda Hutcheon's concept of 'historiographic metafiction' (1989) and Frederic Jameson's critique of postmodern historicity (1991), tended to privilege postmodern instances of the historical novel that make disciplinary, generic and aesthetic boundaries between factual and fictive histories permeable. It is only in recent years that popular neo-historical fictions have been rescued from the stigma of nostalgia and insignificance. They are now theorized as serious attempts to negotiate cultural memory, as attempts that realize the 'potential for radical possibilities in more implicit ways' than earlier postmodern fictions (Rousselot 2014: 5). A recent article about 'exoticising the Tudors' seeks to correct a conventional denigration of historical fictions as interested only in restoring the past and not in 'reflect[ing] on the problematics of such representation' (Mitchell and Parsons 2013: 13). The authors claim that what seems to be 'nostalgia' in recent historical fictions is a means of making available and enacting history in multiple voices (Mitchell and Parsons 2013: 13).

Instead of emphasizing the incommensurability and radical otherness of the past, many present-day historical fictions seek to make their bygone ages vivid and to make readers invest empathetically in the 'foreign country' that is the past (Lowenthal 1985). Like detective fiction, the historical novel faces the problem of making the familiar entertaining, to create suspense where the outcome is clear. Strategies of popular fiction may help to solve this problem, in particular realism, exoticism and suspense. A preference for realist, readable styles over experimental ones is prevalent in recent historical fictions. At the same time, a realist presentation of history can be employed to expose to readers the fallacy of their own impossible desires to possess and inhabit the past. Exoticizing can be an effective strategy for creating simultaneous appeal and fascinating aversion. As Graham Huggan argues, 'wilful exoticism' can be an instrument to repoliticize and unsettle agreed versions of the past (qtd. in Rousselot 2014: 6). Both strategies combine into the production of suspense: exotic details make the past strangely attractive and realism grounds it in sensuous experience and makes it believable. These effects are generated by subtle means in *Wolf Hall*.[2]

In spite of being based on meticulous historical research, the novel foregoes accuracy in favour of generating great emotional sympathy for Cromwell by attributing anachronistic beliefs and convictions to him. In contrast to his Tudor contemporaries, Mantel credits Cromwell with many attributes that we tend to admire today: intercultural competence (he is fluent in many languages), financial and legal genius, psychological insight, physical courage, wit and last but not least a greater interest in others than in himself. He stands for secular scepticism and pragmatic relativism instead of moral principles, for intercultural connections instead of faith in an essential national identity. In terms of world picture, he belongs to the new inquisitive, open-minded and scientifically informed men of his time. Cromwell is something of a cosmopolitan *avant la lettre*, with his knowledge gathered in travels outside England and among people of all walks of life. His interest in new ideas, such as those of Copernicus and Machiavelli, reflects the exploding knowledge systems and the increasing sense of uncertainty in the early modern world, registered in frequent, slightly fantastic references to the shifting nature of reality, this 'quaking world' where 'nothing ... seems steady' and where the ground is shifting under the feet (Mantel 2010: 522, 327, 495).

An unstable world requires flexible minds and '*Wolf Hall* pits the agile mind of Cromwell against unwavering attitudes like More's' (de Bruyn 2012: 92; cf. Mantel 2010: 228). Rather than voice opinions or issue statements when considering the larger context of his times, Cromwell tends to ask questions. He is a foreigner to all the fanaticism and fundamentalism of early-modern England and especially tolerant in religious matters. Mantel's Cromwell is not a pious nor even a religious person. His support for reformers comes from his basic tolerance and from the thoroughly secular grounding of his thought. He is disgusted by superstition and superiority alike, condescending neither to poor people nor to women or children. Male chauvinism is as foreign to his mindset as the outdated feudal arrogance of the privileged. In enduring their jibes at his low birth, Cromwell reflects that:

> The world is not run from where he [Henry Percy, the dull-witted Earl of Northumberland] thinks. Not from his border fortresses, not even from Whitehall. The world is run from Antwerp, from Florence, from places he has never imagined; from Lisbon, from where the ships with sails of silk drift west and are burned up in the sun. Not from castle walls, but from counting houses, not by the call of the bugle but by the click of the abacus, not by the grate and click of the mechanism of the gun but by the scrape of the pen on the page of the promissory note that pays for the gun and the gunsmith and the powder and shot. (Mantel 2010: 378)

Mantel's Cromwell is a clever self-made man in a rapidly changing world where his unprecedented rise from lowly origins is possible. He embodies the cultural shift from religious to secular and from class-bound to meritocratic thinking. He seems confident that noble blood and feats of arms will soon count for less than lines of credit and nicely balanced books (Tayler 2009: n.p.). In such anachronistic reflections Cromwell anticipates the fading of aristocratic power and the dawning of the capitalist system. Unencumbered by strong convictions, he is not impressed by status without intellectual quality. Yet he is also an intimidating physical presence showing no hesitation about using violence and capable of employing quite sinister methods in eliminating his enemies. He is also a transnational economic genius who seems to endorse proto-capitalist ideas: 'Study the market. Increase the spread of benevolence. Bring in better figures next year' (Mantel 2010: 365).

This complex personality of Cromwell's presents a challenge that produces most of the novel's suspense. Mantel has described Cromwell as belonging to a 'chain of literary representation', as well as her impulse to make amends for previous depictions (Simpson 2015: n.p.; cf. also Bordo 2013: 299). In keeping with her long-standing fascination with the occult and the dead, Mantel resurrects the historical figure of Cromwell as an experiencing mind and a feeling and sensing body. This endeavour to make the past familiar territory cannot depend merely on the conventional illusions of fiction (De Groot 2010: 94). Such a resurrectionist approach to historical fiction must privilege 'the private over the public, [focusing on] hearth and home rather than sceptre and sword' (Samuel 1994: 161). Mantel presents us with a private and likable Cromwell behind the notorious public façade.

For her resurrectionist approach Mantel turns Cromwell into the sympathetic and utterly compelling upstart hero of her Tudor story world. In an interview she tells how her interest in Cromwell was piqued by his stupendous advancement from humble origins to counsellor of the king (Wachtel 2016: 184). Without neglecting the strict hierarchical order of Tudor society, she elaborates the scant historical evidence concerning his early life by imagining a miserable childhood as the son of a violent blacksmith in Putney.[3] As events proceed, the novel reminds us again and again of Cromwell's precarious social status through the repeated condescension and mockery he endures from the nobles at court. All these episodes – the childhood depravation and the later discrimination – function to produce empathy. Besides, the abusive fictional parent can serve as a psychological explanation for Cromwell's secretive, conniving personality. At the very beginning he is almost kicked to death by his raging, alcoholic father.

> So now get up.
> Felled, dazed, silent, he has fallen; knocked full length on the cobbles of the yard [...] One blow, properly placed, could kill him now.
> Blood from the gash on his head – which was his father's first effort – is trickling across his face. Add to this, his left eye is blinded; but if he squints sideways, with his right eye he can see that the stitching of his father's boot is unravelling. The twine has sprung clear of the leather, and a hard knot in it has caught his eyebrow and opened another cut. (Mantel 2010: 3)

As this is the novel's first paragraph, we do not even know who 'he' is. The passage makes no allowances for the convention of an accessible beginning, instead, it takes the reader right into Cromwell's experiencing consciousness. Cromwell's mind is the filter for everything that happens, the novel's narrative perspective maintains a strict homodiegetic focalization, so that everything is seen through Cromwell's eyes.[4] It is Cromwell's perception that guarantees textual coherence and defines the vision of the world represented, since it sets the limits of what is possible within this world.

Such a consistent interior perspective stands in direct opposition to traditional conceptions of the historical fiction genre as elaborated by Georg Lukács and Frederic Jameson. However, as Leigh Wilson argues, nowadays a radically subjective perception is a 'reality effect' in response to the contemporary 'crisis of fictionality' (2015: 149). In her view, the serious historical novelist of today does not jettison reality effects but tethers them to modernist narrative strategies that fix the limits of the story world in the interior consciousness of their focalizing characters. Referring specifically to Mantel's Tudor novels, she notes that the use of free indirect discourse allows unmediated access to their main characters' thoughts (154).[5] 'Where the modernists privileged the representation of interiority in order to question and destabilize the question of reality, to make the familiar unfamiliar, and to thin the boundaries between real and representation, the contemporary writer of the historical novel uses them to *secure* the real' (Wilson 2015: 154).

The primacy of individual perception, which Jameson thought detrimental to historical narratives, is the key narrative technique in *Wolf Hall*, as Mantel explains: 'The person on the ground was Cromwell and the camera was behind his eyes' (qtd. in Wilson 2015: 155). The passage quoted above exhibits the fractured syntax and present tense of interior monologue, but interior monologue is normally rendered in first person or elided first person. *Wolf Hall* is written in third person internal perspective. This novel-length free indirect style makes the use of 'he' unusually difficult and confusing as countless commentators on the internet complain.[6] They are right insofar as Mantel breaks the rule that personal pronouns require a referential name in the near vicinity in order to be identifiable. In *Wolf Hall* deixis[7] is obscure because Cromwell's thoughts are given in the third person, and hence 'he' is easily confused with references to other male characters. The confusing use of personal pronouns creates small spaces of dissonance for the reader, who is jolted out of easy immersive reading. Probably in response to her critics, Mantel uses mostly 'he, Cromwell' in *Bring Up the Bodies* instead. This adjustment is disappointing for the discerning reader, for the indeterminate 'he' signals beautifully how Cromwell's mind shifts in and out of external reality, one minute employing his stupendous empathy to imagine what the other 'he' is thinking and the next minute engaged in something else. In this way, his interpersonal mind style produces reading difficulties that train the reader's empathy as well.

Wolf Hall emplots history as a history of the mind, choosing to concentrate exclusively on an imaginative rendering of Cromwell's individual perception, thus creating an engulfing illusion of proximity to the focalizer. The experiencing eye of the reader is limited to the horizon of Cromwell's perception and restricted to his insight into the consequences of his actions. The effect of these strict constraints is to place the reader at a remove from well-known Tudor history into a veritable maelstrom of unpredictable events. *Wolf Hall* thrusts us into history, not as a linear procession of events, but as an ongoing cognitive process accompanied by reminiscences, hopes and speculations. The effect is dramatic irony with a vengeance; as educated readers, we know most of Cromwell's future, his fall from fortune and his execution, yet the protagonist-focalizer knows only the past, the present and possibilities.

Here we encounter a paradox, for the novel's poetics of subjective experience serve to make the personality of Cromwell mysterious rather than to disclose it. On the one hand, homodiegetic focalization turns Cromwell into one of the most appealing and enlightened characters of the period. On the other, it gradually transpires that he is as cunning as legend has it when his flashback memories hint at an unsavoury past. Mantel has called Cromwell '"almost a case study in ambiguity"' (Simpson 2015: n.p.). While we are invited to participate in his perception and 'mind style', we are also intrigued by his ambiguous personality (Semino 2002: 97). This is a strategy familiar from contemporary crime novels, such as Patrick Neate's *City of Tiny Lights*, in which the appeal of the hero rests on his fascinating resemblance to the criminals he is pursuing. In trying to understand Cromwell's enigmatic personality, we are called upon to adjust and readjust our image of this character.

The novel turns characterization into an epistemological challenge, an intriguing and demanding task for the reader. The chapter immediately following the passage quoted above, called 'II: Paternity 1527' (Mantel 2010: 17), gives an impression of the confusion resulting from third person narration:

> So: Stephen Gardiner. Going out, as he's coming in. It's wet, and for a night in April, unseasonably warm, but Gardiner wears furs, which look like oily and dense black feathers; he stands now, ruffling them, gathering his clothes about his tall straight person like black angel's wings.
> 'Late,' Master Stephen says unpleasantly.
> He is bland. 'Me, or your good self?'
> 'You.' He waits.
> 'Drunks on the river. The boatmen say it's the eve of one of their patron saints'.
> 'Did you offer a prayer to her?'
> 'I'll pray to anyone, Stephen, till I'm on dry land.'
> 'I'm surprised you didn't take an oar yourself. You must have done some river work, when you were a boy.'
> Stephen sings always on one note. Your reprobate father. Your low birth [...] The poor orphan boy! (Mantel 2010: 17)

Here, at the very beginning of the story proper, we discover further deictic difficulties that slow the reading process because they demand constant attention to grammatical constructions. For one thing, Cromwell's references to himself ('your reprobate father') are in second person, mentally quoting Gardiner, and therefore do not grammatically match the experiencing narration in third person. While we are turning back pages to make sure we know who said or did what, we are temporarily removed from the fictional world. In a seamless process, while coming to terms with the difficulties in the narration, we gradually unravel the working of his consciousness: we realize that Cromwell is at once the underdog of a condescending and exclusive court in-group and its intellectual superior.

Moreover, in the passage above we may note an unfamiliar combination of tense with the already complicated use of personal pronouns. The present tense is foregrounded by the use of 'now', cf. 'he stands now' (Mantel 2010: 17), so that, we have to step into the shoes of Cromwell, in order to imagine the situation with a sense of immediacy that is his here and now, as it were. Although no longer an experimental technique, narrative in present tense departs significantly from the traditional schemata of the real-world temporality of storytelling (Fludernik 1996: 256). For a historical novel especially, the present tense is still somewhat unusual. To *Wolf Hall*'s experiential approach it is brilliantly appropriate, because it creates a sense of momentariness that seems natural and genuine for an experiencing mind. Noting the obvious fact that a story has to have happened in the past in order to become tellable, Monika Fludernik claims that the present tense produces an unrealistic simultaneity between speaking and doing, since it is not logically plausible that a story is experienced and narrated at the same time; hence present tense narration contravenes schemata of real-life storytelling by foregrounding the process of invention (262).

Present tense is chosen by writers who have rejected the idea of *grands récits* and wish to make their readers aware that they are partaking in one version of (fictional) history only. For this purpose the present tense is ideal because it can undermine the sense of total access to the world of the past recreated in fictional form. It disturbs massively the experience of continuity, making the narrative disjunctive, as it leads us from one moment to the next and excludes a larger temporal reference. The present tense in narrative is more focused on moments or episodes than the past tense; 'it sacrifices the larger time-field to achieve keen, close focus' (Le Guin 1998: 73). Therefore, the present tense implies discontinuity; it could be called a narrative tense of less authority. By giving us the past in present tense, *Wolf Hall* immerses us in uncertainty, suggesting that we cannot yet know which detail or marginal person will become important. The unordered, associative impressions of lived experience align the reader with the focalizing Cromwell since both share the task of having to discover significance and coherence in a seemingly chaotic world. In short, the functions and effects of Mantel's use of focalization and deixis, including confusing use of pronouns, present tense and interior perspective, are ambiguous or even contradictory. On the one hand, the grammatical and linguistic difficulties have a defamiliarizing effect, because they undermine the sense of illusion and demand concentrated attention. On the other, interior focalization in present tense immerses us in Cromwell's disjunct and momentary experientiality and reinforces the strong bond between reader and focalizer.

Participating in the mental life of a character in this way can lead to identification, but then Cromwell's mind style is very different from our contemporary individualist thought. In the quote above from chapter 2, for instance, he might have wondered why Stephen Gardiner is always insulting him, he might have admitted to being hurt. None of that is mentioned: his mind is busy imagining the point of view of others, a mental occupation so prominent and central to his character that it prevents him from thinking about himself. In spite of the dominant interior monologue mode, the narrative does not reveal Cromwell's interiority or allow inferences about his 'subconscious'.

We never exit his consciousness, but this consciousness is not an isolated egocentric Freudian underground chamber. He is not given to acts of pure self-expression or self-examination but is interested mainly in the observation and awareness of others; he is constantly engaged in reading and judging other minds. *Wolf Hall* seems determined to demonstrate Alan Palmer's contention that 'thought is consummately social: social in its origins, social in its functions, social in its forms, social in its applications. At base, thinking is a public activity' (2004: 11).

It is one of his likeable characteristics that Cromwell intuitively performs this imaginative identification with others. It is a less endearing aspect of his character that he explicitly realizes the manipulative advantage this kind of imagination may bring: 'Possibly it's something women do: spend time imagining what it's like to be each other. One can learn from that, he thinks' (Mantel 2010: 44). In many scenes we are allowed to watch him making good use of this knowledge, because we are privy to his command of insight into the minds of his enemies. Cromwell is assigned the superiority of a detective: his views of other characters are presented as intellectually superior, emotionally detached, ironically amused as well as rational and intuitive. The other characters are made to seem not only prevaricating and deceitful, but also inept in attempting to pull the wool over Cromwell's eyes.

In consequence, this Cromwell remains a disconcerting mystery for the people around him: his own sister cannot comprehend him; rumours about dangerous activities during his lost years abroad make it easy for courtiers to believe in the earnestness of his threats. The novel stresses his unstable personality not only through the use of the confusing personal pronoun 'he', it suggests multiple selves in the many variants of Cromwell's common name: 'Thomas, also Tomos, Tommaso and Thomas Cromwell' (Mantel 2010: 71). That 'half the world is called Thomas' (68) presents itself as an opportunity to Cromwell: 'The compound nature of this formidable figure that intrigues Wolsey and King Henry himself, [...] scares the noblemen [...], and ultimately renders him a blank to himself, as well as to others' (Caines 2009: n.p.). And for the reader it produces a fascinating postponement in recognition about the nature of this mystery hero, as Mantel uses focalization through Cromwell's consciousness not only to secure reality effects but also to create suspense.

His opaque nature is foregrounded in a startling use of ekphrasis, which the novel utilizes for giving an outside view of Cromwell.[8] It describes Hans Holbein's famous portrait now in the Frick collection in New York, which offers the reader a powerful aid to visualization. 'Hans has made his skin smooth as the skin of a courtesan, but the motion he has captured, that folding of the fingers, is as sure as that of a slaughterman's when he picks up the killing knife' (Mantel 2010: 525). The grim simile is reinforced in the dialogue that follows, in which everyone agrees that Cromwell looks like a murderer in the painting (527). This *consensus* late in the novel may come as a shock to readers, because thus far they have been largely screened from any negative judgement of Cromwell's character by his positive self-appraisal.

Commenting on this passage, Wilson notes that Cromwell's crimes are 'forgotten acts' in the novel. For her the question arises 'what is the reason for the absence of his villainous acts from the consciousness that constructs Mantel's narrative?' (2015: 163). Once we have ascertained the novel's narrative technique, the answer is self-evident: interior focalization records his actions and manoeuvres without disapproval and prevents moral judgement, as Cromwell is not given to regrets or guilty feelings that might creep up on him unawares. Naturally, given his advantage as the first voice in the hierarchy of discourses, we succumb to the charm and wit of his omnicompetent and witty personality.[9] Hence, the portrait scene is pivotal to the suspense effect of the novel's gradual unveiling of the puzzle of Cromwell's personality.

Since the narrative makes significant demands on readers to perform a mind-reading activity similar to Cromwell's own, the process of relativizing the characterization is gradual. What Colin Burrow puts down to character change, a 'long slow toughening', I would regard as a long slow revelation in which we become increasingly aware that we are being misled by seeing only his side of things (2009: 5). In one scene at court, for instance, we glimpse his brutal manhandling of an unwelcome follower, but the narrative glosses over the violence of his action because focalization does not deliver an outside perception:

> Francis Bryan follows him out.
> 'Please feel you can leave me now, Sir Francis.'
> 'I thought I would go with you. I want to learn what you do.'
> He checks his stride, slaps his hand flat into Bryan's chest, spins him sideways and hears the thud of his skull against the wall. 'In a hurry,' he says. (Mantel 2010: 376)

Even in this rare moment of physical violence on the part of Cromwell, we cannot be sure, how far the 'thud of his skull on the wall' was intended. For a large part of our reading experience, then, the novel tricks us into believing that he is not only an intimidating, but also a generous and considerate personality. *Wolf Hall* exploits the common desire for narratives with a hero, which postmodern historiographic metafiction eschewed. Through the emphasis on the present moment Cromwell becomes an object of sympathy, but the careful reading which the narrative technique necessitates gradually dissolves the hero figure into a thoroughly ambiguous personality, so that it dawns on us that we may have been misled in trusting his first person ascriptions. Only slowly in the course of reading this long novel do readers – some admit to only realizing it at the very end – accept the novel's accumulating hints and clues that the character of Cromwell may not be to his outside world what he appears to be on the inside to himself. The foreshadowing of the portrait scene will be confirmed when it becomes unavoidable to face the fact that in the fictional world of the novel Cromwell must look like a murderer because he is one.

Besides the challenges of point of view, Mantel's virtuosity in creating sympathy with a humanized and enlightened Cromwell depends on a vividly imagistic rendering of his inner life in a succession of pictures and dreamlike sequences in which he observes, remembers or imagines. In both novels – *Wolf Hall* and its sequel – the compelling visuality consists in unforgettable *tableaux vivants* that encapsulate the episodic process of history as it is lived. As Burrow claims, 'the process of history seems to be fixed in a series of stills, of moments when the king's or Cromwell's attention is suddenly caught by something or someone, and time stops with their gaze' (2009: 3). Every now and then an event surfaces indistinctly at the edges of Cromwell's awareness that we as readers are neither shown nor clearly told. This ambiguous visuality is beautifully effective in bringing to life the superstitions of early-modern times when history itself shades off into the supernatural. It is also appropriate psychologically for Cromwell's subjective perception of unconsciously repressed or deliberately blurred memories of his own past. The delay this causes in readerly understanding of his complex personality is due to what cognitive literary scholars call 'primacy effect'. Since first impressions prove more resistant to revision than information given at a later stage, things mentioned first in a narrative possess an advantage over information received later ('recency effect') (Stockwell 2002: 19). Mantel's strategy of slow disclosure profits from this rule of privileged position in the sequence of narrative. In *Bring Up the Bodies*, in which the mystery of Cromwell's person is no longer central, he is increasingly a haunted man, haunted by the ghosts of dead loved ones and haunted by his own past.

Another strategy for mystifying readers about the protagonist is the gaps in narrative chronology. After the beating which opens *Wolf Hall*, Cromwell runs away from home and we meet him next thirty years later. Of the years in between we only learn what Cromwell's recollections reveal, which is not much: some years as a mercenary in France, some more with bankers in Florence, some time as a clothier, some more as a lawyer. As we follow his lost history in vivid flashbacks, what surfaces in fragments from the past are often acts better forgotten. In an early episode we see him evading an imagined attack by Wolsey with the swiftness of somebody who is used to assassins lurking in the shadows (Mantel 2010: 71–73). We witness the working of memory as flashes of visual images surfacing without conscious reflection.

On the continent, Cromwell has mastered an Italian technique that allows him to store stunning amounts of information in his memory (79). In another ekphrastic scene his skill is linked to classical descriptions of *ars memoria*. He memorizes the seating of guests at a dinner table, as in the famous legend of Simonides, signalling to the educated reader the future downfall of aristocratic society. Thus the protagonist performs acts of memory and of strategic forgetting that are at the core of his self-fashioning. His intrusive visual memories reflect the novel's engagement with the past, reminding readers how dependent they are on iconic items from cultural memory, and how refreshing it can be to rearrange these. Without the more overt postmodern techniques of multiple narration and metafictionality, these scenes are subtle self-reflexive hints at the task of reconstructing history, in which the reader is involved as much as the novel. According to Mantel's idea of the novel as 'a cooperative effort, a joint venture between writer and reader', the reader participates in the historiographical intervention and is made to reflect on the process (qtd. in De Groot 2016: 23).

Ultimately Cromwell emerges as a complicated compound of likable and legendary, presentist and historical, characteristics. Readers willing to tackle the novel's dense, complex and sometimes opaque narrative style are rewarded with massive affective involvement. Yet, they are also disabused of their initial exaggerated esteem for its hero. In offering this compelling indeterminacy at the centre of its construction of character, the novel not only rejects the notion of a psychologically rounded character, but also educates its readers that identity is unstable, a process rather than an entity, and – above all – that it depends on interpersonal relations. We meet a historical figure that is not a definitively circumscribed identity but a 'work in progress', a performance that requires our participation in the process (Mantel cf. Wachtel 2016: 181). As Levinasian philosophy has taught us, identity cannot be constituted without an Other who affirms and questions its existence. In this case the position of the Other is filled by the reader who completes, empathizes, hypothesizes, casts into doubt and reconceptualizes Cromwell's identity. A commonly assumed roundness and unity of subjectivity is undermined by our own very act of reading. Thus the novel rejects the traditional 'subjectivity first' model of the mind – polemically called 'the Robinson Crusoe model of epistemology' (Jones 1995: 27) – and educates its readers to not only perceive but exercise the mind as an instrument of interpersonal awareness and cultural learning capable of 'dialogic, intermental engagement with other minds' (Trevarthen 2001: 417).

It seems to be the hallmark of serious historical novels to direct some message to the present day via its description of the past, since the two time-planes of historical fictions – the protagonist's present and the reader's present – are joined in a cause-and-effect relationship. At the level of historical content,

Wolf Hall tells the success story of capitalism and the transformation of the incipient nation state's financial administration. This affirmative message is undermined, however, by the psychology of an intersubjective reading of its proto-capitalist hero's character. Realizing that we, as readers, have been complicit in constructing a hero to our liking, we are reminded that our judgements can be misled, and that they may be based on false values. *Wolf Hall* encourages us to examine our values in the construction of identity. By casting us in the role of the Other, the novel makes us aware of the moral responsibility involved in interpreting other people and the past. Instead of the limited postmodern project of juggling alternative histories, *Wolf Hall* asks us to transcend what Jameson calls 'monadic relativism' and interrogate the ethics we value in literary and historical 'heroes' (1991: 412). I believe that the novel not only deals with intersubjective processes but that its reading promotes intersubjectivity: its outstanding achievement is to captivate the reader with the enormous appeal of entering the mind of its hero, only to ultimately reject such an investment in egocentric subjectivity in favour of an intersubjective construction of identity.

Notes

1 Philippa Gregory's *The Other Boleyn Girl* (2001) is an example as well as the TV series *The Tudors* (BBC 2007–2010).

2 Mantel mentions this combination of modes in an interview with Mona Simpson: 'There is the Cromwell of popular history and the one in academic history.... What I have managed to do is bring the two camps together' (Simpson 2015: n.p.).

3 That his father was a blacksmith as well as a shearer of cloth and kept a hostelry and brewing house in Putney is confirmed by the *Oxford Dictionary of National Biography* ('Cromwell, Thomas' 1986: 192).

4 According to Gérard Genette's categories, a homodiegetic narrator is one who exists as a character within the fictional story world; as opposed to a heterodiegetic one who tells the story from an outside perspective (Genette 1980: 248).

5 Free indirect discourse (FID) is a narratological term for the dual voice of interior focalization: although narrated in third person the vocabulary and style of language are those of the character whose thoughts are represented.

6 See user reviews on amazon, the first to come up when accessed in March 2017 refers to this complaint as 'the "he" issue': https://www.amazon.com/Wolf-Hall-Hilary-Mantel/dp/1250077583

7 The term 'deixis' refers to all those linguistic and grammatical elements which help to orient the reader in the story world and cannot be understood out of context, for example personal pronouns like 'he' and 'me', spatial and temporal adverbs like 'here' and 'now' as well as tense and aspect of verbs.

8 Ekphrasis is commonly understood as the verbal representation of a work of visual art.

9 Hierarchy of discourse refers to the difference in importance among the voices that constitute a narrative: in an omniscient novel the narrator is obviously at the top of this hierarchy, followed by the main character.

Bibliography

Bordo, S. (2013), *The Creation of Anne Boleyn: A New Look at England's Most Notorious Queen*, New York: Houghton Mifflin Harcourt.

Burrow, C. (2009), 'How to Twist a Knife', *London Review of Books* 31 (8), 30 April: 1–5. Available online: http://www.lrb.co.uk/v31/no8/colin-burrow/how-to-twist-a-knife (accessed 20 October 2016).

Caines, M. (2009), 'Arrange One's Face', Rev. of *Wolf Hall*, by Hilary Mantel, *Times Literary Supplement*, 15 May. Available online: http://entertainment.timesonline.co.uk/tol/arts_and_entertainment/the_tls/article6279083.ece (accessed 6 June 2012).

'Cromwell, Thomas, Earl of Essex [1485?-1540]', (1986), in Leslie Stephen and Sidney Lee (eds), *Dictionary of National Biography*, vol. 5, 192–202, Oxford: Oxford University Press.

De Bruyn, B. (2012), *Wolfgang Iser: A Companion*, Berlin: de Gruyter.

De Groot, J. (2010), *The Historical Novel*, The New Critical Idiom, London: Routledge.

De Groot, J. (2016), *Remaking History: The Past in Contemporary Historical Fictions*, London: Routledge.

Fludernik, M. (1996), *Towards a 'Natural' Narratology*, London: Routledge.

Genette, G. (1980), *Narrative Discourse: An Essay in Method*. Ithaca: Cornell University Press.

Hutcheon, L. (1989), 'Historiographic Metafiction: Parody and the Intertextuality of History', in P. O'Donnell and R. Con Davis (eds), *Intertextuality and Contemporary American Fiction*, 3–32, Baltimore: John Hopkins University Press.

Jameson, F. (1971), *Marxism and Form: Twentieth-Century Dialectical Theories of Literature*, Princeton: Princeton University Press.

Jameson, F. (1991), *Postmodernism, or, the Cultural Logic of Late Capitalism*, London: Verso.

Jones, P. (1995), 'Philosophical and Theoretical Issues in the Study of Deixis: A Critique of the Standard Account', in K. Green (ed.), *New Essays in Deixis: Discourse, Narrative, Literature*, 27–48, Amsterdam: Rodopi.

Laing, O. (2009), 'The Tudors' Finest Portraitist Yet', *The Guardian*, 26 April 2009. Available online: https://www.theguardian.com/books/2009/apr/26/hilary-mantel-wolf-hall (accessed 1 December 2017).

Le Guin, U. (1998), *Steering the Craft: Exercises and Discussions on Story Writing for the Lone Navigator or the Mutinous Crew*, Portland: The Eighth Mountain Press.

Lowenthal, D. (1985), *The Past Is a Foreign Country*, Cambridge: Cambridge University Press.

Lukács, G. (1983), *The Historical Novel*, translated by Hannah Mitchell and Stanley Mitchell, Lincoln: University of Nebraska Press.
Mantel, H. (2010), *Wolf Hall*, London: Fourth Estate.
McIntyre, D. (2006), *Point of View in Plays: A Cognitive Stylistic Approach to Viewpoint in Drama and Other Text-Types*, Amsterdam: Benjamins.
Mitchell, K. and Parsons, N. (2013), 'Reading the Represented Past: History and Fiction from 1700 to the Present', in K. Mitchell and N. Parsons (eds), *Reading Historical Fiction: The Revenant and Remembered Past*, 1–18, Basingstoke: Palgrave Macmillan.
Palmer, A. (2004), *Fictional Minds*, Lincoln: University of Nebraska Press.
Rigney, A. (2001), *Imperfect Histories: The Elusive Past and the Legacy of Romantic Historicism*, Ithaca: Cornell University Press.
Rousselot, E. (2014), 'Introduction: Exoticising the Past in Contemporary Neo-Historical Fiction', in Elodie Rousselot (ed.), *Exoticising the Past in Contemporary Neo-Historical Fiction*, 1–16, Basingstoke: Palgrave Macmillan.
Samuel, R. (1994), *Theatres of Memory. Vol. 1: Past and Present in Contemporary Culture*, London: Verso.
Semino, E. (2002), 'A Cognitive Stylistic Approach to Mind Style in Narrative Fiction', in E. Semino and J. Culpeper (eds), *Cognitive Stylistics: Language and Cognition in Text Analysis*, 95–122, Amsterdam: Benjamins.
Simpson, M. (2015), 'Art of Fiction', *The Paris Review*, vol. 212, spring no. 226. Available online: https://www.theparisreview.org/interviews/6360/hilary-mantel-art-of-fiction-no-226-hilary-mantel (accessed 12 July 2012).
Stockwell, P. (2002), *Cognitive Poetics: An Introduction*, London: Routledge.
Tayler, C. (2009), 'Henry's Fighting Dog', Rev. of *Wolf Hall*, by Hilary Mantel, *The Guardian*, 2 May. Available online: http://www.guardian.co.uk/books/2009/may/02/wolf-hall-hilary-mantel (accessed on 12 July 2012).
Trevarthen, C. (2001), 'Intersubjectivity', in Robert A. Wilson and Frank C. Keil (eds), *The MIT Encyclopedia of the Cognitive Sciences*, 415–419, Cambridge: MIT Press.
Vermeule, B. (2010), *Why Do We Care about Literary Characters?* Baltimore: Johns Hopkins University Press.
Wachtel, E. (2016), *The Best of Writers and Company: Interviews with 15 of the World's Greatest Authors*, Windsor, Ontario: Biblioasis.
White, H. (1973), *Metahistory: The Historical Imagination in Nineteenth-Century Europe*, Baltimore: Johns Hopkins University Press.
White, H. (1978), *Tropics of Discourse: Essays in Cultural Criticism*, Baltimore: Johns Hopkins University Press.
Wilson, L. (2015), 'Historical Representations: Reality Effects: The Historical Novel and the Crisis of Fictionality in the First Decade of the Twenty-First Century', in N. Bentley, N. Hubble and L. Wilson (eds), *The 2000s: A Decade of Contemporary British Fiction*, 145–171, London: Bloomsbury.
Wineburg, S. (2001), *Historical Thinking and Other Unnatural Acts: Charting the Future of Teaching the Past*, Philadelphia: Temple University Press.

5

Subjectivity in Process: Writing and the I in *Giving Up the Ghost* and *Ink in the Blood*

Victoria Bennett

There is a popular conception of Hilary Mantel's thought as blurring boundaries, as rebellious. This chapter will examine this notion in detail, by investigating how Mantel's texts create a 'cosmology', in which 'other' ways of seeing, knowing and being are brought to the fore. This cosmology allows for the magical, for the unseen, for those aspects of life that are 'felt' and experienced but are not privileged as 'real'. Through exploring Mantel's 2003 memoir *Giving Up the Ghost* and her 2010 hospital diary *Ink in the Blood*, this chapter will attempt to show how Mantel plays with autobiographical and realist forms in order to disrupt the reader's ways of seeing. This chapter thus demonstrates how in Mantel's work, particularly in her life-writing, there is always the play of something other to the text, an excess which positions her writing as 'provisional', holding any possibility of 'closure' in suspension, and that this sense of 'provisionality' has significant consequences for objectivity, realism and autobiography.

*****

Hilary Mantel's versatility as a writer is often remarked upon; John Mullan, for example, characterizes her work as 'rich and strange' (2015).[1] The strangeness stems partly from how each novel seems to belong to a different genre: for example, *Bildungsroman* (*An Experiment in Love*); Gothic horror (*Eight Months on Ghazzah Street*); and her successful historical novels, the third volume of which is forthcoming. A fertile resource for critical attention, Mantel's oeuvre also revels in probing creative and critical boundaries. This essay explores Mantel's 2003 memoir *Giving Up the Ghost* and how she tests the limits of fiction, autobiography and, to some extent, what might be called reality itself. Mantel's choice of the memoir form is already problematic, in that the form has certain assumptions inbuilt. An example from David Lodge's review of *Giving Up the Ghost* illustrates such assumptions. In 'Little Miss Never Well Triumphs', Lodge writes:

> In short there has always been something of an enigma about the person behind Hilary Mantel's novels, as if each of them were a mask held up to disguise herself in a new and unpredictable way. Now she has dropped or discarded the masks of fiction by writing an autobiographical memoir, focusing particularly on her childhood. (2004: 42)

For Lodge, autobiography acts as a form of revelation, a means by which we might learn something startling about the enigmatic author. Autobiography becomes a personal history with an ontology that differentiates it from the fictional, a history of childhood which can be used to glean facts about the life of the author which will stand as guarantor over the work.[2] A clear demarcation emerges between autobiography as truth, pertaining to real life, and fiction as created and untrue. If we take as read that *Giving Up the Ghost* is somehow part of the creation of what Mantel calls her 'self', it is possible to read the rich and strange in her work in a much less reductive way. Not only does she dispute orthodox notions of what 'autobiography' is or should be, her work also challenges traditional assumptions of writing as the translation of psychological experience into a concrete medium of expression. Reading Mantel demands that we attend both to her desire to 'seize the copyright in myself' (2010a: 71), and to the assumptions which underpin the critical work on literary autobiography.

The setting of *Giving Up the Ghost*, published in 2003, begins in 2000 with the author and her husband deciding to sell their cottage; a seemingly innocuous moment in their lives, until the reader understands that this house has 'a ghost in it' (5). Mantel uses this event to launch her memoir of 'mid-life' which is also the story of her childhood, complete with strange hauntings and family secrets. Writing about her misdiagnosed pain from endometriosis, and the medical procedures which dominated much of her young adult life, Mantel describes in harrowing detail her hysterectomy at the age of twenty-seven. The memoir is thus a story about childhood and childlessness; as such, how it has been read so far is indicative of the interesting place Mantel occupies as a woman writing. Amy Prodromou, for example, rightly recognizes Mantel's work as subversive and pushing boundaries: she writes about *Giving Up the Ghost* and its 'inbetween-ness' as part of the grief memoir sub-genre she terms 'memoir of textured recovery' (2012: 58). In this article Prodromou identifies Mantel's place 'in how these narratives of loss invoke and produce a gendered self' (60), arguing:

> so while ... Mantel on the one hand engender[s] a whole, solid sense of self through the autobiographical act, the tension between self as either fragmented and discontinuous or whole and continuous (a tension never fully reconciled) is the basis for this nuanced, 'textured recovery' that I am arguing forces us to rethink theories of the self, narrative and healing. (71–72)

'Textured recovery' works as a metaphor to a point, emphasizing as it does the messy bodily functions and ways in which Mantel seems to draw the lines of her body through writing. I would argue however, that there is never a 'solid sense of self' in Mantel that is not also at the same time in a process of decay. What Prodromou takes to be a 'solid sense of self' is the textual residue of Mantel's narrative voice that puts meat on the bones of her words. For instance, Prodromou quotes Mantel writing about writing, 'when you have committed enough words to paper you feel you have a spine stiff enough to stand up in the wind' (68). Continuing, Mantel says, 'But when you stop writing you find that's all you are, a spine, a row of rattling vertebrae, dried out like an old quill pen' (2010a: 223). In the act of writing Mantel builds a sense of self that can 'stand up' to scrutiny, but the act is the very thing that sustains the body's solidity. Without writing, she seems to say, she is dry bones and old feathers, and could blow away in a puff of dust.

This intimate and strange connection between the body and writing occurs even more powerfully in Mantel's hospital diary of 2010, *Ink in the Blood*. She writes, 'I am fascinated by the line between writing and physical survival' (2010b: 28). This short diary is full of parallels between the written word and Mantel's descriptions of her body. The description of her wound, 'it has a spiral binding, like a manuscript' is written with her inimitable humour and self-deprecation: 'On the whole I would rather be an item of stationery than be me' (5). She describes the new line she discovers on her palm, and the 'lines' of the drip going into her wrist: 'The iambic pentameter of the saline stand, the alexandrine of the blood drain, the epidural's sweet sonnet form' (7–8). When she has to stay longer in hospital due to complications, she invents stories in her head, 'the novel is composed in elaborate Jamesian circumlocutions, and I breathe along with the punctuation' (24). Text and body combine in this diary to form an unusual symbiotic entity. Leaving aside the references to Woolf,[3] Mantel's commitment to writing and its connection with the inside of her body, its most intimate spaces, is less a space of recovery than of exploration. Mantel goes exploring in her own abdominal cavity, in effect. She makes the body metaphorical to investigate her own insides, and through writing thus problematizes the relationship between the inside and outside. Looking at *Ink in the Blood* thus enriches the reading of *Giving Up the Ghost* by showing how Mantel intervenes in autobiography: not as a predetermined subject representing oneself in writing, but as a subject whose physical existence cannot be separated from its textual existence. As Sidonie Smith trenchantly states, 'Life narrative is a site of embodied knowledge … life narrative inextricably links memory, subjectivity, and the materiality of the body' (Smith and Watson 2010: 49). Mantel makes the explicit link in *Giving Up the Ghost*:

> I have been so mauled by medical procedures, so sabotaged and made over, so thin and so fat, that sometimes I feel that each morning it is necessary to write myself into being – even if the writing is aimless doodling that no one will ever read, or the diary that no one can see until I'm dead. (222)

Writing, for Mantel, allows her to make her self recognizable. The mention of her diary as hidden until death suggests that what is at stake is visibility: the episode of the 'magic slate' in *Giving Up the Ghost* adds weight to Smith's claim that writing is inextricably linked to the production of the self.

Mantel writes about her first writing as a child, 'letters from an imaginary me to an imaginary someone' which 'could be disappeared in an instant' (69). These attempts take place on a child's toy, the 'magic slate', a piece of equipment well known to Freud as the 'Wunderblock' or 'Mystic Writing Pad' (Freud 1957). Consisting of a thin sheet of paper over a waxy surface, writing upon the paper with a stylus causes writing to appear: lifting up the paper makes the writing disappear. The secrecy of this writing is a comfort to the child Mantel, all the time she is unaware that it is visible to others: 'I could write anything I liked, but if someone loomed into view I could disappear it in an instant' (69); 'I believed I was doing it in perfect safety' (69). On closer inspection, however, the imprint of what has been written is still visible. When the child Mantel discovers that the 'pen left marks on the plastic sheet' (69–70), the magic slate is changed for her forever. She thus gives up writing on the magic slate, for fear that her words could be deciphered, 'I didn't dare to risk it' (70). What disconcerts the author Mantel so much about this episode is the feeling of a safe space being invaded or violated: the word 'loomed' suggesting an adult overlooking the child Mantel's writing. The reader is left with the sensation of the interruption as a negative event, a precursor to judgement or censorship.

The tension created throughout this passage allows us to experience the child Mantel's fears. The continuing 'horror' the adult Mantel feels if someone reads her work in the drafting stages is translated into pragmatic writing advice, 'don't show your work before you're ready' (70). This fear of exposure not only betrays the persistence of the child's 'habit' of 'concealment' (71), it also demonstrates the power of writing to create the self. Writing brings order to the chaotic interior world, but at the same time creates a vulnerability. Jacques Derrida writes about this vulnerability and the threat of exposure in 'Freud and the Scene of Writing' in *Writing and Difference*:

> There is no writing which does not devise some means of protection, to protect against itself, against the writing by which the 'subject' is himself threatened as he lets himself be written: as he exposes himself. (Derrida 2001: 281–282)

This is the author Mantel's dilemma: to write is to court the threat of exposure, and flirt with judgement. To not write, however, means the dissolution of the self, the inability to draw one's boundaries tightly enough. Writing delimits the boundaries of the body, and marks off what is inside from what is outside, but this process is always unstable: writing is a risky activity. Mantel's description of her body as 'a shabby old building in an area of heavy shelling' (Mantel 2010a: 222) emphasizes the ever-changing nature of her attempts to 'write myself into being' (222).

This fluctuation is underscored when she writes about a mirror in her dream, '[But] what happens, when you face the mirror, is that its surface melts, and the self walks into the glass. You step through it, and into a different dream' (224). In this dream, the mirrored surface does not reflect back the image, but 'melts', letting the undefined outline of the body go unreflected, unpinned. The mirror in the dream dissolves to create a further dream, representing the instability of the dreamer's reality. The mirror brings to the surface a myriad of associations within Mantel's oeuvre and in wider culture; Jacques Lacan's work, for example, affirms the primacy of the real and metaphorical mirror in the development of the infant, the 'jubilant assumption of his specular image' (1977: 76). The infant is overjoyed at the appearance of his image in the mirror and being able to take on his reflection as 'his'. The reflection of the small child's image in the mirror is for Lacan the 'root-stock of secondary identifications' (76), and the point from which the subject is instituted in language, as it grows and learns the rules of the symbolic order. The visual image of oneself in the mirror is the primary identification, from which all others flow, and it underwrites (however imperfectly) the sense of self. For the self in culture then, according to Lacan, the mirror is its foundation, the apprehension of one's reflection through a clear and focused look. The image corresponds to its real-life referent in an uncomplicated visual relationship; the human subject is reflected faithfully back to itself. As Eileen Pollard's interview '"Mind what gap?"' attests, Mantel is fascinated by mirrors and the ways they function, drawing Pollard into a discussion of the mirror that hangs over her writing table (Pollard 2015: 1042). The mirror bears witness to the non-coincidence between the self and how it is perceived in the world, and how the self is perceived by the self and others. 'I live by metaphor', Mantel writes in the Foreword to Jane Haynes's memoir *Who Is It That Can Tell Me Who I Am?* (2009) and what better symbol of metaphor is there than the mirror? There is always a gap between the reflection and the reflected; the word and the thing; the experience and its expression in language. As with the 'magic slate', the mirror behaves in unpredictable ways. What one expects to see is never what one gets. Not only this; the mirror can only reflect the surface and leaves the interior untouched.

The unpredictable nature of the mirror, and how it relates to writing, is reflected in Mantel's evocation of George Orwell's essay 'Why I Write' (2000), from which she paraphrases, 'good prose is like a window-pane' (2010a: 5). Words are tools that deceive from the beginning: Mantel relates how, when she learns to write, the letters 'slip off' the slate at school. When she is finally given modelling clay to make them with, her desire to make them stand up slows her down. Words continue to come with caveats for the reader, warnings to beware of so-called transparency:

> And as for transparency – window panes undressed are a sign of poverty, aren't they? How about some nice net curtains, so I can look out but you can't see in? How about shutters, or a chaste Roman blind? Besides, window-pane prose is no guarantee of truthfulness. Some deceptive sights are seen through glass, and the best liars tell lies in plain words. (Mantel 2010a: 5)

Just as the unpredictability of the mirror fails to reflect back an acceptable image, so the clarity of the window-pane is 'deceptive'. Mantel's preoccupation with the appearance of the window is to some extent a rhetorical device, a *caveat lector*. but at the same time belies her consideration of social class. The 'net curtains' seem to function as a signifier of middle England suburban taste; aspiring lower-middle-class gentility, as typified by the inhabitants of Fetherhoughton in Mantel's 1989 novel *Fludd*, for example. They also act as a clue to the dilemma of writing for Mantel. 'So I can look out but you can't see in?' sounds like a plea: echoing the impossible desire to write but also to remain private and unseen by the world. If by writing, then, Mantel is drawing and redrawing the limits of herself, the remaking that takes place 'each day' (2010a: 222) is a social act. This may seem paradoxical, given the tension that judgement invokes, but her explicit statement of intent, to 'write herself into being', shows that by writing autobiography Mantel is grappling with identity, and this engagement is absolutely implicated in the wider social implications of class and gender, in particular. As Leigh Gilmore writes in the preface to *Autobiographics: A Feminist Theory of Women's Self-Representation*, 'self-representation' is a 'contradictory code whose interruptive effects can be located in other genres' (1994: ix). The contradiction of 'self-representation' Gilmore identifies is played out in Mantel's autobiography as a dialogue between the I who writes and the 'myself' whose story the 'I' is attempting to tell.

This contradictory practice can also be read as a social act. To explore this further, Marianne Dekoven's essay 'The Literary as Activity in Postmodernity' reimagines the literary as a practice within postmodernity, rather than simply denoting certain kinds of texts. 'The literary' thus becomes a doing with a social and cultural application, with implications for what Dekoven calls the 'non-hegemonic constituencies empowered by the opening of the canon' (Beaumont-Bissel 2002: 105). For Mantel, a woman from a working-class background, writing is a way of creating and delimiting the self. If the literary offers a site of resistance, as Dekoven argues, Mantel's writing is a revolutionary act that calls into question accepted ideas of who should write, and what they should write about. Mantel's attempt to 'seize the copyright in myself' not only puts the stability of the I into question, it also exposes the workings of the narrative self-in-the-world, the self that writes in order to be a part of the world and the social (dis)order. This ordering and disordering of the self, the making of 'something fit to be seen in … to go out in and face the world' (Mantel 2010a: 223) refers back to the suggestion of writing for Mantel as a space less of recovery (as Prodromou argues) than of exploration. Moreover, this exploration into the self demonstrates the primacy of visibility and the network of inescapable social connections that exist in *Giving Up the Ghost*. Mantel's attempts to redraw herself through writing constitute a revolutionary literary act that reconfigures the way bodies and writing are represented and created in the social. Her need to create a 'spine stiff enough to stand up in the wind' (222) is only assuaged through writing. Writing her-self is a kind of defiance, a way of breaking out of socially prescribed ideas of what that self should be, whether these are mediated through her stepfather's proscriptions or the doctor who forbids her to write.

If the 'truth' of Mantel's autobiography rests in its value to the reader as a document of lived experience, then the reading of her autobiography becomes 'an intersubjective process that occurs within a dialogic exchange between writer and reader' (Smith and Watson 2010:16). Taking this into account, moreover, means that the 'authority of the autobiographical, then, neither confirms nor invalidates notions of objective truth, rather it tracks the previously uncharted truths of particular lives' (Smith and Watson 2010: 16).

Mantel has spoken about the 'texture' of lived experience in her Reith lectures (2017),[4] referring to the process of writing about historical characters. This attention to 'texture' creates a relationship to writing and meaning which is predicated upon a different kind of reading; a reading that elucidates how Mantel challenges both autobiography and literary realism. The dialogue created through writing, between writer and reader, informs the process of creating and representing identity. In her essay '"Fiction" and the experience of the other', Peggy Kamuf (Beaumont-Bissell 2002) writes about what she calls the fictional operation, characterizing it as 'the irreducible possibility of fiction that is brought to bear in such a way as to shift the ground on which any theoretical discourse may claim validity' (157). Mantel's creation and representation of identity makes use of such a 'fictional operation' in the places where she self-consciously references her own writing practice. For instance, 'Eat meat. Drink blood. Give up your social life and don't think you can have friends. Rise in the quiet hours of the night and prick your fingertips, and use the blood for ink' (2010a: 5). By presenting the writer in hyperbolic fashion, and showing an aesthetic sensibility clearly worked over by the fictional, Mantel creates a kind of hybrid which invests the memoir's narrative with rhetorical value. This traversing of limits between fact and fiction does not sit well with traditional autobiographical conventions, as David Lodge's reading shows. But the emphasis on the visceral and bodily nature of the writing process opens up the autobiographical to reading, and reading in a way that I call provisionality. By making problematic the relationships between all the different modes of life that are represented in the autobiography, and her openness to 'other' ways of seeing and knowing, Mantel takes up a provisional stance. This is the source of Mantel's power: the ability to say 'yes' to all kinds of experience. Yet this quality in her writing does not allow the reader a firm ground from which to understand 'reality', as her emphasis on dreams, hallucinations and bodily experience demonstrates. By privileging the 'ghost' which haunts the cottage, provisionality has an integral connection to the spectral.[5] A ghost is an appearance of something which in usual circumstances remains hidden, but for the time being is manifested to the ordinary vision:

> About eleven o'clock, I see a flickering on the staircase. The air is still; then it moves. I raise my head. The air is still again. I know it is my stepfather's ghost coming down. Or, to put it in a way acceptable to most people, I 'know' it is my stepfather's ghost. I am not perturbed. I am used to 'seeing' things that aren't there. Or – to put it in a way more acceptable to me – I am used to seeing things that 'aren't there'. (1)

By using quotation marks for 'know' and 'aren't there', Mantel makes problematic the ways in which it is possible to 'know' something is 'real', and signals from the outset that the reader is not on solid foundations, epistemologically or ontologically. The movement of the air and the 'flickering on the staircase' are attempts to write about an experience that is 'perturbing', but not for Mantel, who from the beginning of the memoir demonstrates the different ways of being and knowing. She continues by describing how she has greeted her stepfather on the stairs, and how, 'it was in this house that I last saw my stepfather Jack, in the early months of 1995: alive, in his garments of human flesh' (1–2). The eerie effect of this sentence is then undercut by the breezy, impossibly light style of the next: 'It may be, of course, that the flicker against the banister was nothing more than the warning of a migraine attack' (2). Mantel then describes in unswerving detail the visions, hallucinations and aural disturbances that accompany these attacks, treating them all as if their epistemological status was the same, not stopping to demarcate clearly the different types of experience, including dreams. She describes the:

> strange dreams, from which I wake with hallucinations of taste. Once, thirty years ago, I dreamt that I was eating bees, and ever since I have lived with their milk-chocolate sweetness and their texture, which is like lightly cooked calves' liver. (3)

Mantel places the dreams, hallucinations and visions into the context of her migraines, the day-to-day illness which impairs her cognition. However, this context is placed into question by the paragraph that begins directly after she describes seeing her stepfather's ghost in the cottage: 'It *may be*, of course, that the flicker against the banister was nothing more than the warning of a migraine attack … I *don't know* whether, at such vulnerable times, *I see more than is there; or if things are there, that normally I don't see*' (emphasis added, 2). The equivocation in these words shows a lack of definitive attribution, and the repetition of seeing what may or may not be 'there' is a powerful indicator of the questioning of reality that starts with the 'ghost'.

Again, in her narration of the dream of eating bees, the reader is invited to share and revel in the synaesthesic sensation, as Mantel evokes a materially solid experience of an event (in this case the dream) that is somehow insubstantial. The taste and texture of the bees thus described opens up the reading, contrary to the specificity of 'milk-chocolate' and 'lightly cooked calves' liver'. The identification of particular flavours and textures situates Mantel's dream within the context of her outward experience, while also remaining necessarily subjective and unverifiable. The power of the dream, which stays with Mantel, suggests that the strangeness of the taste, itself a hallucination within a dream, somehow overrides the pleasure of the eating. To dream of eating is a common enough thing, as is savouring the pleasure of the taste on waking, yet the flavour invariably fades soon after, and for

Mantel the weirdness of being able to remember the exact taste mitigates the pleasure. Mantel is writing her own experience, a non-verifiable aspect of her subjective world, which is neither exclusively real nor fictional. This is the heart of provisionality, what Sidonie Smith calls 'the paradoxical status of self-reference' (Smith and Watson 2010: 17). The powerful image of eating bees suggests the webs of experience that Mantel will explore, creating a mythology around the 'synaesthesia' for which words are not enough (23).[6]

The physical sensations of taste and sight Mantel explores relate both to childhood fantasy and to the telling of her life story. Thus, the reader's sense of chronology in the text is influenced by the intertwining voices of the adult and child narrators. For example, whereas the dream of eating bees is narrated by Mantel from a retrospective viewpoint, the episode in which she fears she has swallowed a fly is narrated from the child's perspective, and employs present tense narration. Mantel is writing about learning to walk, 'in the house, but [I] don't remember that' (28), and moving outside onto the street, she turns left, 'I don't know it's left' (28). She describes how there is a 'rusty iron ring' in the stone of the house, near the front door:

> I always slip my finger into it, though I should not. Grandad says it is where they tied the monkey up, but I don't think they ever really had one; all the same, he lurks in my mind, a small grey monkey with piteous eyes and a long active tail. (28)

The thought of the monkey is given real status by the child Mantel, filling in as she does all the details of its appearance. She knows there is no monkey, but the thought and the image of the monkey continues to exist within her consciousness, until she states, 'Two things not to believe: the monkey. People who say, "I have eyes in the back of my head"' (31). The change in tone signals a kind of transition for the child Mantel, in learning to differentiate between what is real and what is not; but the next episode demonstrates the limited extent of this differentiation:

> I sit on the stairs, which are steep, box-like, dark. I think I am going to die. I have breathed in a housefly, I think I have. The fly was in the room and my mouth open because I was putting into it a sweet. Then the fly was nowhere to be seen. It manifests now as a tickling and scraping on the inside of my throat, the side of my throat that's nearest to the kitchen wall. (31)

The short sentences, the repetition of I, and the use of 'and' and 'then' as connectives show the reader that this event is being presented to us by the child Mantel. She has not yet learned which way is left, and can only identify the affected side as nearest to the kitchen wall. The episode continues as the child's internal monologue, where she resolves to die quietly, is asked what is wrong and says nothing, although 'my resolve to die completely alone has faltered' (32). The sweet that the child Mantel was eating when the fly disappeared represented an act of considerable courage on the part of the child, knowing as she did that to hesitate over the box would mean no sweet at all, but 'now I'm on the stairs not knowing whether it's green sweet or fly' (32). The child's perception of causality is exposed here, the fact that if the fly is no longer in the room it must be buzzing inside her throat, causing the rasping. The tragic-comic nature of the scene is alluded to, by author Mantel, in her mention of the word 'absurdity'. The adult is intruding, here, although the scene is narrated in the present tense, and continues to be as the adult narrator slowly takes over the child's urgent telling of her story:

> The dry rasping in my throat persists, but now I don't know if it is the original obstruction lodged there, or the memory of it, the imprint, which is not going to fade from my breathing flesh. For many years the word 'marzipan' affects me with its deathly hiss, the buzz in its syllables, a sepulchral fizz. (32–33)

The imprint of the fly becomes connected in the infant Mantel's vocabulary with the word 'marzipan', the name of the sweet she did not get to choose in the first place, knowing that her hesitation in the choice would cost her the choice altogether. It is the choice *not made* that leaves the imprint. The fear of imminent death is forgotten, and all that's left is 'marzipan', the sense of death having been displaced onto this word, with its 'deathly hiss' and 'sepulchral fizz' (33). A sweet paste used to decorate cakes is now associated with death, assonance completing the connection with the fly as a signifier of decay. This moment marks a kind of education for the child Mantel, who is learning to differentiate between reality and fantasy; yet these lessons are not entirely absorbed by the child or the adult, and never completely for any of us. A bit like the sweet/fly, they stick in the throat, are not swallowed whole or completely taken in. It is the word 'marzipan', seemingly innocuous, that continues to denote the child's feeling of imminent death: not entirely ingested, words stick in the throat, like the fly she may or may not have swallowed.

It is fitting that we end with the child's way of making itself, for this is Mantel's own sense of her writing practice:

> The inner process, the writing life, it doesn't change at all. Every day is like the first day, it's like being a beginner. There's no time for complacency. You need to be extending your range all the time. (Elmhirst 2012: 43)

Writing is mandatory for making and remaking the self, this much is clear. What lies beneath, however, is always to some extent obscured: the interior that the mirror does not reach. Mantel writes this obscurity, which necessitates the provisional stance, by redrawing the connections between dreams, reality and writing. She does this in subtle ways to not only represent her experience ('seize the copyright') but to move beyond the crude differentiation of experiences that takes place in narrative, the theoretical cul-de-sac of 'did this or that really happen?' Mantel's writing, by troubling the boundaries set by 'truth' opens up possibilities for critical readings. Moreover, she blurs the boundaries between fact and fiction, a distinction that she holds in reserve throughout. In writing about Mantel's writing, indeed any writing, metaphors of depth, of truths to be gleaned or uncovered keep making themselves known. As I have shown, however, Mantel's writing complicates this. By thinking about her life, her self as a story to be read and thought about and discussed she crosses and re-crosses the boundaries dividing fact/fiction/dream, fantasy, reality. As Christa Wolf states, 'writing can only begin for those to whom reality is no longer a matter of course', (Hirsch 1989: 158) which expresses simply the truth of writing the singular experience of self. But this formulation also exposes the tension remaining between the 'I' who writes and the 'myself' to be represented through writing, which comes from writing itself. There is a force within the movement of writing which evades the writer's desire to 'seize the copyright'. Not only that the writer's desire to 'seize' control is undermined by the hesitation provoked by writing, but that writing itself can only provide part satisfaction of that desire. Something other always haunts. As Mantel herself writes, 'All your houses are haunted by the person you might have been' (20). The spectral presences of these other lives demand openness to their existences, and this openness is what Mantel does so well.

Notes

1 An allusion to Ariel's song in *The Tempest*, Act 1 Scene 2: 'Full fathom five thy father lies;/Of his bones are coral made;/Those are pearls that were his eyes./Nothing of him doth fade,/But doth suffer a sea-change/Into something rich and strange./Sea-nymphs hourly ring his knell' (964) William Shakespeare, *The Tempest* in *The Complete Oxford Shakespeare*, Wells, Stanley and Gary Taylor eds, Oxford: Oxford University Press, 1987.

2 Barthes's formulation of the 'reality effect', in which the writer's 'useless detail' offers a verification of the writing's adherence to reality, operates in a similar way. Like the literary detail (Flaubert's barometer) that underpins the 'real', details in autobiography are used to explain and inform readings of the writer's novels, and offer a guarantor of authenticity. See Roland Barthes 'The Reality Effect', in *The Rustle of Language*, 141–148, Los Angeles: University of California Press, 1989.

3 Stella Bolaki discusses the connections between Mantel and Woolf in '"When the Lights of Health Go Down": Virginia Woolf's Aesthetics and Contemporary Illness Narratives', arguing that Mantel's critique of Woolf threatens to reinstate the hierarchy between mental and physical illness. In Ryan and Bolaki eds.

4 'Your real job, as a novelist, is not to be an inferior sort of historian, but to recreate the texture of lived experience: to activate the senses, and deepen the reader's engagement through feeling' (Mantel 2017).

5 See for example the work of Lucy Arnold, and Wolfgang Funk in Adiseshiah and Hildyard eds.

6 Neil Vickers suggests, 'what Mantel calls her synaesthesic perception could equally be described as a capacity to disperse her emotional experience into different sensory fields' (63). 'Hilary Mantel and the Space of Life Writing', In Killan and Wolf eds.

Bibliography

Adiseshiah, S. and Hildyard, R. eds. (2013), *Twenty-First Century Fiction: What Happens Now*, Basingstoke: Palgrave Macmillan.

Barthes, R. (1989), 'The Reality Effect', in *The Rustle of Language*, 141–148. Los Angeles: University of California Press.

Beaumont-Bissell, E. ed. (2002), *The Question of Literature: The Place of the Literary in Contemporary Theory*, Manchester and New York: Manchester University Press.

Chambers Dictionary, (2014), 13th edn, London: Harrap Publishers.

Derrida, J. (2001), *Writing and Difference*, London and New York: Routledge.

Elmhirst, S. (2012), 'The Unquiet Mind of Hilary Mantel', *New Statesman*, 3 October 2012. Available online: http://www.newstatesman.com/culture/culture/2012/10/unquiet-mind-hilary-mantel (accessed 19 January 2017).

Freud, S. ([1925] 1957), 'A Note upon "The Mystic Writing Pad"', in Strachey, J. (ed.), *Collected Papers: Volume 5*, 175–180, London: Hogarth Press.

Gilmore, L. (1994), *Autobiographics: A Feminist Theory of Women's Self-Representation*, Ithaca, NY and London: Cornell University Press.

Haynes, J. (2010), *Who Is It That Can Tell Me Who I Am?* London: Constable.

Hirsch, M. (1989), *The Mother Daughter Plot: Narrative, Psychoanalysis, Feminism*, Bloomington, IN: Indiana University Press.

Kamuf, P. (2002), '"Fiction" and the Experience of the Other', in Elizabeth Beaumont Bissell (ed.), *The Question of Literature: The Place of the Literary in Contemporary Theory*, 154–173, Manchester and New York: Manchester University Press.

Kilian, E and Wolf H. eds. (2016), *Life Writing and Space*, Farnham: Ashgate.

Lacan, J. (1977), *Ecrits*. New York and London: W.W. Norton.

Lodge, D. (2004), 'Little Miss Never Well Triumphs', *Commonweal* 131 (19): 42–45.

Mantel, H. (2005), *Fludd*, London: Harper Collins.

Mantel, H. (2010a), *Giving Up the Ghost*, London: Fourth Estate.

Mantel, H. (2010b), *Ink in the Blood: A Hospital Diary*. Kindle edition.

Mantel, H. (2017), 'Fourth Reith Lecture: Can These Bones Live?' BBC, 4 July 2017. Available online: http://downloads.bbc.co.uk/radio4/reith2017/reith_2017_hilary_mantel_lecture%204.pdf (accessed 17 July 2017).

Mullan, J. (2015), 'The Strange and Brilliant Fiction of Hilary Mantel', *The Guardian*, 17 January. Available online: https://www.theguardian.com/books/2015/jan/17/-sp-hilary-mantel-profile-adaptation-wolf-hall (accessed 21 February 2015).

Orwell, G. (2000), *Essays*, London: Penguin.

Pollard, E. J. (2015), '"Mind What Gap?": An Interview with Hilary Mantel', *Textual Practice* 29 (6): 1035–1044. Available online: http://dx.doi.org/10.1080/0950236X.2015.1024729 (accessed 17 July 2017)

Prodromou, A. (2012), '"That Weeping Constellation": Navigating Loss in "Memoirs of Textured Recovery"', *Life Writing* 9 (1): 57–75.

Ryan, D. and Bolaki, S. eds. (2012), *Contradictory Woolf*, Clemson: Clemson University Press.

Smith, S. and Watson J. (2010), *Reading Autobiography: A Guide for Interpreting Life Narratives*, Minneapolis,MN: University of Minnesota Press.

Vickers, N. (2016), 'Hilary Mantel and the Space of Life Writing', In Killan and Wolf eds.

6

Becoming Ghost: Spectral Realism in Hilary Mantel's Fiction

Wolfgang Funk

In her review of Hilary Mantel's 2005 novel *Beyond Black* in *The Guardian*, Fay Weldon claims that Mantel has 'taken that ethereal halfway house between heaven and hell, between the living and the dead, and nailed it on the page'. This chapter makes a case for the central significance of this eerie territory between life and death in Mantel's writing in general. It examines how many of her works suggest an anti-modernist epistemology to counteract the simulated hyper-realism and rampant consumerism agenda of the late twentieth and early twenty-first centuries by 'privileging the unseen', in other words, by taking seriously manifestations of the supernatural which exceed the scope of objectivist and logical discernment.

*****

> And soon the fragments dim of lovely forms
> Come trembling back, unite, and now once more
> The pool becomes a mirror.
> (Coleridge)

In Hilary Mantel's short story 'Terminus' (2014: 193–202), the unnamed narrator briefly catches a glimpse of her dead father on a train running parallel to her own. This chance encounter prompts her to ponder the question, if, in a manner of speaking, everyone is potentially more spectral than we usually assume: 'For how many of all these surging thousands are solid, and how many of these assumptions are tricks of the light? How many, I ask you, are connected at all points, how many are utterly and convincingly in the state they purport to be: which is, alive?' (198). This projection and protrusion of the spectral into everyday reality pertains just as well to a wider context of cultural theory, where, following the publication of Derrida's *Specters of Marx* (1994), the metaphor of the spectre and the epistemological mode of hauntology have come to figure as a compelling symbol for late-postmodern thinking. According to Julian Wolfreys, 'any medium through which we seek to communicate today that involves a narrativization of our identities in relation to others not immediately present is inescapably spectral' (2002: 2), and Roger Luckhurst even identifies a 'spectral turn' in contemporary literature (2002: 527). It would seem as if the more unreal or simulated the world appears to us and the more detached from physical materiality individual identities are becoming, the more we turn to images of disembodied spectrality for counsel. It is to ghosts we turn in order not to become too ghostly to ourselves.

This essay investigates the current appeal of the ghost specifically as a literary metaphor. It attempts to sharpen the conceptual acuity and epistemic validity of this metaphor by examining how the critical and popular success of Mantel's Tudor novels can be attributed to specific narratological techniques which apply this spectral sensitivity to the writing of historical fiction. I will show how Mantel formally collapses the seeming dichotomy between the reality of history and the fictionality of its representation by embodying and eventually sublating this conflict in spectral images. If a term should be required to designate this approach, I would tentatively suggest 'spectral realism', a phrase which, like the metaphors it describes, tries to give substance, in however disembodied a form, to an oscillation between absence and presence, between past, present and future, between form and content. In order to contextualize Mantel's spectral realism, I will first provide an overview of the different forms and functions that spectres assume in literature in general. Hamlet, one of the most prominent ghost-seers in English literary history, famously muses how the appearance of a ghost indicates that 'time is out of joint' (Shakespeare 2001: 228, I,v). Accordingly, my analysis of literary spectres initially focuses on the temporal dimension of this metaphor, the various aspects, in other words, of how ghosts in fiction symbolize the relationship of past, present and future.

When asked in an interview by one of the editors of this volume if she herself believes in ghosts, Mantel's answer is that she indeed does so, 'for practical purposes'. Recalling how she had once been asked this question before by a teenager, she remembers weighing the alternatives: 'if I say no I close down this conversation ... and if I say yes, it opens the whole world of possibility' (Pollard 2015: 1042). This very pragmatic answer neatly summarizes the appeal of spectres in critical theory and their more specific function in the fiction of Mantel: they are not, or at least not primarily, symptoms of a present out of tune with its past, who require to be dealt with in order to achieve some kind of closure. Quite to the contrary, Mantel's spectral metaphors defy closure and demand discourse. They represent things left unsaid and call for further engagement. They come bearing the promise of possibility rather than brandishing unsettled accounts. They are elliptic in the sense that they do not point towards the settlement of such accounts but rather (dis)embody the openness and in(de)terminability of the account per se. In the same interview, Eileen Pollard identifies the three dots which are used to indicate a textual ellipsis as 'a theoretical tool' which signifies 'the burst full stop' (2015: 1044). The spectres in Mantel's books, and in particular in her Tudor novels, are employed in similar fashion. They are very decidedly textual phenomena, which nevertheless gesture beyond the mere materiality of the text. They are both an effect of and a challenge to representation. It is precisely this undecidability, this oscillation between presence and absence, between the once-upon-a-time, the here-and-now and the not-yet, which makes the ghost such a potent tool for renegotiating the relationship between the past and its representation, a negotiation which has always been at the heart of the genre of historical fiction.

Haunting presences: The functions of the literary ghost

Before addressing Mantel's ghosts in more detail, it is necessary first to ask why ghosts appear in writing at all. Answers to this question traditionally start out from the assumption that every period in (literary) history has its own way with the supernatural, that the image of the revenant is employed at different times to address different issues. Just as Hamlet's fateful procrastination in carrying out his dead father's mandate to revenge his murder reflects an awakening humanist consciousness emancipating itself from medieval superstition, every literary ghost is both a projection and a reflection of the fears and premonitions which beset its age. Explaining the spread of the 'Gothic' mode around and after 1800, Fred Botting writes for example, that the 'new concern inflected in Gothic forms emerged as the darker side to Romantic ideas of individuality, imaginative consciousness and creation' (1996: 10). In this traditional configuration, Botting argues, the fear induced by the liminal figure of the ghost stages this transgression only to eventually solidify and consolidate the legitimate bounds of experience and representation; 'the terrors and horrors of transgression', he claims, 'become a powerful means to reassert the values of society, virtue and propriety' (7).

The ghosts that haunt the pages of Mantel's Tudor novels are of a rather different order. They do not challenge boundaries in order to safeguard social propriety nor do they spread fear in order to conserve the status quo. Their aim is to break the representational mould as such. They throw open the limits of experience because the future, rather than the past, is their concern. In order to appreciate the novelty of Mantel's use of the spectral metaphor, I will first provide a brief outline of traditional features and aspects of literary ghosts. Showing how Mantel has employed more traditional ghosts throughout her work, I will argue that the spectral realism that manifests itself so strongly in the Tudor novels is in fact the culmination of Mantel's extensive exploration of the literary allure of ghosts.

The intrusion of a revenant from the past into the present often gives evidence that the conventional sequence of past, present and future and the irresistible inevitability attached to this sequence are being challenged. Lisa Kröger and Melanie P. Anderson's statement that 'with ghosts, the past is never over, the present is never secure, and the future is certain only of the spectral return' (2013: x) denotes precisely this disruptive effect of spectral appearances on a traditional, linear conception of time. Expanding Botting's argument that the Gothic originally clarified and policed the limits of the socially acceptable in an age of revolution, it seems more than just coincidence that the heyday of the literary ghost story also coincides roughly with the solidification of the concept of time as an arrow at the expense of time as a cycle (cf. Gould 1987). Their status as untimely reminders of a past that – to quote Faulkner – is neither dead nor even past (cf. 2012: 73) explains why ghosts disrupt the ordinary flow of time in the first place. They are emblems of unfinished business; they intrude into the present because it has failed to answer questions of the past. In her study *Night Visitors* (1977), Julia Briggs provides this succinct summary of the motives of the traditional literary ghost: 'If a person returns from beyond the pale, it can be because he was not buried properly; he has unfinished business; he must atone for some sin or guilt; he must warn the living or provide important information [...]; or finally, he could be seeking vengeance' (15–16).

In Mantel's work, such spectres with a mission from the past appear for example in the shape of the insubstantial tenants who haunt the home of Evelyn and Muriel Axon in *Every Day Is Mother's Day* (1985) and *Vacant Possession* (1986): 'Without eyes and ears, they made themselves known by shuffling; by the sucking of their breath, in and out; but they had no lungs. They were malign intentions, Mother said, waiting to be joined to bodies; they were the notions of the dead, expecting flesh' (Mantel 1986: 37). In a textbook

Freudian reading of ghosts as symbolizing the return of the repressed, these spirits are desperately trying to embody both the unspoken mechanisms of the abuse Muriel has been suffering at the hands of her mother and the obscure but potentially horrific doings of her late, apparently paedophilic father. Matthew, the abducted child of Anna and Ralph Eldred in *A Change of Climate* (1994), whose unacknowledged existence continues to haunt the family in numerous ways, also belongs here, as does the mysterious woman haunting a department store in the story 'Third Floor Rising' from the collection *Learning to Talk*, who disturbs staff members 'by noises from the bricked-in cavity above their heads: by footsteps' (2003b: 116). All of these spectral apparitions are very much in the vein of Hamlet's father as individual beings seeking redress for past injustice.

Recent scholarship has shifted the focus towards more collective forms of haunting. Avery Gordon, for instance, reminds us that 'haunting and the appearance of spectres or ghosts is one way [...] we are notified that what's been concealed is very much alive and present, interfering precisely with those always incomplete forms of containment and repression ceaselessly directed toward us' (2008: xvi). She associates these forms of repression with oppressive political practices or institutions when she claims that 'haunting is one way in which abusive systems of power make themselves known and their impacts felt in everyday life, especially when they are supposedly over and done with (slavery, for instance)' (2008: xvi). Implicit in this political variety of haunting is, of course, an exhortation to restore moral order, to address the unanswered demands and redress unexpiated wrongs. The most obvious case in point of such a spectre in Mantel's work is the eponymous protagonist of the 1989 novel *Fludd*, who manages to liberate the inhabitants of the fictional village of Fetherhoughton from the shackles of an oppressive Catholic structure of feeling and thinking (cf. Funk 2013: 152–155).

Colin Davis links the moral force commanded by the spectre with the fact that it transcends conventional methods of making sense of the world. He claims that 'the spectre's ethical injunction consists ... in not reducing it prematurely to an object of knowledge' (2005: 379). Ghosts, in their (a)temporal aspect, disrupt not only the customary sequence of past, present and future; by collapsing the binary opposition of presence and absence, they express an even more comprehensive challenge to traditional forms of ordering the world. It is commonly assumed that the main achievement of Derrida's notion of 'hauntology' is to have established the spectre as the prime metaphor for this alternative configuration of knowledge. For Derrida, hauntology figures not as an epistemological practice, but rather as the underlying condition of knowability as such. Not unlike its more well-known sibling *différance*, it indicates that every presence must always be haunted by its constitutive absences. Martin Hägglund shows how this fundamental hauntology is itself a function of the temporal condition of existence. Since, so he argues, 'time – the disjointure between past and future – is a condition even for the slightest moment, spectrality is at work in everything that happens' (2008: 82). Due to this oscillating position between life and death, between presence and absence, 'the ghost functions as the paradigmatic deconstructive gesture, the "shadow third" or trace of an absence that undermines the fixedness of such binary oppositions' (Weinstock 2004: 4). In other words, the spectre presents a chronological anomaly as well as an ontological paradox and can thus figure as symbolic of 'this other *thinking of knowledge*' (Derrida 1994: 34).

Mantel's work repeatedly hints at this alternative form of knowledge. Evelyn in *Every Day Is Mother's Day* tries to induce spectral sensitivity into her daughter Muriel by telling her that if 'people did learn to look out of the corners of their eyes, they would see a great deal that at present they miss' (1985: 28). Most prominently, however, Alison Hart in Mantel's 2005 novel *Beyond Black* symbolizes and channels this spectral epistemology (cf. Funk 2013: 155–157). As a travelling medium, Alison is in the business of tuning in to and making her audiences aware of a world beyond the known and the knowable. Her part-time friend and full-time manager Colette exemplifies the confounding and literally mind-blowing effect this can have: 'Like the punters out there, [Colette] could entertain simultaneously any number of conflicting opinions. They could believe in Al, and not believe in her, *both at once*'. (31; my emphasis) Alison, in other words, is a living proof that there is indeed a world beyond black-and-white, that things need not be either one or the other but can sometimes be both true and untrue at the same time. Agreeing from the sidelines of cultural theory, Gordon likewise attests to this potentially life-changing aspect of cultural hauntings, when she claims that 'being haunted draws us affectively, sometimes against our will and always a bit magically, into the structure of feeling of a reality we come to experience, not as cold knowledge, but as a transformative recognition' (2008: 8).

By dragging ghosts from the old-fashioned epistemological realm of the 'either-or' into a bewildering new order of the 'both-and', hauntology also transforms the standard *gestus* of the metaphorical spectre. While in its traditional configuration it would point backwards, summoning the present from an unacknowledged past, it now very much seems to hail from the future, pointing us forward into the unknown. Since, according to Derrida, the spectre 'no longer belongs to time, if one understands by this word the linking of modalized presents' (1994: xx), the 'spectral moment' severs the present from the past. Only because ghosts are free from any binding ties with the past, they can embody 'the impatient and nostalgic waiting for a redemption' (1994: 136). The late Mark Fisher very powerfully endorsed this forward-looking and redemptive mode of haunting. Taking up Derrida's challenge to 'endeavour to speak and listen to the spectre, despite the reluctance inherited from our intellectual traditions' (Davis 2005: 376), Fisher writes that in our days 'what haunts is the spectre of a world in which all the marvels of communicative technology could be combined with a sense of solidarity much stronger than anything social democracy could muster' (2014: 26), adding that what 'should haunt us is not the *no longer* of actual existing social democracy, but the *not yet* of the futures that popular modernism trained us to expect, but which never materialised' (2014: 27; emphasis in the original).

Mantel's fiction features a number of spectres which beckon towards the future and transform the worldly beings they come in touch with. Here belong the uncanny goings-on in the gated community in *Eight Months on Ghazzah Street* (1988), which prompt Frances Shore to reassess her identity as a female expat in Saudi Arabia, as well as the above-mentioned encounter on the train in 'Terminus', an encounter which eventually leads the narrator to 'tear up the timetable and take some new routes' (2014: 201). The quintessential example in this context, however, is again the revenant alchemist Fludd, who, true to his erstwhile Earthly occupation, explicitly states that 'transformation is my business' (2010: 55). In the novel, he sets to work by freeing the hitherto slightly repressed and fearful Sister Philomena from her Catholic constraints and compulsions and transforming her, via sexual intercourse, into the altogether more happy-go-lucky and free-spirited Philly (cf. Mantel 2010: 141–144).

Ghosts writing: Spectral realism in *Wolf Hall* and *Bring Up the Bodies*

If the categories I have so far introduced have one aspect in common it is to show that ghosts are literally neither here nor there. Just as they collapse easy categorizations of past, present and future, so they can neither be placed comfortably in the realm of pure invention – if this were the case, the ghost story would very often miss its point – nor do they partake of the hard-and-fast certainty of observable reality. By dint of this liminal status they come to symbolize in and of themselves the thin red line separating belief from knowledge and fact from fiction. My subsequent analysis of *Wolf Hall* and *Bring Up the Bodies* will focus on this aspect of the ghost as a metaphor for the process of writing as such. On first view, the parallels between the acts of writing and haunting are obvious: both entail the conjuring of something out of nothing; both rely on and demand the suspension of disbelief; both employ registers of imaginative symbolism in order to convey a message.

The literary text, in other words, in its very nature takes the form of a haunting, as it can be understood as a cipher communicating between past and present, between the fictional and the factual, between depiction and imagination.

In her book *On Form* (2007), Angela Leighton provides a comprehensive delineation of the notion of literary form, which shows noticeable parallels with the characteristics of literary ghosts outlined in this first part of this chapter. Literary form, she writes, constitutes 'an abstraction from matter, removed and immaterial; but it is also subtly inflected towards matter' (1). Like the spectre, the notion of 'form' itself seems to oscillate between absence and presence, between the material and the imagined, it is 'a go-between, an interval, an interrupter, breaking the norms of representation and obstructing the passage from thing to name' (20). There is also a restlessness adhering to form, as it 'suggests in itself something of the very multi-dimensionality, the unsettled busyness, of the artwork' (3). Like the ghosts invoked by Derrida and Fisher, form in its very undecidability as 'not a fixed shape to be seen, but the shape of a choice to be made' (16), gestures towards promises of an as yet unredeemed future. And finally, Leighton argues, addressing the form of an artwork implies an ethical injunction, since form can be seen as 'the distribution of space caused by edging one thing against another, so that each calls attention to the other' (2007: 16). These formal parallels between haunting and the literary text will now provide the basis for an appreciation of Mantel's spectral realist approach to historical fiction.

Mantel herself explicitly claims this link between writing and haunting for her work. In her pertinently titled memoir *Giving Up the Ghost* she declares that 'I am writing in order to ... locate myself, if not within a body, then in the narrow space between one letter and the next, between the lines where the ghosts of meaning are' (2003a: 222).[1] By fashioning herself as a writer, Mantel coerces the shapeless forms of her haunted imagination into the order of a narrative. Writing ghosts is an attempt to address the spirits that haunt her by imposing the form of fiction onto them. This might also explain *en passant* another spectral feature in her oeuvre: the regular intertextual revisitations that occur across her corpus. The narrator of the short story 'Sorry to Disturb' (2014: 3–36), could well be said to be attending to unfinished business from *Eight Months on Ghazzah Street*, while the anorexic girl Morna, who in 'The Heart Fails without Warning' (2014: 169–190) dies and returns to haunt her sister, could herself be seen as a *revenant* of Carmel McBain from *An Experiment in Love*. Seen in this light, Mantel's art of fiction, by itself, performs continued and ever-changing returns of the repressed. Applying this diagnosis to the analysis of her Tudor novels, the remainder of this essay will now try to illustrate how the parallel structures of writing (fiction) and haunting inform her groundbreaking renegotiation of historical fiction in *Wolf Hall* and *Bring Up the Bodies*.[2]

If literature is in its very form always already a site of haunting, historical fiction is of course even more so. The ghosts appearing in its pages are spectral not merely due to their uncertain status in-between the immaterial imagination of author and reader and their material reality as words on the page. More to the point, they are revenants of actual living beings, so that what matters in historical fiction is always to an extent 'the ability to summon up ghosts' (Greenblatt 2009: n.p.). As Simon Hay indicates (2011: 13), the ghost story and the historical novel alike can be understood as negotiating two rivalling conceptions of relating the past to the present: the notion, for one, that the past is not only a foreign country, as L. P. Hartley famously had it, but that it is hermetically sealed off from the present, that the present has literally no business in the past and vice versa. Contrasted to this view is the Faulknerian assumption that the present can never really outlive its past, that the past needs to be seen and can only be told in the light of what it subsequently engendered. Leigh Wilson (2015) places this apparent dichotomy at the heart of her discussion of whatever happened to literary realism in the twenty-first century. In this context she argues that Mantel's historical fiction can be said to contribute to a reinstitution of realism as a pertinent category for literary analysis, since it 'reassert[s] the ability of realism to connect the reader with the real' (157). This new version of realism is not straightforward, however; it is haunted by the real rather than indulging in it. It is, in Wilson's words, 'a realism that strains against itself, and reveals in its techniques a profound discomfort' (147). I would argue that the particular success and persuasiveness of Mantel's spectral realist approach to the historical novel can be attributed to the fact that it is firmly inscribed both in the (hi)story recounted in the books (what Gérard Genette calls *histoire*) and in the (literary) form in which it is being related (*narration*).

Mantel's protagonist, Thomas Cromwell, is himself a liminal character in many senses. Arguably like few other historical figures, he presents the spirit of a new age. He has financial and social capital invested all over Europe. His network of dependants and informants ignores all barriers of class, gender, nationality, faith and political allegiance. His is a composite identity among Universal Men: 'He Thomas, also Tomos, Tommaso and Thomaes Cromwell, withdraws his past selves into his present body and edges back to where he was before' (Mantel 2009: 71). As a global player, performance artist and smooth operator *avant la lettre*, Cromwell is both an established presence (in terms of actual influence) and a glaring absence (in terms of conventions and decorum) among Henry's courtiers. He is a politician among patricians, a contrast which Mantel highlights by setting his pragmatism and tactical flexibility against 'Uncle' Norfolk's haughty parochialism and Suffolk's testosterone-driven laddishness.

Even though Cromwell seems immune to any form of personal or political nostalgia and sentimentality, this does not mean that he is not haunted by his own ghosts. The past that he so rigorously expunges in his politics – he is after all the driving force behind the break with Catholicism and the Dissolution of the Monasteries – still finds its way into his personal system. The potential ramifications of Henry's divorce from Katherine of Aragon, for example, register with Cromwell in the spectral shape of the king's dead brother, and first husband of Catherine: 'On his left side, a hand touches him: fingers without flesh. A ghost walks: Arthur, studious and pale. King Henry, he thinks, you raised him; now you put him down' (147). Even when Henry has achieved his goal, with Anne Boleyn on the throne and Katherine safely in her grave, ghosts are still invoked to give explanation to the vicissitudes of the present. When Anne suffers a miscarriage, it is because 'Catherine is too fresh in her tomb to lie quiet. She has reached out and shaken Anne's child free, so it is brought untimely into the world' (Mantel 2012: 180–181). Cromwell shows himself well aware of the essential paradoxicality of his attitude towards such revenants from the past, when he claims that he 'doesn't believe that the dead come back; but that doesn't stop him from feeling the brush of their fingertips, wing-tips, against his shoulder' (Mantel 2009: 154). At certain points the businessman in him manages to economize this fundamental undecidability along the lines laid out a century later by Pascal's Wager: 'He doesn't believe the dead need our prayers, nor can they use them. But anyone who knows the Bible as he does, knows that our God is a capricious God, and there's no harm in hedging your bets' (Mantel 2012: 83).

The most persistent of his spectral visitations are those of his wife Liz and their daughters Anne and Grace, who all succumb to the sweating sickness within the space of a year. Reading from Liz's prayer-book, Cromwell realizes that 'Grace, silent and small, turns the page with him' (Mantel 2009: 155); the peacock feather wings he had made for his daughters speak to him and remind him that 'we are here: a whisper, a touch, a feather's breath from you' (Mantel 2012: 119); in the blurry shapes of a cloud he encounters a 'flash of his wife Elizabeth's white cap, as she follows him to the door on her last morning' (413). Again, the practical part of his character attempts to explain away these apparitions by blaming them on an intricate mnemonic aid he is in the habit of using, whereby memories are retained, organized and recalled by linking them with specific images. Perhaps, he reasons, it is 'because of this practice that he tends to glimpse his dead wife lurking in a stairwell, her white face upturned, or whisking around a corner of Austin Friars, or the house at Stepney' (216). Immediately it becomes evident, however, that this rationalization of the spectral appearances as memories gone awry more likely than not derives from the fact that Cromwell has by this time set his eyes on his sister-in-law. The image of Liz 'is beginning to merge with that of her sister Johane, and everything that belonged to Liz is beginning to belong to her: her half-smile, her questioning glance, her way of being naked. Till he says, enough, and scrubs her out of his mind' (216–217). Yet, Liz's ghost will not be banished. Despite all his attempts, 'she neither stays nor goes. She is always with him and not with him' (584).

In keeping with what has been said before concerning the parallels between historical fiction and spectral epistemology, Cromwell's own interpretation of the spectres that haunt him finds its formal analogy in Mantel's narrative channelling of Cromwell's voice in consistent and uninterrupted free indirect discourse. This perplexing and, for some, confounding device of what is in fact a first person perspective told in third person form is usually cited as the secret behind the novels' accomplishment. Stephen Greenblatt applauds the 'powerful hallucination of presence, the vivid sensation of lived life' which this device engenders (2009: n.p.), and Irmtraud Huber notes how 'in its close proximity to Cromwell, the narrative perspective foregoes any historical distance' (2016: 78). This short-circuiting of temporal dissociation, the making present of the historical past in what Wilson calls 'the "reality effect" of the familiar mind' of the focal character Cromwell (2015: 157), is the formal correlative Mantel uses to render perceptible the spectral effect that the ghosts have on Cromwell himself. Both the content of the story, and Mantel's technique of representing it, collapse any meaningful distinction between past, present and future, between reality, fiction and representation.

Mantel's use of the 'unprecursed pronoun when referring to Cromwell' (Wilson 2015: 156), as, for example, in a sentence such as 'He, Cromwell, eyes the other half of himself, as if through a mirror' (Mantel 2012: 184), marks the most striking formal manifestations of this narrative short-circuiting. One effect of this interiorization of narrative authority is that the readers themselves are forced to adopt a spectral position towards the events narrated. By being limited to the thoughts and perspective of Cromwell, they are palpably and immediately present to the events as they unfold, an effect which is also greatly abetted by the rather less advertised device of Mantel's present tense narration throughout (cf. Huber 2016: 76–79). At the same time, however, the third person perspective forces readers to distance themselves from the action. Huber very elegantly summarizes the narratological paradox which I see as central to Mantel's spectral realism, when she argues that 'Cromwell is both central to the narrative and remains opaque to the reader, who is confronted with a clearly subjective representation, but gains only a very limited insight into the mind of the narrative's reflector' (2016: 79). Markku Lehtimäki describes this ambiguous amalgamation of first and third person perspective in terms of a literary variation on the visual practice of anamorphosis, which requires the onlooker to adopt an oblique angle in order to be able to see an image 'correctly'; a famous contemporary example for this is Holbein's painting *The Ambassadors*. Similarly, in anamorphic readings, Lehtimäki claims, 'the object can be perceived only when it is viewed from the side, in a partial, distorted form' (2011: 47). For Mantel's characters, the seeing of ghosts is frequently the result of not looking at things directly or consciously; Cromwell, for example, feels 'when he is on the verge of sleep the cardinal's large scarlet presence flits across his inner eye' (2012: 24). The spectral, anamorphic effect generated by Mantel's formal innovation of the historical novel, likewise results from the oblique narrative perspective in which past and present become one, and the reader simultaneously is and is not Cromwell, is there and here at the same time.

What is it then that Mantel's realist spectres have to convey to us? Why the need to dispel the pastness of the past? Why now? I have tried to show how in Mantel's Tudor novels, the reader partakes of Cromwell's struggle to separate the factual from the spectral. When 'at the edge of his inner vision, behind closed eyes, he [Cromwell] senses something in the act of becoming' (2012: 26), we can read this as an invitation to join in and address this vision of the future. Zygmunt Bauman describes our contemporary condition as 'liquid' in so far as it is characterized by a 'collapse of long-term thinking, planning and acting, and the disappearance or weakening of social structures in which thinking, planning and acting could be inscribed for a long time to come' (2007: 3). This, he continues, results in 'a splicing of both political history and individual lives into a series of short-term projects and episodes which are in principle infinite, and do not combine into the kinds of sequences to which concepts such as "development", "maturation", "career" or "progress" (all suggesting a preordained order of succession) could be meaningfully applied' (2007: 3). Towards the end of *Bring Up the Bodies*, the appearance of ghosts is related to a deep disruption in the present order of things: 'A queen is locked in a tower, accused of incest. The commonwealth, nature itself, is perturbed. Ghosts are glimpsed in doorways, standing by windows, against walls, hoping to overhear the secrets of the living' (Mantel 2012: 364). In an age, when the perpetual present has destroyed their natural habitat between past and present, the ghosts themselves seem to have lost the plot and now turn to the living for advice. Fundamentally Other to what Fredric Jameson calls 'the end of temporality' (2003), they are no longer emblematic of the wrongs of yesterday but of the abuses of tomorrow. If they seek to remind us of something, it is not the unfinished business from the past but the fact that there is such a thing as the future at all – and that it will be our unfinished business.

Notes

1 Even granted that every literary text is per se a site of haunting, Mantel's writing is arguably even more so than many others, as many of her works display significant autobiographical traits, from her upbringing in rural Catholic Cheshire and Derbyshire (*Fludd*) via her student days in London (*An Experiment in Love*) to living in Botswana (*A Change of Climate*) and Saudi Arabia (*Eight Months on Ghazzah Street*).

2 It needs to be acknowledged here that any discussion of Mantel's Tudor novels will necessarily remain provisional until the final instalment in the series will have been published. Its title, *The Mirror and the Light*, as well as the fact that Mantel will have to come to narratological terms with the demise of her central focal character, suggest that the relationship of historical reality and its representation/reflection in fictional form will be crucial. On the other hand, however, the experience of writing (and reading) on Cromwell's ghost from a perspective of a historically defined and yet narratologically undetermined future, of being stuck with the immediate presence as it were, neatly parallels the spectral narrative perspective this chapter tries to argue.

Bibliography

Bauman, Z. (2007), *Liquid Times: Living in an Age of Uncertainty*, Cambridge: Polity.

Botting, F. (1996), *Gothic*, London: Routledge.

Briggs, J. (1977), *Night Visitors: The Rise and Fall of the English Ghost Story*, London: Faber.

Davis, C. (2005), '*État Présent*: Hauntology, Spectres and Phantoms', *French Studies* 59 (3): 373–379.

Derrida, J. ([1993] 1994), *Specters of Marx: The State of the Debt, the Work of Mourning, and the New International*, translated by P. Kamuf, New York: Routledge.

Faulkner, W. ([1951] 2012), *Requiem for a Nun*, New York: Vintage.

Fisher, M. (2014), *Ghosts of My Life: Writings on Depression, Hauntology and Lost Futures*, Winchester: Zero Books.

Funk, W. (2013), 'Ghosts of Postmodernity: Spectral Epistemology and Haunting in Hilary Mantel's *Fludd* and *Beyond Black*', in S. Adiseshiah and R. Hildyard (eds), *What Happens Now: 21st Century British Fiction – The First Decade*, 147–161, Houndmills: Palgrave Macmillan.

Gordon, A. ([1997] 2008), *Ghostly Matters: Haunting and the Sociological Imagination*, Minneapolis, MN: University of Minnesota Press.

Gould, S. J. (1987), *Time's Arrow, Time's Cycle: Myth and Metaphor in the Discovery of Geological Time*, Cambridge, MA: Harvard University Press.

Greenblatt, S. (2009), 'How It Must Have Been', *The New York Review of Books*, 5 November. Available online: http://www.nybooks.com/articles/2009/11/05/how-it-must-have-been/(accessed 27 November 2016).

Hägglund, M. (2008), *Radical Atheism: Derrida and the Time of Life*, Stanford, CA: Stanford University Press.

Hay, S. (2011), *A History of the Modern British Ghost Story*, Houndmills: Palgrave Macmillan.

Huber, I. (2016), *Present-Tense Narration in Contemporary Fiction: A Narratological Overview*, London: Palgrave Macmillan.

Jameson, F. (2003) 'The End of Temporality', *Critical Inquiry* 29 (4): 695–718.

Kröger, L. and M. R. Anderson (2013), 'Introduction', in L. Kröger and M. R. Anderson (eds), *The Ghostly and the Ghosted in Literature and Film*, ix–xvi, Newark, DE: University of Delaware Press.

Lehtimäki, M. (2011), 'Anamorphic Narrativity: Hilary Mantel's *Wolf Hall* in the Renaissance Perspective', in M. Salmela and J. Toikkanen (eds), *The Grotesque and the Unnatural*, 43–66, Amherst, NY: Cambria Press.
Leighton, A. (2007), *On Form: Poetry, Aestheticism, and the Legacy of the Word*, Oxford: Oxford University Press.
Luckhurst, R. (2002), 'The Contemporary London Gothic and the Limits of the "Spectral Turn"', *Textual Practice* 16 (3): 527–546.
Mantel, H. (1985), *Every Day Is Mother's Day*, London: Fourth Estate.
Mantel, H. (1986), *Vacant Possession*, London: Fourth Estate.
Mantel, H. (1988), *Eight Months on Ghazzah Street*, London: Fourth Estate.
Mantel, H. (1994), *A Change of Climate*, London: Fourth Estate.
Mantel, H. (1995), *An Experiment in Love*, London: Fourth Estate.
Mantel, H. (2003a), *Giving Up the Ghost*, London: Fourth Estate.
Mantel, H. (2003b), *Learning to Talk*, London: Fourth Estate.
Mantel, H. (2005), *Beyond Black*, London: Harper Perennial.
Mantel, H. (2009), *Wolf Hall*, London: Fourth Estate.
Mantel, H. ([1989] 2010), *Fludd*, London: Fourth Estate.
Mantel, H. (2012), *Bring Up the Bodies*, London: Fourth Estate.
Mantel, H. (2014), *The Assassination of Margaret Thatcher*, London: Fourth Estate.
Pollard, E. J. (2015), '"Mind What Gap?": An Interview with Hilary Mantel', *Textual Practice* 29 (6): 1035–1044.
Shakespeare, W. (2001), *Hamlet*, The Arden Shakespeare, ed. Harold Jenkins, London: Thomson Learning.
Weinstock, J. A. (2004), *Spectral America: Phantoms of the National Imagination*, Madison, WI: University of Wisconsin Press.
Wilson, L. (2015), 'Historical Representations: Reality Effects: The Historical Novel and the Crisis of Fictionality in the First Decade of the Twenty-First Century', in N. Bentley, N. Hubble and L. Wilson (eds), *The 2000s: A Decade of Contemporary British Fiction*, 145–171, London: Bloomsbury.
Wolfreys, J. (2002), *Victorian Hauntings: Spectrality, Gothic, the Uncanny and Literature*, Basingstoke: Palgrave.

7

Walking the Dead: Unruly (Re)Animation in *A Place of Greater Safety*

Ginette Carpenter

This chapter claims that Hilary Mantel's strategies of reanimating the past offer unruly and challenging conceptions of both history and the historical body. In *A Place of Greater Safety*, as well as in Mantel's work more generally, the conventionally accepted stability of history and boundaries of bodies are recalibrated to articulate more disruptive and porous potentials. The chapter argues that the form of *A Place of Greater Safety* demands new ways of thinking about history and that its representations of dis/embodiment further destabilize conventional binaries whereby both the past and the body are bounded and fixed. The chapter deploys Michel de Certeau's model of walking in the city as analogy for Mantel's strategies as historical novelist in order to position the past as a space that can be actively traversed and to demonstrate how Mantel metaphorically walks with and raises the dead.

*****

In the opening paragraphs of her first Reith Lecture Hilary Mantel states that 'we sense the dead have a vital force still – they have something to tell us, something we need to understand' (2017a: 2). In the same lecture Mantel identifies a gap, a lacuna, between the explanatory contexts of history and science and the comforts of art in which we can 'meet the dead looking alive'

(2017a: 2). Art promises the impossible: a reconnection to the losses of the past, a communication with the 'vital' dead. It is this idea of Mantel as re-animator that is the concern of this chapter as I argue that in *A Place of Greater Safety* (*APOGS*) (1993) Mantel relocates history and history's bodies as unruly. In 'Walking in the City' (1988: 91–110) Michel de Certeau identifies a gap in perception between the systemic overview of the city, viewed panoptically from above as 'gigantic mass' (1988: 91) and illusory whole, and the activities of the 'ordinary practitioners of the city [who] live "down below"' (93). The paths these 'practitioners' take – the myriad conflicting ways in which they walk the city – are not visible from above as they become lost in 'the dark space where crowds move back and forth' (92). De Certeau compares these diverse spatial practices to the proliferation of numerous individual texts that both elude and interrupt the overarching script of the planned city. It is this concept of the embodied traversing of space that is mobilized here to argue that Mantel walks history and its archived bodies differently. I argue that Mantel reanimates the past to construct both patchwork histories and patchwork bodies that refute the idea of a coherent whole. This chapter thus operates within a series of spatial metaphors that revolve around the concept of navigation as Mantel is characterized as walking with the dead. Mantel's formal and representational strategies are identified as weaving a new 'urban fabric' (de Certeau 1988: 103) that challenges the myth of coherence in regard to the monolithic narratives of both the body of history and historical bodies.

In a relatively early career interview with Rosario Arias, long before the literary media spotlight turned full-beam upon her, Mantel claims that she regards *APOGS* as her 'best achievement' (288). Earlier in the same interview she has revealed that 'I didn't start out to be a writer really. I started out to write one novel, that novel is the novel about the French Revolution' (1998: 281). Mantel wrote *APOGS* between 1974 and 1979 and then, unable to find a publisher, shelved it until 1991 when it was rapidly re-worked in the wake of the critical success of her first four novels (Arias 1998: 288). In her opening Reith Lecture for the BBC Mantel explains that 'I wanted to find a novel I liked, about the French revolution. I couldn't, so I started making one' (2017a: 5). The novel narrates the origins and key events[1] of the first French Revolution from the perspectives of Georges Jacques Danton, Maximilien Robespierre and Camille Desmoulins, and their families, friends and associates. It covers the years from 1763 until the execution of Desmoulins and Danton, at Robespierre's instigation, in April 1794, although over 700 pages of the 872-page text are devoted to July 1789 and after. The cast of characters takes eight pages to detail and can at times be dizzyingly diverse, as are the complex and internecine accounts of the shifting loyalties and betrayals in the revolutionary governing Assemblies, but the focus upon the ebb and flow of the triumvirate's friendship is the rudder that steers the novel's course. Mantel's research is very extensive and she has acknowledged that her original aim was to 'write a sort of documentary fiction, guided entirely by the facts' (Simpson 2015). The key occurrences of the revolution – the calling of the Estates-General in May 1789, the storming of the Bastille, the women's march on Versailles, Louis and Marie Antoinette's interrupted escape to Varennes and the ensuing Champs de Mar massacre, the August 1792 rebellion and the deposing of the king, the September prison killings, the formation of the Committee of Public Safety and the implementation of the Terror – are all detailed and skilfully navigated alongside the peaks and troughs of the characters' personal lives. Mantel admits, however, that she 'came to a point where the facts about a certain episode ran out' and that she had to start 'making things up'. Although she steadfastly refuses to alter retrievable knowledge – 'I don't try to improve on the facts' (Simpson 2015) – Mantel recognizes that it was the 'erasures and silences' she encountered while composing *APOGS* that 'made me into a novelist' (2017a: 5).

Mantel's recent, unparalleled, success with her Tudor fictions means that she now, arguably, occupies an unassailable position as Grande Dame of historical fiction, yet the reception of her first-penned work still clearly rankles. Mantel continues to raise the spectre of *APOGS* in numerous articles, describing her struggles both to get it published and to have it taken seriously: 'By December of '79, I had finished *A Place of Greater Safety*, but I couldn't sell it, I couldn't get anywhere with it at all' and admits that 'writing a contemporary novel [*Every Day Is Mother's Day*] was just a way to get a publisher. My heart lay with historical fiction, and I think it still does' (Simpson 2015). She confesses that 'I had no idea how little the British public knew or cared or wished to know about the French Revolution. And that's still the case. They want to know about Henry VIII' (Arias 1998: 288). This lack of attention to *APOGS* is also applicable to scholarly interest in the text. Mantel's oeuvre in general has garnered far less academic notice than the work of many of her contemporaries but to date *APOGS* has only been explored critically as a staging post en route to the final destination of the Cromwell texts (Arias 2014; de Groot 2016). The notable exceptions to this are Pilar Hidalgo's useful comparison of the novel to Dickens's and Carlyle's representations of the same period (2002) and Edwin Frank's account of the text as about 'transformation', with regard to both its private and public narratives (1995). Both Hidalgo and Frank commend Mantel's complex interweaving of the private and the political, the former arguing that this imbrication is 'one of the most original traits of this original work' (205). This resonates with Mantel's own comments that 'my concern as a writer is with memory, personal and collective' (2017a: 2).

However, despite winning the *Sunday Express* Book of the Year, the critical attention garnered by the novel's publication was sometimes scathing and often patronizing. In the *London Review of Books*, P. N. Furbank admitted that

'Hilary Mantel is a formidably talented novelist, exceedingly well-informed about the Revolution and resourceful in all sorts of modes and genres' yet also complained that the novel was often too 'flip' and '"amusing"' and that the horrors of the French Revolution 'cannot be reduced to the personal' (1992: 4). Furbank begins his article quoting Henry James's account of the historical novel as reliant upon '*escamotage*' (trickery) (3) and seems concerned that *APOGS* may be little but smoke and mirrors, downplaying the seriousness of major historical events with fabrication. Joan Smith also raises what she observes as 'the novel's trivialising tendency, its fatal attraction to slickness', arguing that it 'draw[s] too heavily on the stereotypes of romantic fiction' and represents the French Revolution 'as upmarket soap opera' (1992). James Saynor's review is more generous in terms of the aims of Mantel's project, recognizing that 'we're prisoners of a schoolroom vision that sees history as a pageant of strutting and bombast', but nevertheless viperously mocks Mantel by crass imitation of what he identifies as her 'Jeffery-Archer-ish saga of three precocious pals'. He claims the text 'falls in an unfortunate gap between history writing and fiction-writing' and is thus guilty of 'reducing some of the most awesome, paradigm-shattering moments in European history to a mosaic of homespun moments' (1992).[2]

What these critics cling to is a series of binaries that privilege history over historical fiction: true/false, serious/trivial, political/personal, public/private. What Mantel does in *APOGS* is to smash these apart:

> The novelist ... works away at the point where what is enacted meets what is dreamed, where politics meets psychology, where private and public meet. I break through the false wall. On the other side I connect my personal story with the collective story. I move through the domestic space and emerge into the buzzing economic space of the mill yard – the market place, the gossip shop, the street and the parliament house. (Mantel 2017a: 5)

The 'wall' that Mantel identifies here has, of course, been challenged by theorists[3] like Hayden White, whose seminal *Metahistory* famously disrupts the certainties of history by resituating it as a form of 'narrative prose discourse' (2014: xxix). In *Heterologies* de Certeau argues that 'Western history struggles against fiction' and that the 'internecine strife between history and storytelling is very old' as historiography's purpose is to 'efface[s] error from the "fables" of the past' (2000: 200). De Certeau observes 'the historian's representation ... mends the rents in the fabric that joins past and present' and 'assures a "meaning" which surmounts the violence and divisions of time ... which guarantee a sense of unity ... as Michelet once said, it's the work of the living to "quiet the dead"'(2000: 205). By contrast, Mantel's historical fiction does the opposite: it wakes and walks the dead. By virtue of its very form, with its narrative eclecticism and its sprawling length, *APOGS* refuses any invisible mending, any smoothing over of the absences, inconsistencies or 'obscenity' (Mantel 2009) of the past. Mantel's strategy is to refute the simplicity of binarisms and therefore to highlight the porous quality of these mythic demarcations that are overly deployed to promote a coherent and untroubling (and distanced) account of the past. In Mantel's oeuvre, far from needing quietening, the dead are unshuttupable, clamouring for attention and space. This in turn disrupts the myth that the past is fixed, frozen and immoveable. This characterization of history as anchored, as somehow settled, speaks to a desire for linear narrative coherence but is repeatedly interrupted by the spatial metaphors that are applied in articulations of the past. Mantel herself locates history as a space that can be walked anew: 'The past is not dead ground, and to traverse it is not a sterile exercise. History is always changing behind us, and the past changes a little every time we retell it. The most scrupulous historian is an unreliable narrator' (2009).

Repositioning the past as a place of activity, of recalibration and recomposition, can be theorized through de Certeau's conception of the city. In 'Walking in the City' (1988: 91–110) he argues that the myriad paths trodden by the inhabitants of the city challenge the fixed and panoptic overview of prescribed place. He describes this overview as a 'texturology', as a coherently woven whole that can be seen from above and 'read'. By contrast, the walkers of the city 'whose bodies follow the thicks [*sic*] and thins of an urban "text" … write without being able to read it' (93). De Certeau continues by claiming that these individual 'writings' create '[a] *migrational*, or metaphorical, city [that] … slips into the clear text of the planned and readable city' (de Certeau 1988: 93). His point is that however carefully the city is planned and administered, the people that live in it will use it differently and that these 'singular and plural practices' enacted by its walkers evade any type of overarching regulation to become a 'proliferating illegitimacy' (96). In de Certeau's model, the act of traversing city places creates 'spatial practices' that 'elude discipline without being outside the field in which it is exercised' (de Certeau 1988: 96). In other words, it is possible to resist and perform 'otherwise' while within the framework that is being imposed: the walker can resist by creating 'shortcuts' and 'detours' or by refusing the sanctioned route (98). Mantel's formal strategies in *APOGS* can be seen as analogous to de Certeau's characterization of the city as a potential space of disruption whereby the past is 'walked' differently to create new conceptions that interrupt the accepted stories, the predetermined paths. Mantel debunks the myths of the revolution, the nailed-down narratives of heroism, counter-insurgency and betrayal, to tell new stories and open-up a space for contestation and reappraisal. As Hidalgo observes, her 'choices are revelatory' (204). The result is an extraordinarily polyvalent text that creates a type of historical bricolage, refusing to privilege one source or one viewpoint above others. As such, this novel's narrative differs dramatically from the Tudor novels (Mantel 2010; 2013) where the account is focalized solely through Thomas Cromwell. However, its imagining of the domestic lives of the famous agents of history, its insistence upon the private and personal alongside the public and political, similarly disrupts any notion of history as securely anchored. Mantel convincingly casts loose the moorings that secure history as grand narrative (as overarching linear sequence of cause and effect) to offer varied and competing perspectives.

Thus, for all its immersive qualities, *APOGS* simultaneously insists upon uprooting the reader[4] with sudden changes of narration, pace, form and voice, as well as carefully placed anachronisms, for example Lucille's abandoning of prayers for the dead: 'Now she thought, what the fuck's the use' (1993: 483). The effect of all of this is often discombobulating and the novel can seem unwieldy and difficult to navigate without occasionally feeling uncomfortably at sea. Arguably, this sense of imbalance is due to readers' expectations, of both fiction in general and the historical novel specifically. Like many British writers since the 1970s (John Fowles, Angela Carter, Salman Rushdie, Ian McEwan, Jeanette Winterson, to name but a few) Mantel refuses to adhere to the conventions of classic realism whereby the fictional is accepted as an unproblematic representation of the phenomenal world. To use Roland Barthes's terminology in *S/Z*, Mantel's work is very *writerly*, demanding that the reader be an active participant in the creation of meaning, not merely a passive recipient of the storyteller's tale (Barthes 1990: 4). Mantel's opening 'Author's Note' to *APOGS* echoes this idea of the text as a space of mutual creativity: 'I am very conscious that a novel is cooperative effort, a joint venture between writer and reader … I have tried to write a novel that gives the reader scope to change opinions, change sympathies: a book that one can think and live inside' (1993: x). This motif of textual occupation resonates with de Certeau's conception of the text as 'habitable, like a rented apartment' (1988: xi), whereby the reader is simultaneously both *at home* and *not at home*, in 'a space borrowed by a moment by a transient' (de Certeau 1988: xi). This conceit of the reader as temporary textual inhabitant means that the text is reanimated anew each time it is read and that the practice of reading can actively alter interpretation, something that Mantel is keen to emphasize the 'facts change according to your viewpoint' (Mantel 1993: x). This changing perspective is made explicit in *APOGS* via the frequent shifts in naming. An example is the trial and execution of Marie Antoinette where over less than five pages she is labelled 'the woman' (712), 'the prisoner' (711, 713) 'The Austrian' (714), the 'She-Tyrant' (717), the Queen (717). These rapid switches of appellation foreground the complexity of subjectivity as Marie Antoinette occupies multiple roles in the cultural imaginary, but also disorientate the reader, reinforcing a sense of being directionless or unanchored.

The discomforts of reading *APOGS*, the dis-ease with which it infects its readers, forcefully and deliberately challenges the sense that history is unproblematically accessible or relatable. Mantel destabilizes the familiarities of reading and the certainties of history in the same way that de Certeau's 'urban life' (1988: 95) disrupts the planned city. The novel's formal strategies insist that the reader engages directly with the unreliability of the record, the gaps in the archive and thus the unruliness of history as discourse. The novel's narrative eclecticism sees it moving back and forth between third person omniscient and varied first person accounts (with some passages of second person address at crucial points) as well as moving between past, present and future tense. An example of this is the chapter 'Conspirators', which relates the events following the 10 August 1792 coup, which finally overturned the monarchy. It opens with a present tense, third person narration focalized through Camille who wistfully, and wishfully, imagines delivering his father news of his appointment as secretary to Danton's Minister and thereby countering his father's repeated disappointment in his son's career and publicly-chewed-over indiscretions (Mantel 1993: 493–495). The chapter then turns to a more sustained, third person, past tense account that begins with Danton and his wife Gabrielle's response to his being instructed to 'take charge of the nation' (495) and segues into a sustained conversation between Danton and Robespierre (497–501) about problems of state. This move from married intimacy to political dilemma is rapid, underlining Mantel's strategy of intercutting between the private and public to demonstrate their inextricable interweaving: 'When I write about a household, I'm not simply writing about someone's domestic set-up. I'm writing about them as a reflection of politics in the wider world ... this is probably most overt in *A Place of Greater Safety* [...] where the power politics and the sexual politics are so directly connected' (Arias 1998: 281). Furthermore, even when the focus changes to public matters, the solidity offered by the third person, past perfect is contrapuntally undercut by the predominance of direct speech interspersed with details of Danton's thoughts on Robespierre: 'Did you imagine, Danton thought, that I wanted to make you into a functionary? Of course I didn't' (Mantel 1993: 496).

This uneasiness conveyed by Danton's internal counter-narrative is further reinforced by their dialogue being immediately succeeded by both men enquiring separately of Camille how each is viewed by the other: '"I wonder what Robespierre really thinks of me?" ... "I'd like to know how Danton really regards me"'(501). This is followed by an abrupt, and disorientating, shift to second person, the disorientation further augmented by an attendant sense of collusion: 'Life's going to change. You thought it already had? Not nearly as much as it's going to change now. Everything you disapprove of you'll call "aristocratic"' (501). This section oscillates between present and future tense to inform the reader of some of the changes wrought by the transference of power from king to National Assembly. The deployment of the future tense allows Mantel to prefigure mythologized events of the French Revolution such as the Terror – 'the scientific beheading machine will be set up there; it will become known as the "guillotine"' (501) – and the brutal assassination of Marat in his bath: 'And in the fullness of time, the rue des Cordeliers will become the rue Marat' (502). The clinical distance used to describe these horrors interrupts the informality of the second person address with an arch insouciance and the reader thus feels simultaneously hailed and dismissed. Mantel is at her most menacing when combining imagined character detail with such prefiguring: 'Cravats grow higher, as if they mean to protect the throat. The highest cravats in public life will be worn by Citizen Antoine Saint-Just, of the National Convention and the Committee of Public Safety' (Mantel 1993: 502). Prior to this point Saint-Just's role in the novel has been as a figure of ridicule, ceaselessly mocked, particularly by Camille, for his 'interminable, violent, faintly salacious' poetry (257). This juxtaposition of his unsurprisingly pretentious sartorial excess with his future public role as signatory to genocide is uncannily disquieting; we don't know whether to laugh or cry.

These rapid transitions of perspective and voice (I have detailed only the first eleven pages of a forty-one-page chapter) make explicit what Jerome de Groot labels the 'double effect' (2016: 23) of historical fiction. The genre exists in a paradox whereby the suspension of disbelief that is essential to the construction of realism is in constant tension with the knowledge of *how things end*, that however the story may be told and retold the result is not only already determined by history but already known by the reader. Thus, the reader is, to quote Mantel, 'in two places at once. He [*sic*] is at the foot of the cliff, wise after the event, and he is also on the path, he is before the event; he is the observer, and he is also the person who steps into air' (2017c: 6). If *APOGS*, and historical fiction more generally, forcefully disrupts the blanket 'texturology' (de Certeau 1988: 91) of history as totalizing whole and the reader as passive receptacle, these are disruptions that, according to Mantel, frequently fall foul of reader scepticism: 'No other sort of writer has to explain their trade so often. The reader asks, is this story true?' (2017a: 4). The inconsistencies that erupt in the reanimation of the past, and particularly in Mantel's emphasis upon its continuing malleability, engender anxieties about the role of the novelist: Is she archivist or fantasist? Again, the 'Author's Note' to *APOGS* addresses this directly: 'The reader may ask how to tell fact from fiction' (Mantel 1993: x). However, the answer provided does little to reassure the nervous: 'A rough guide: anything that seems particularly unlikely is probably true' (Mantel 1993: x).

At the close of the first chapter of *APOGS* Mantel cites Robespierre's famous adage: 'Maximilien Robespierre, 1793: "History is fiction"' (29); over 500 pages later, when the novel reaches 1793, she incorporates it into a conversation between Robespierre and Desmoulins: "Camille, history is fiction" (566). This movement between the record and the imagined is the balance beam of the historical novelist's craft. For the narrator of *APOGS* history is not entirely fictional but it is 'a corpse candle to the intellect ... error-breeding, sand-blind and parched' (29). Nevertheless, although Mantel may loosen the grip of the archive she does not refuse its lessons, as evinced by her incorporation of archive material and repeatedly professed refusal to bend the facts: 'People say to me – and with good reason – why don't you just make things up? It's just not in my nature, if the facts are to be found. It's very perverse of me to be a novelist because I really don't like making things up' (Simpson 2015). Thus, although she argues that this strategy means that readers are forced 'to live with the ambiguities' (Simpson 2015) exposed by the archive's absences, it also emphasizes that the paths of history walked in the text are, ultimately Mantel's. The collusion offered by the selective use of the third person plural – 'We are now in 1790' (Mantel 1993: 280) – is counterbalanced by that fact that the reader's interpretive choices and textual interventions are limited: to return to de Certeau's metaphor of the reader as textual inhabitant, s/he is only renting space on a short-term lease.

To a certain extent, of course, authors are always 'voyeur-gods' (de Certeau 1988: 93), they are knitting their own 'texturology' and have their own overview: to harness de Certeau's analogy they are like Dedalus, 'transform[ing] the bewitching world ... into a text' (92). Yet, as we have seen above, Mantel's formal strategies repeatedly interrupt any pretence of seamlessness, her textual blanket is a patchwork fabric of 'plural practices' (96) whose weave allows for pockets of 'proliferating illegitimacy' (96). *APOGS*'s re-animation of revolutionary Paris is criss-crossed with exposed needlework that undermines the myth of 'imaginary totalizations', be these of history or text (93). In Mantel's oeuvre, it is the pull 'of the restless dead asserting their claims' (Mantel 2017a: 2) that is used to repeatedly undermine the misdiagnosed stability of the past. As such, her role as historical novelist is akin to that of her character Alison in *Beyond Black* (2005): she is a medium, a channel to the dead but one which is full of jamming interference, the signal is neither consistent nor clear. The in/famous dead – Danton, Robespierre, Desmoulins, Cromwell, Henry, Anne Boleyn – are constantly clawing and clammering for voice in the same way that Maurice Warren, Keith Capstick and their associates in *Beyond Black* ceaselessly harass Alison. The past is always there snapping at our heels, waiting to trip us up while simultaneously, provocatively (impossibly) offering up its secrets. De Groot claims that Mantel's work 'highlights something about the oxymoronic corporeal spectrality of the encounter with the past' and that it is this craving for 'encounter', this 'desire to somehow raise the dead [that] brings us to historical fiction' (2016: 20). De

Groot's characterization is echoed by Mantel herself who has recently argued that 'in imagination, we chase the dead, shouting, "Come back!"' (2017a: 2).

The historical novelist, then, as well as a medium, is not only a reanimator of the past but also of the dead, someone who puts flesh back on the skeletal remains of the archive: 'You become profoundly involved in this effort to clothe old bones' (Mantel 2007). Therefore, the familiar Mantelian trope of the ghost might be joined by the dead-but-walking spectacle of the zombie: the spectral made 'flesh' by way of the text. Mantel observes that as historical novelist she 'frees the people from the archive and lets them run about, ignorant of their fates, with all their mistakes unmade' (2017a: 7). In this evocation, as she gleefully releases past characters from their imprisonment in dry and dusty tomes, the historical novelist becomes a Frankensteinian re-animator, populating her fictions with the walking dead; she is 'working in the crypt' (Mantel 2017c: 9)-The historical novelist is a grave-robber, an exhumer not only of the sacred ground of history but also of its silent corpses. Thus, the model of the patchwork text is echoed in the piecing together of the bodies of the past. When, following his brutal and bloody assassination, Jean Paul Marat's body is paraded through the streets of Paris, the narrator of *APOGS* notes that his trailing arm, the only part of his body that is in plain view, is 'sewn on from a better class of corpse' (Mantel 1993: 679; see also Schama 1989: 742). This is necessitated by the fact that Marat's body was already decomposing in life due to a degenerative skin condition – 'it's as if he were decaying while he was still alive' (Mantel 1993: 678)- and therefore both more *and* less complete in death. This image of Marat's dismembered and recomposed corpse serves as analogy for Mantel's reanimation of the corpses of history who walk the text.

These re-awoken corpses are fictional bodies which are always *other* to their historical referents, painstakingly constituted from a combination of archival scraps and imaginative industry. As such, they misbehave, their seams burst and tear. Bodies in Mantel's work are repeatedly unreliable. They slip and slide around all over the place, fail and fall short, disappear and reappear. They are equally sites of wonder and frustration. The instances are numerous: Carmel's collapse from anorexia in *An Experiment in Love* (2010b); Alison's fleshly struggles from being filled-to-bursting with jabbering spectral communications in *Beyond Black* (2005); the kidnap of the Eldred's child in *A Change of Climate* (2010a) and its symbolic recomposition as monstrous other in the novel's closing pages. Intimations and descriptions of dismemberment are also common, see, for example, the boxes being carried to and from the garage in *Beyond Black* (2005: 108); John Hunter's ceaseless accruement of body parts for medical experimentation in *The Giant, O' Brien* (2010c). Mantel's characters' lack of compliance with the conventions of embodied coherence and order is echoed in the fact that the boundaries of their bodies are often fluid; they ooze and they reconstitute. Conversely, there is also an emphasis upon the restrictions imposed by certain categories of embodiment as opposed to others such as Frances's confinement as a woman in *Eight Months on Ghazzah Street* (2004a) and O'Brien's enfreakment, whereby he is positioned, judged and valued solely on the basis of his physical deviations from the 'norm' in *The Giant, O' Brien*. Bodies are troublesome, disobedient and largely unbiddable. Mantel herself has been very explicit about the unruliness of her own body and has publicly documented her struggle with endometriosis in, among other sources, her memoir *Giving Up the Ghost* (2004b: 168–232) and a chapter for a collection on infertility (2003).

Endometriosis is a literal wandering womb: the sufferer's endometrium cells migrating to other parts of the body where 'wherever they are found, they obey their essential nature and bleed' (Mantel 2004b: 191). Mantel's experience, once finally diagnosed following years of extreme ill-heath, made her painfully aware of the ways in which one's own body can become a site of otherness, changed beyond (self) recognition by the effects of surgery and drugs: 'perpetually strange to myself, convoluted, mutated, and beyond the pale' (2004b: 54). Like subjectivity, bodies too morph and move, perform differently: 'All of us can change … we can be made foreign to ourselves, suddenly by illness, accident, misadventure, or hormonal caprice' (Mantel 2004b: 54). The ramifications of Mantel's endometriosis, of this 'caprice', was, that her 'dead womb' was categorized as 'clinical waste' (2003: 21). This matter of waste, waste matter, that which the body expunges or that which is excised from it, underscores the fiction of corporeal limits and experiences: bodies lie and transgress and wander off-course and off-message. Both the internal workings of the body and the way in which the body is enacted upon by external forces, can be seen analogous to de Certeau's urban walkers 'proliferating illegitimacy' (1988: 96). The walkers' 'urban eruptions' (91) and the trampling of the city's planned places to create new spaces, new 'texts' is echoed in Mantel's bodies' refusal to adhere to their prescribed limits. However insistent the 'texturology', the mapping, the body will rebel in both overt and covert ways. In Mantel's work, the visibility of these transgressions varies but the trope of bodily eruption, dislocation and general disorderliness maintains.

Mantel's historical fictions rehearse and reinforce this Mantelian convention of the unruly and often disobedient body. Women's bodies are doubly jeopardized in *APOGS*, victim to the vagaries of their female embodiment (Danton's wife Gabrielle, for example, dies in childbirth [609]) but also at risk of execution due to status or association; Camille's anguished cry of 'they are going to murder my wife' (863) recognizes the inevitability (albeit beyond the confines of Mantel's text) that his fate will also determine Lucille's. Despite the freedoms granted by the revolution, women's bodies are not yet awarded an agency in separation from their husband's or father's. Similarly, Katherine of Aragon and Anne Boleyn in *Wolf Hall* (2010d) and *Bring Up the Bodies* (2013), respectively, are both confined by their embodied status as women, unable, fatally in Boleyn's case, to direct their bodies to perform to the script that is written for them. The dissenting body of Boleyn is, of course, itself a (mis)functioning component of the divine body of the king and its failure to comply condemns not only her but also her alleged suitors. The very title of *Bring Up the Bodies*, drawn from the cry that was given at the Tower of London as prisoners were brought to trial, implies processes of disinterment, of un-burying, and that Weston, Brereton, Smeaton and Norris are now literally dead men walking (Mantel 2013: 432–433). *APOGS* positions its three protagonists as similarly doomed; the corpse-candle that provides such a dim light to the archive is also lighting their stumbling walk to the scaffold. Danton's, Desmoulins's and Robespierre's entrances onto the public stage signal the countdown to their untimely executions, whichever way they decide to cross and re-cross the city, their bodies will end up as dismembered meat. The titular 'place of greater safety' is located by Camille as '"the grave"' (Mantel 1993: 651).

In revolutionary France, then, bodies are safer dead than alive and walking the city is rife with the possibility of being caught up in casual massacre à la Champs de Mar (362) or vigilante-style misdirected attack, or worse. For example, during the fall-out from Champs de Mar, Robespierre is rescued from mob-justice by Duplay (369–370) and Prudhomme (also a young Jacobin journalist) is severely beaten instead of Camille for whom he is mistaken. The power shift from the divine body of the king to the body politic – 'Louis must die so the nation can live' (586) – happens at a very high price in terms of body count. However, Mantel's narrative patchwork means that the recurring violence of the revolution can be often driven to the edges of the text, lurking as the horrific endgame of decisions taken behind the closed doors of offices and homes. Occasional, yet precisely detailed, descriptions of the visceral reality of revolution and terror are juxtaposed with the familiar and often domestic situations in which decisions are made about the perpetuation (or not) of flesh and blood and tissue and bone. The 1792 prison massacres, which, according to Schama, saw 'the killing of at least fourteen hundred people in cold blood' (1989: 631) are enacted on the basis of judgements made by revolutionary comrades as they sit up all night drinking and compiling lists of whom to cull and whom to spare (Mantel 1993: 516–517). Responsibility for the massacre is devolved – 'It was thought advisable to recruit a number of butchers' (518) – as bodies become, by virtue of the panoptic distance of power, little more than carcasses for disposal.

This transformative journey, from revolutionary agent to state administrator, or, in de Certeau's terms, from street walker to urban planner, is illustrated by

Camille's response to the massacre he and his colleagues have instigated. His internalized sense of horror at their collective responsibility – 'We will never, now, know an hour free from guilt' (519) – is rapidly overwritten by his inability, less than a page later, 'to transpose Prudhomme's fading scars onto his own face' (520): something humane has been lost in the mistranslation. But state-orchestrated genocide brings its own problems: how to maximize turnover and dispose of the mess. In revolutionary Paris this is countered, at least in part, by the invention of the guillotine. The chapter entitled 'Three Blades, Two in Reserve' (407–426) includes a detailed breakdown of the precise cost of more mechanized execution (417) and a droll (highly Mantelian) remark by Guillotin himself as he proudly promotes his device to the National Assembly: 'With this machine I can have your head off in a flash and you won't suffer at all' (Mantel 1993: 417). However, despite its implementation as a method of bodily control and containment and as a way of efficiently curtailing the fleshly inconveniences of mass-murder, in dismembering the body the guillotine reinforces the very corporeal unruliness it seeks to erase. Decapitated corpses become symbols of the fragility of the body's coherence ('too too solid flesh' is revealed to be anything but) and of the body's refusal to behave within delimited boundaries even in death. The guillotine might expedite the killing process but it is attended by the mess of murder on this scale, as articulated by an unidentified executioner: 'Do the powers-that-be understand just how much blood comes out of even one decapitated person? The blood ruins everything, rots things away, especially his clothes. People down there don't realize, but he sometimes gets splashed right up to his knees. It's heavy work' (724). This image of transgressive overspill serves as a final anarchic riposte to the punitive management of the body by the architects of T/terror. Bodies, it seems, are reluctant to conform even in death. Thus, in *APOGS*, rewriting the body as carcass is positioned as simultaneously effortless and onerous. The gore of the guillotine serves as metaphor for Mantel's work as reanimator of both historical bodies and history: there will always be collateral damage and there will always be resistance.

APOGS's representation of unruly bodies and, specifically, dismemberment rehearses Mantel's repeated defamiliarization of history, whereby the past is a potentially porous space that can be occupied differently and patterned anew by the novelist's interventions. Mantel's formal and representational practices are analogous to the inhabitants of de Certeau's city who 'compose a manifold story … shaped out of fragments of trajectories and alterations of spaces', a story that 'remains daily and indefinitely other' (de Certeau 1988: 93). To redeploy de Certeau's paradigm of city walkers as constructing their own textual fabrics: the paths along which Mantel walks her dead do not deny the overall texturology, the panoptic patterning of the spaces of the past but they do expose the weave. In other words, seamlessness is exchanged for exposed stitching that demands the reader attends to ambiguity, contradiction and ellipses. In this reading both history and the bodies of the past are untethered from more conventional narratives that anchor them solely to specific positions. Discussing the past and its dead via the prism of spatial metaphors allows for a re-calibration that contradicts fixity and allows for resistance and change; it (re)positions the past as mutable and history as re-walked and rewritten by both its writers and readers. This way of reworking the past requires courage as it eschews the reassurances of monolithic meanings and refuses the ease of binary polarizations. It also recognizes the past as a different country rather than rehearsal for the present, yet simultaneously acknowledges its constant presence. It asks us to walk with the unruly dead. In the epigraph to *The Giant, O'Brien* Mantel cites George Macbeth's 'The Cleaver Garden': 'All crib from skulls and bones who push the pen./Readers crave bodies. We're the resurrection men' (Mantel 2010c). It is perhaps this process of working with the dead in order to make them walk anew that makes some readers queasy: these processes are not for the fainthearted.

Notes

1. For a comprehensive historical account of the French Revolution (although not without its revisionist biases) that was published contemporaneously to *APOGS* see Simon Schama's *Citizens* (1989).
2. Saynor also cites Mantel's references to 'wallpaper' which perhaps makes this the source that she so frequently berates when speaking about the attachment she maintains to this first book. See for example, Mantel (2008); Mantel (2017a: 6).
3. The relationship between history and fiction has, of course, also been extensively discussed by literary critics, from Linda Hutcheon's groundbreaking concept of historiographic metafiction (1988: 105–123) to more recent work such as that by Peter Boxall (2013: 40–83), Leigh Wilson (2015), Jerome de Groot (2016).
4. The term reader is used for stylistic purposes but does not assume a homogeneous response to the text.

Bibliography

Arias, R. and H. Mantel (1998), 'An Interview with Hilary Mantel', *Atlantis* 2 2: 277–289.

Arias, R. (2014), 'Exoticising the Tudors: Hilary Mantel's Re-Appropriation of the Past in *Wolf Hall* and *Bring Up the Bodies*', in E. Rousselot (ed.), *Exoticising the Past in Contemporary Neo-Historical Fiction*, 19–36, Houndmills: Palgrave.

Barthes, R. (1990), *S/Z*, translated by Richard Miller, Oxford: Blackwell.
Boxall, P. (2013), *Twenty-First Century Fiction*, Cambridge: Cambridge University Press.
De Certeau, M. (1988), *The Practice of Everyday Life*, translated by Steven Rendell, Berkeley, CA: University of California Press.
De Certeau, M. (2000), *Heterologies: Discourse on the Other*, Minneapolis, MN: University of Minnesota Press.
De Groot, J. (2016), *Remaking History: The Past in Contemporary Historical Fictions*, Abingdon: Routledge.
Frank, E. (1995) 'Writing about Revolution', *Boston Review: A Political and Literary Forum*, Summer. Available online: http://bostonreview.net/archives/BR20.3/frank.html (accessed 27 July 2017).
Furbank P. N. (1992), 'Falling for Desmoulins', *London Review of Books* 14 (16): 3–4.
Hidalgo, P. (2002), 'Of Tides and Men: History and Agency in Hilary Mantel's *A Place of Greater Safety*', *Estudios Ingleses de la Universidad Complutense*, 10: 201–216.
Hutcheon, L. (1988), *The Poetics of Postmodernism: History, Theory, Fiction*, Abingdon: Routledge.
Mantel, H. (1993), *A Place of Greater Safety*. London: Penguin.
Mantel, H. (2003), 'Clinical Waste', in Jane Haynes and Juliet Miller (eds), *Inconceivable Conceptions: Psychological Aspects of Infertility and Reproductive Technology*, 19–26, London: Routledge.
Mantel, H. (2004a), *Eight Months on Ghazzah Street*, London: Harper Perennial.
Mantel, H. (2004b), *Giving Up the Ghost: A Memoir*, London: Harper Perennial.
Mantel, H. (2005), *Beyond Black*, London: Harper Perennial.
Mantel, H. (2007), 'Ghost writing', The Guardian, Saturday 28th July. Available online: https://www.theguardian.com/books/2007/jul/28/edinburghfestival2007.poetry (accessed 27 July 2017).
Mantel, H. (2008), 'Author, Author', *The Guardian*, 24 May. Available online: https://www.theguardian.com/books/2008/may/24/1 (accessed 30 July 2017).
Mantel, H. (2009), 'Booker Winner Hilary Mantel on Dealing with History in Fiction' *The Guardian*, October 17. Available online: https://www.theguardian.com/books/2009/oct/17/hilary-mantel-author-booker (accessed 27 July 2017).
Mantel, H. (2010a), *A Change of Climate*, London: Fourth Estate.
Mantel, H. (2010b), *An Experiment in Love*, London: Fourth Estate.
Mantel, H. (2010c), *The Giant, O'Brien*, London: Fourth Estate, 2010.
Mantel, H. (2010d), *Wolf Hall*, London: Fourth Estate.
Mantel, H. (2013), *Bring Up the Bodies*, London: Fourth Estate.
Mantel, H. (2017a), 'First Reith Lecture: The Day Is for the Living', BBC, 13 June 2017. Available online: http://downloads.bbc.co.uk/radio4/reith2017/reith_2017_hilary_mantel_lecture%201.pdf (accessed 21 July 2017).
Mantel, H. (2017b), 'Third Reith Lecture: Silence Grips the Town', BBC, 27 June 2017. Available online: http://downloads.bbc.co.uk/radio4/reith2017/reith_2017_hilary_mantel_lecture%203.pdf (accessed 21 July 2017).
Mantel, H. (2017c), 'Fourth Reith Lecture: Can These Bones Live?' BBC, 4 July 2017. Available online: http://downloads.bbc.co.uk/radio4/reith2017/reith_2017_hilary_mantel_lecture%204.pdf. (accessed 21 July 2017).
Saynor, J. (1992), 'Three Precocious Pals', *The Observer*, 30 August, 50.

Schama, S. (1989), *Citizens: A Chronicle of the French Revolution*, London: Penguin.

Simpson, M. (2015), 'Hilary Mantel, Art of Fiction No. 226', *Paris Review* 212. Available online: https://www.theparisreview.org/interviews/6360/hilary-mantel-art-of-fiction-no-226-hilary-mantel (accessed 27 July 2017).

Smith, J. (1992), 'The Rough and Tumbril of History: *A Place of Greater Safety*', *The Independent*, 5 September. Available online: http://www.independent.co.uk/arts-entertainment/book-review-the-rough-and-tumbril-of-history-a-place-of-greater-safety-hilary-mantel-viking-pounds-1549781.html (accessed 27 July 2017).

White, H. (2014), *Metahistory: The Historical Imagination in 19th-Century Europe*, 2nd edn, Baltimore, MD: John Hopkins University Press.

Wilson, L. (2015), 'Reality Effects: The Historical Novel and the Crisis of Fictionality in the First Decade of the Twenty-First Century', in N. Bentley, N. Hubble and L. Wilson (eds), *The 2000s: A Decade of Contemporary British Fiction*, 145–172, London: Bloomsbury.

8

Holy Ghost Writers: Spectrality, Intertextuality and Religion in *Wolf Hall* and *Fludd*

Lucy Arnold

From an early age, Hilary Mantel's conception of the Catholic faith was predicated upon an understanding 'that the world is not what you see; [...] beyond appearances there is another reality'. It is this framing that provides the impetus for her work, the urge to see 'beyond' manifesting itself perhaps most potently in the various spectres and phantoms that populate much of her writing. While the ghosts of Mantel's literary project frequently find themselves uncoupled from an overtly religious context, the sacred and the spectral find striking intersections in two of her novels in particular: *Fludd* and *Wolf Hall*. My chapter interrogates the ways in which Mantel uses haunting and spectrality to meditate on authorship and authority, ultimately positing that *Fludd* and *Wolf Hall* powerfully assert intertextuality as a mode of haunting in its own right.

*****

'It's the living that turn and chase the dead. The long bones and skulls are tumbled from their shrouds, and words like stones thrust into their rattling mouths: we edit their writings, we rewrite their lives' (2010a: 649). So concludes Thomas Cromwell at the close of *Wolf Hall* in a gesture which acknowledges accusations frequently levelled at writers of historical fiction. Mantel herself 'hold[s] up [her] hands' and states 'you might think that what I am doing in this book is dubious – it might even be thought to be reprehensible' (6). Nevertheless, the two Booker prizes awarded to her Tudor novels clearly evidence a positive critical reaction. Certainly, the novel has been received by the popular press primarily as a paradigm-shifting example of historical fiction (Holland 2009). Christopher Taylor describes *Wolf Hall* as 'a non-frothy historical novel', situating the text in opposition to a prevalent critical discourse in which the genre is 'frowned on' and 'disapproved of' (2009: 9). Meanwhile, the limited academic attention the novel has garnered has focused on the text as a seminal example of its genre, using *Wolf Hall* as a vehicle through which the tropes of historical fiction can be analysed (Stoker 2012: 308–318). Contrastingly, those studies which depart from this generic approach display a tendency to decry the text for a lack of historical veracity while neglecting its status as literary production (O'Reilly 2010: 164–193). In attempting to aggressively situate *Wolf Hall* as an account of the Tudor period without meaningfully recognizing its status as a work of literature, or else in using the book as an exemplar through which historical fiction as a genre can be validated, these critical approaches act to neutralize and simplify a literary text whose project, I will argue, is both more subtle and more expansive than these previous viewpoints have allowed. I posit that to define the text as 'simply' – or, as A. S. Byatt puts it, 'innocently' (2000b: 38) – an example of the realist historical novel, is to fail to appreciate the subtle and nuanced discussions orchestrated within the text, discussions whose impact exceeds questions of genre and historical veracity.

In this chapter I explore how *Wolf Hall*, in conversation with its literary predecessor, *Fludd*, understands the written word as capable of producing myriad spectres and facilitating a variety of hauntings. I begin with an analysis of the novel's representation of material books and the texts which they contain, demonstrating Mantel's assertion of a complex relationship between textuality and the dead subject. I then consider how *Wolf Hall* represents Reformation print culture as incubating a spectral textuality, putting pressure on how Mantel articulates the manner in which the advent of print culture radically altered both the ways in which texts could circulate and textual practice itself, heralding new and significant modes of intertextual play. Finally, I consider the haunting and haunted relationship which exists between *Fludd* and *Wolf Hall*, demonstrating how Mantel's corpus is structured through spectral acts of self-quotation.

In the body of the text: Corpses and corpora

'We are always dying – I while I write, you while you read' (Petrarch in *Wolf Hall*, 648). In response to the use of printed material within Christian religious practice, the seventeenth-century oration priest, Bernard Lamy complained that 'the words on the page are like a dead body stretched out on the ground' (quoted in Eisenstein 2011: 47). Lamy argued that the use of typography 'devocalized' and 'desocialized' Christian teaching (47). Yet his striking statement also provides a formulation of how the posthumous is implicated by all acts of writing, the fact of the inscription being reproducible in our absence, rendering us, as Derrida observes, 'haunted by [a] future which brings our own death' (2002: 117). This interaction between physical inscription and death is powerfully present in *Wolf Hall*, positioning the act of writing as involving the passage from subject (the author) to object (the document they produce).[1] This interaction is strikingly inscribed through the complex relationship between corporeal bodies and physical books within *Wolf Hall*.

The historical moment of the Protestant Reformation provides an ideal crucible within which the various linkages between writing and dying can be explored. Before a detailed analysis of the concomitance between books and the dead in *Wolf Hall* can be undertaken it is useful to establish one of the two contextual points which drive the text's intellectual project: the changing status of the dead in Reformation England. As Cromwell confirms early on, *Wolf Hall* depicts a period in which 'with every month that passes, the corners are knocked off the certainties of this world: and the next world too' (Mantel 2010a: 39) as debates around previous theological certainties gathered pace. In the words of Anthony Low, while 'many things were repudiated at the English Reformation [...] [f]ew things were ended as absolutely as Purgatory' (1999: 450). The abolition of Purgatory wrought a drastic change in the relationship between the subjects of Reformation society and their dead, as they no longer had recourse to this intermediate space which, to quote Stephen Greenblatt, 'enabled the dead to be not completely dead – not as utterly gone, finished, complete, as those whose souls resided forever in Heaven or Hell' (2001: 17). *Wolf Hall* is concerned with the period immediately antecedent to this abolition, a time when the writings of reformist thinkers like Martin Luther were beginning to put pressure on Purgatory as a concept and to question previously 'legitimately sanctioned belief in ghosts' (152). Yet, rather than rendering the division between the living and the dead impenetrable, as they were intended to, these reforms apparently had the effect of increasing rather than decreasing the permeability of the barrier between the living and the dead. As the rejection of the doctrine of Purgatory gathered pace, the regulatory structure whereby the dead could appear to the living was beginning to give way, not to a ghost-less landscape, but rather to an unregulated ingress of the dead into the world of the living. In *Wolf Hall* this questioning of the location of the dead through religious literature is deftly acknowledged with physical books repeatedly providing the conduits through which the dead return:

> Halloween: the world's edge seeps and bleeds. This is the time when the tally-keepers of Purgatory, its clerks and gaolers, listen in to the living, who are praying for the dead. (Mantel 2010a: 154)

In this way Mantel introduces the religious practices that surrounded the Catholic feast of All Hallows day, capturing how Purgatory accommodated the admission of the dead into the world of the living while also facilitating the partial entry of the living, their prayers and pleas, into the world of the dead. Initially it is not the individual dead that trouble Cromwell but rather 'a solid aggregated mass, their flesh slapping and jostling together, their texture dense like sea creatures, their faces sick with an undersea sheen' (154–155). Then comes a moment of transition as Cromwell 'stands in a window embrasure, Liz's prayer book in his hand' (155); the Book of Hours which 'his daughter Grace liked to look at' (Mantel 2010a: 155). The homogenous dead fall away to leave the individuated phantoms of Cromwell's wife, Elizabeth, and his daughter, Grace. In this moment, when the dead stand alongside the living, it is a manuscript book that is placed at the centre of the scene, the provocation for the return of Cromwell's familial dead. As he progresses through the various religious offices he 'feel[s] the imprint of [Grace's] small fingers under his own' (Mantel 2010a: 155). The materiality of the book produces a post-mortem materiality for Grace, whose fingers seem to combine with the page under Cromwell's hands. Through their invocation alongside the vividly illustrated Book of Hours, the phantoms of Liz and Grace become symbols of a religious status quo about to be changed forever. The Reformation's emphasis upon print transformed religion for the laity, performing a 'shift from image towards word' (Rex 2006: xvi). As Cromwell puts it, '[The laity] have seen their religion painted on the walls of churches, or carved in stone, but now God's pen is poised, and he is ready to write his words in the book of their hearts' (Mantel 2010a: 516).

This is not the only moment in *Wolf Hall* when the presence of a material book belonging to a deceased subject provokes their spectral apparition. However, the second extract examined here marks a movement from manuscript to print productions and concerns another Book of Hours, this time belonging to Thomas More.[2] *Wolf Hall*'s account of More's execution moves quickly back and forth between the present moment, in which Cromwell waits to learn of More's death, and his trial for treason. As Cromwell waits More's phantom appears to stand before him, 'more solid in death than he was in life' (644). Yet this apparition has significantly less impact within the text than the approach and appearance of More's book:

> The window rattles; it startles him, and he thinks, I shall bolt the shutter. He is rising to do it when Rafe comes in with a book in his hand. 'It is his prayer

> book, that More had with him at the last.'
>
> He examines it. Mercifully, no blood specks.[…].
>
> More has written his name in it. There are underlinings in the text: *Remember not the sins of my youth.* […]
>
> The whole house is rocking about him; wind in the eaves, wind in the chimneys, a piercing draft under every door. (646)

As the invasive wind creates an instance of pathetic fallacy, stressed almost to the point of cliché, More's book comes to stand in for him posthumously, the analogue all the more powerful because of the presence of his annotations. These annotations are crucial when we consider that, unlike Liz Cromwell's prayer book, the volume in the above passage is a printed text. Certainly, the presence of annotations in both passages underscores the posthumous quality implicated in all modes of inscription. However, if we compare the two scenes of haunting, one serene, if poignant, taking place within the contained space of the window embrasure, the other unsettling and disruptive, a contrast can be seen between the kinds of haunting that print and manuscript technologies are able to provoke. It is the printed book whose presence is depicted as capable of causing disruption. The space of Cromwell's house is destabilized by its presence while the wind, which penetrates ubiquitously, captures the unsettling and uncontainable quality of print. The unruliness of print will be examined in more detail below but for the moment I would like to address the corporeality implied by the 'merciful' absence of the blood specks tentatively sought by Cromwell above.

Alongside the linkages already analysed between books and haunting, present in *Wolf Hall* is a persistent analogue between the physical body and the object of the book that articulates the play the novel is engaging with through the various meanings of the word 'corpus' and its relationship to the 'corpse'. We saw above how More's book arrives on Cromwell's desk as evidence of his death, a substitute for More's corpse. A further striking manifestation of the corpse-like book is found in the account given of the confiscation of Cardinal Wolsey's books in the wake of his fall: 'They are packing [the cardinal's] gospels and taking them for the king's libraries. The texts are […] awkward as if they breathed; their pages are made of slunk vellum from stillborn calves, re-veined by the illuminator in tints of lapis and leaf-green' (48–49). In this description there is a sense of the books hovering phantasmally between life and death which is made particularly striking by Mantel's description of the vellum binding being produced from the flesh of 'stillborn' calves, creatures whose entry into the world of the living takes place only in death. The volumes appear to breathe and struggle against their removal, the veins of the original material suggested through the artifice of the illuminator's brush. While in the previous two examples the book's owner is deceased, in this passage, the undead quality of the cardinal's library acts as a harbinger of the cardinal's own death, the confiscation of the books a precursor to the forfeit of the cardinal's body. Within the emphasis on vellum can be detected a tongue-in-cheek inversion of the notion of 'the word made flesh' as the 'flesh' of the binding is obscured by the words inked upon it. This inversion, which implies that flesh can also be reduced to words, that it can offer (or be rendered) a surface of inscription, has profound implications which are realized in *Wolf Hall*'s representation of the relationship between an author and their work, as distinct from the relationship between a book and its owner or owners.

The relationship between the doomed Cardinal Wolsey and his undead gospels exemplifies how *Wolf Hall* depicts books and bodies as having a consonant relationship. Considering Rembrandt's painting *The Anatomy Lesson of Dr Nicholas Tulp*, Derrida observes how the focus of the figures within the painting is not upon the body being dissected but the open book lying at its feet. He comments, 'This book stands up to, and stands in for, the body: a corpse is replaced by a corpus, a corpse yielding its place to the bookish thing' (2001: 176). This form of 'standing in' is active within *Wolf Hall*'s presentation of the relationship between authors and their texts. An equivalence is repeatedly drawn between an author and their works through the use of the writer's name to refer also to their written output, an equivalence captured by Thomas More's observation: 'I hear they are burning the books from the city libraries. Erasmus has gone into the flames. What kind of devils would burn the gentle Erasmus?' (Mantel 2010a: 591). Likewise, giving an account of how Cardinal Wolsey will respond to the influx of heretical texts arriving in England from Germany it is stated that 'Wolsey will burn books, but not men' (40). This refusal carries within it an acknowledgement that the destruction of the book could stand in for the destruction of its author, an equivalence which has significant consequences as the novel progresses and men are burned in the place of their books.

In the context of this analogue between the book and the body, the harbouring of ideas and beliefs within the body of the subject comes to parallel the inscription of those ideas and beliefs within the pages of the book. The depiction in *Wolf Hall* of an inscription whose ideational content remains though its material form no longer persists, points towards the unpredictable circulation of ideas, and more specifically, the texts that express those ideas, whose existence is not predicated upon 'cheap parchment' or 'slunk vellum'. It is to the unbound or, perhaps, disembodied text that this analysis now moves.

Pressing matters: Technology, textuality and ghosts from the machine

Thus far I have discussed the undead lives of books and the hauntings those books facilitate, examining how the image of book as corpse articulates the act of writing as negotiating the boundaries between pre- and post-mortem, with the writer creating a bibliographic cadaver that anticipates the physical body in death. Yet, a material book is merely the physical container for a text whose existence is not prescribed by bindings and pages but has a disembodied quality which renders it unregulatable and unruly. What then is the status of the *text* in *Wolf Hall* and how does it develop the linkage that has already been established between writing and death? To answer these questions it is necessary to outline the second contextual element upon which the novel grounds its intellectual and creative project: the advent of print.

The Protestant Reformation is a period inextricably linked with the proliferation of print culture. In Germany in the 1500s the rapid expansion of print enabled unprecedented access to education among urban populations, significantly increasing levels of functional literacy (Biller 1994: 35). This in turn allowed, in Peter Biller's words, an 'astonishing wave of religious heterodoxy to sweep across [Germany]' (Scribner 1994: 257), and subsequently England. As is observed in *Wolf Hall*:

> When the last treason act was made, no one could circulate their words in a printed book or bill, because printed books were not thought of. [Cromwell] feels a moment of jealousy towards the dead, to those who served kings in slower times than these; nowadays the products of some bought or poisoned brain can be disseminated through Europe in a month. (Mantel 2010a: 492)

Cromwell's envy of those living in the 'slower times' of the pre-print era articulates a broader association between print, heresy and sedition. As Jesse Lander points out, '[A] printed book cannot be dismissed as the solitary ravings of a singular heretic, disgruntled reader or political dissident' (2006: 15) and as Loewenstein notes, the 'Henrician Reformation of the 1530s' perceived heresy 'in terms of proliferating texts [...] capable of quickly disseminating dangerous and unorthodox doctrine and seditious opinion to the people' (2006: 15–16). Indeed, as Richard Rex observes, the flood of reformist literature into England so concerned Henry VIII that in 1538 '[he] issued a proclamation banning the importation of any book printed in English' (2006: 93). The strategy failed and Protestant texts continued to be printed, imported and circulated (2006: 93).

Circulation, proliferation, dissemination; these words emerge repeatedly in the literature that has grown up around early print culture.[3] Cromwell's mournful jealousy of his pre-print predecessors articulates all three concepts either implicitly or explicitly but it also captures another common quality attributed to print technology at this time – that of being contagious or else poisonous. Harold Weber observes how 'the printed word becomes [...] a power unhealthy, infectious, subtly and mysteriously contagious [...]. A plague has invaded the body of the kingdom [...], a dark and secret realm of books which mysteriously propagate themselves' (1996: 137–139). Despite pertaining to the reign of Charles II, Weber's analysis of various proclamations responding to print culture offers a picture of print that is instantly recognizable within *Wolf Hall* with the novel acknowledging how the press emphasized the disembodied nature of textuality and in so doing 'gave new vitality to ghosts' (Raymond 2003: 204–205). The novel presents print culture as changing the nature of spectrality and by doing so generating new forms of haunting.

'The Castile soap came. And your book from Germany. It was packaged as something else. I almost sent the boy away' (Mantel 2010a: 37): here Liz Cromwell informs her husband of the delivery of a copy of William Tyndale's testament, printed in English. This seemingly off-hand comment captures Mantel's nuancing of the compromised presence of material books in *Wolf Hall* through an acknowledgement of how, during the Reformation, banned religious texts were frequently smuggled into the country by European textile merchants under false titles. By examining how these objects are established as only partially present, it becomes clear how, through compromising the physical forms of the books which contain them, Mantel sets the scene for an understanding of text as spectral. *Wolf Hall* does not foreground scholarly descriptions of the printed products of the Reformation, rather, the occult life of Reformation publications is emphasized as Cromwell is described 'keep[ing] up with what's written and with what's smuggled through the Channel ports, [...], the tidal creeks where a small boat with dubious cargo can be beached and pushed out again, by moonlight, to sea' (39–40). The vernacular religious books of the Protestant Reformation flicker in and out of the novel, alluded to, yet hidden and compromised, frequently destroyed by the time they appear within the narrative. This representation is exemplified by the fate of the books belonging to Humphrey Monmouth, the master draper thought to have sheltered William Tyndale:

> When Monmouth's house is raided, it is clear of all suspect writings.[...]. There are neither books nor letters that link him to Tyndale and his friends. [...] They have to let him go, for lack of evidence, because you can't make anything of a heap of ashes in the hearth. (125)

The physical presence which confronts the reader is that of 'a heap of ashes' rather than a complete book, and is paralleled in a later passage in which the wife of John Peyt, another Protestant Reformer arrested for heresy, recounts the raid upon their house by Thomas More. Lucy Peyt describes her husband 'cast[ing] his Testament under his desk': 'Tyndale lying there, like a poison stain on the tiles' (300). Ashes, stains; this pre-occupation with remains sits alongside the compromised physical presence of Protestant texts more generally depicting a process of disembodiment with regard to texts and ideas. By occulting the material object of the book, showing it burned, hidden and smuggled, and in doing so creating a parallel with the fates of their readers and writers, Mantel provokes her readers to ask what is left over when book and body are destroyed? The answer can be found in Protestant reformer Hugh Latimer's explanation of how he evaded his heresy charge: 'bare walls my library. Fortunately, my brain is furnished with texts' (360). Latimer's description of his mind as 'furnished with texts' reaffirms an understanding of the text as exceeding the physical bounds of the book and possessing a discarnate persistence, a spectrality which is given potency by its production in print. Having examined how print allowed for a medium-specific spectralization of text, it is necessary to examine what impact this bibliographic development had upon textual practice and how this spectral quality manifests itself in specific textual hauntings.

Paratextual activity: Textiles, (inter)textuality and haunting

> Suppose within every book there is another book, and within every letter on every page another volume constantly unfolding; but these volumes take no space on the desk. (Mantel 2010a: 482)

These 'volumes [that] take no space on the desk' attest to the phantasmal quality given to textuality in *Wolf Hall*, their 'volume' seeming to refer more to a billowing and voluminous textual mass rather than to any physical binding. Furthermore, these lines adeptly capture the supposition which drives not only *Wolf Hall* but many of Mantel's other works: that all works of literature harbour within them myriad moments where the influence of, or references to other texts make, or attempt to make themselves known. In short, this scene of discarnate textual multiplication refers to the notion of intertextuality. It is essential to recognize the relationship between print technology and intertextual practice in *Wolf Hall*. This relationship affords Mantel the opportunity to critique intertextuality while establishing the multiplicity of intertextual drivers which exceed marked quotation and encompass allusion, translation, paraphrase, unmarked and mis-quotation.[4] When read alongside *Fludd*, the treatment of intertextuality in *Wolf Hall* establishes intertextuality as an inherent quality of textuality itself and Mantel's intertextual play as a potent and deliberate mode of haunting, with her intertexts acting 'as ghosts passing through the text'.[5]

The medium of print profoundly influenced the message of the texts it produced, particularly in terms of how print accommodated and amplified intertextuality. With the advent of print, the practice of textual quotation was significantly altered. Lander usefully reminds us that in the pre-print age quoted material was indicated by a change in font (2006: 29), an unavoidable visual indicator of the presence of a voice discrete from that of the author of a text. The invention of print brought with it, as recognized by Douglas McMurtrie, the invention of the quotation mark (1934: 4), and while the symbol's usage differed from contemporary convention, this formal change should be seen as significant, denoting a partial occlusion of quoted material which made it less immediately identifiable. Secondly, the printed material of the Protestant Reformation should be understood as predominantly paratextual. As Scribner notes, 'expanding lay-interest in printed works of piety' was satiated by the publication in print of texts 'recycled from the predominantly scribal pre-print era' (1994: 256). These recyclings sat alongside vernacular translations of the Bible which were 'increasingly filtered through marginal glosses, sermons, catechisms and devotional literature' (276). The printed texts of the Protestant Reformation were crucially multi-vocal, re-working texts in a way which was neither as pronounced nor as commonplace before the advent of the press.[6] This is not to deny the intertextual play already present in the texts of the pre-print era but rather to acknowledge that the 'borrowings, re-workings and enhancements that manuscript took for granted as its very substance became the problem of intertextuality' following the advent of print (Orr 2003: 148).

In what ways, then, is intertextuality, as concept and as technique, at work within *Wolf Hall*? This question can be addressed in part through an examination of the way in which Mantel uses textile imagery within the novel to elegantly articulate the unavoidably 'textile' nature of text, its availability for re-purposing and transformation:

> October comes, and his sisters and Mercy and Johane take his dead wife's clothes and cut them up carefully into new patterns. Nothing is wasted. Every good bit of cloth is made into something else. (120)[7]

The quotation above, while referring to a poignant act of recycling, also serves as an example of how textiles are predominantly foregrounded in the novel in order to discuss acts of repurposing and remaking. Earlier I noted *Wolf Hall*'s acknowledgement of the role played by European textile traders in importing banned Reformation texts. This link to the textile industry is expanded throughout the novel from a contextual detail to a significant metaphorical vehicle which allows the reader to think about what Barthes terms 'the generative idea that the text is made, is worked out in a perpetual interweaving' (1975: 64) producing a fabric composed of many strands, capable of being re-cut and re-fashioned to fit the taste of the times. The most notable manifestations of this use of the textile metaphor are the discussions of the deceased Cardinal Wolsey's clothes. After the Cardinal's death it is observed:

> The cardinal's scarlet clothes now lie folded and empty. They cannot be wasted. They will be cut up and become other garments. Who knows where they will get to over the years? Your eye will be taken by a crimson cushion or a patch of red on a banner or ensign. You will see a glimpse of them in a man's inner sleeve or in the flash of a whore's petticoat. (265–266)

This brief passage provides an elegant metaphor for the kinds of intertextuality that became recognizable during the Reformation, some borrowing obvious and attributed (the banner or ensign), some decorative, like the marked quotation (Orr 2003: 130) (the 'crimson cushion') while still others are allusive and easy to miss ('a man's inner sleeve', 'the flash of a whore's petticoat'). Furthermore, this recruitment of the language of textiles is not limited to providing an (albeit nuanced) analogy for intertextual play. The circulation of the dead Cardinal's clothing in a variety of new forms constitutes not merely a description of Tudor household practice but an articulation of how recycled 'material', be it textile or textual, possesses a spectral presence for Mantel. In the case of literary productions, the intertextual material has the effect of haunting the primary text, unavoidably drawing past utterances into the present, permitting the creation of new meanings. This exploration of text as textile in *Wolf Hall* is valuable in that it makes licit an awareness within the novel not only of the changing nature of Reformation textual practice but also of the structures created through textuality's intrinsically intertextual quality. Yet Mantel's consideration of intertextuality exceeds an articulation of the phenomenon as a structural property of writing. To more fully appreciate the complexities of her intertextual strategy, it is necessary to examine one of *Wolf Hall*'s most striking intertexts.

Après Moi, Le Deluge: *Wolf Hall* as the great *Fludd*

One of the crucial elements that gives the use of intertextuality in Mantel's work its unique quality is the way in which she utilizes self-quotation. In accordance with the re-workings of Liz Cromwell's clothes, previous works are 'cut up carefully into new patterns'. In turning to look at *Wolf Hall*'s intertexts it is necessary to bring another of Mantel's novels to the fore: her 1989 text *Fludd,* identifying two moments of intertextual resonance in which it is apparent that *Fludd* anticipates *Wolf Hall*'s concerns, not only intellectually but textually. *Fludd* coalesces around the life of parish priest, Father Angwin, depicting the spiritual upheavals which take place in the religious communities associated with the Roman Catholic Church of St Thomas Aquinas and its convent.

Before moving to examine the status of *Fludd* as intertext for *Wolf Hall* it is useful to acknowledge that *Fludd* is a text whose intertextual strategy bears consideration in its own right, concerned as it is with drawing out a matrix of connections between textuality, spectrality and the dead. From the novel's first moments the reader is aware of multiple intertextual presences hovering at the text's peripheries. Mantel's description, placed before the opening of the novel's first chapter, of Sebastiano del Piombo's painting *The Raising of Lazarus* serves as one example among many where, in a doubly haunted gesture, the intertexts invoked throughout *Fludd* frequently re-animate and resurrect narratives concerning the dead. Perhaps one of the most striking manifestations of the density of *Fludd*'s intertextual strategy comes early on in its first chapter when Fetherhoughton, its environs and inhabitants, are initially described:

> The people of Fetherhoughton kept their eyes averted from the moors with a singular effort of will. [...] They were not Emily Brontë, nor were they paid to be [...]. The moors were the vast cemetery of their imaginations. Later, there were notorious murders in the vicinity, and real bodies were buried there. (Mantel 2010b: 12)

The second sentence of this passage is a mis-quotation of the line 'I am not Prince Hamlet, nor was meant to be', taken from T. S. Eliot's 'The Lovesong of J. Alfred Prufrock' (1963: 13). This revision invokes three separate literary texts (taking in Emily Brontë's *Wuthering Heights* and Shakespeare's *Hamlet* in addition to the Eliot poem) and the cultural narrative of the Moors Murders and creates a potent, if highly compressed, tapestry of texts which crystallize around vexed relationships with dead subjects and their disruptive post-mortem presences.

As is the case in Mantel's Tudor London, it is a heterodox religious scene we are confronted with in *Fludd,* the faith displayed by the novel's protagonists being presented as complex and compromised. Father Angwin has lost his faith in God but still believes in the devil (53) while Agnes, his housekeeper, holds a plethora of superstitious beliefs. To make matters worse, the vicarage in which they live is seemingly haunted: '[Agnes] heard footsteps above, in the passage, in the bedroom. It is ghosts, she thought, walking on my mopping' (23). Against this background of lapsed and heretical faith, Mantel orchestrates a parodical playing out of the debates which structured the Reformation.

Yet the connection between *Wolf Hall* and *Fludd* is not merely thematic but formal. The first moment in which the intertextual relationship between these two novels is made manifest takes place during a meeting between Father Angwin and a nun, Sister Philomena, in which they discuss the life and death of her aunt, Dymphna (37–38). Following their conversation the nun and the priest return home:

> As they left the church, [Angwin] thought that a hand brushed his arm. Dymphna's bar-parlour laugh came faintly from the terraces; her tipsy, Guinness-sodden breath, stopped by the earth these eleven years, filled the summer night. (39)

This moment of haunting is resurrected structurally in *Wolf Hall,* as Cromwell returns with his ward from a meeting with Cardinal Wolsey and is prompted to write his will:

> 'Rafe,' he says, 'do you know I haven't made my will? I said I would but I never did. I think I should go home and draft it'.
> [...]
> On his left side, a hand touches his: fingers without flesh. A ghost walks: Arthur, studious and pale. (147)

These *mains mortes* (dead hands) are performing an analogous purpose. In both cases the ghost in question appears to a stranger, their manifestations partial and apparently prompted by discussion of their lives and the manner of their deaths. Even so, this provocative instance of self-quotation could be dismissed as incidental if it were not for a further passage in which the spectre of *Fludd* seems to be attempting to manifest itself within the space of *Wolf Hall.* In the following passage Thomas Cromwell is standing in the house belonging to the Master of the Rolls and left all but vacant for years:

> He rests his hand on the banister of the great staircase, looks up into the dust-mote glitter from a high window. When did I do this? At Hatfield, early in the year [...]. If he himself went to Hatfield, must not Thomas More have gone up too? Perhaps it was his light footstep he expected, overhead?
> [...]
> Whoever will come downstairs and claim him, must do it now. His daughter Anne with her thundering feet [...] Grace skimming down like dust, drawn into a spiral, a lively swirl ... going nowhere, dispersing, gone.
> Liz, come down.
> But Liz keeps her silence; she neither stays nor goes. (Mantel 2010a: 583–584)

This temporally ambivalent moment, in which a ghost's presence is signalled by footsteps from above and their identity is guessed at, finds itself reanimated from the moment in *Fludd* recalling the ghostly footsteps which pace the upper floor of the vicarage, unsettling Agnes Dempsey and interfering with her mopping. When Agnes confesses her experiences of these disturbances to Father Angwin, he attributes these ghostly perambulations to 'a forerunner. Someone who is to come'. Mantel's use of self-quotation here, in which a scene of haunting from one novel spectrally erupts through the text of another, generates an uncanny resonance, as *Wolf Hall* takes the place of the 'someone who is to come' in relation to *Fludd*'s 'forerunner'. These moments are composed of miniature ghost stories and, when lifted from their original context and resuscitated in *Wolf Hall,* the hauntings they depict become compounded by their status as spectral intertextual fragments.

To conclude, the occluded books and spectral texts that populate *Fludd* and *Wolf Hall* nuance the 'literal' ghosts that manifest within the atmosphere of pervasive haunting that characterizes the two novels. Yet it is vital to acknowledge that these hauntings are not only thematic but structural. The rich and complex treatment of intertextuality present in *Wolf Hall* and its textual predecessor *Fludd* is constantly engaged in producing moments of formal haunting in which the surface of the primary text is disrupted by intertextual phantoms which work to disorganize and destabilize readerly perception. Mantel's intertextual strategy prompts the reader to recognize that, to quote A. S. Byatt, 'a text is all the words that are in it, and not only those words, but the other words that precede it, haunt it and are echoed in it' (2000b: 46) and to understand these peripheral words and texts as constituting that place 'where the ghosts of meaning are' (Mantel 2003: 22).

Notes

1 This linkage between inscription and the dead is also present in *Fludd.* Here the presence of a vernacular religious text (*Faith and Morals for the Catholic Fireside: A Question-Box for the Layman* (157) forms a spectral presence within the novel, being quoted from extensively (in the context of establishing obscure intricacies of Catholic doctrine) before being revealed to be a pre-existing text and to contain an inscription by the book's former owner, now deceased. The mysterious circulation of this religious text combines with its annotated indications of past ownership to act as a parodic prototype for the kinds of annotated prayer books we will encounter in *Wolf Hall.*

2 For a transcription of More's Book of Hours see Martz and Sylvester.

3 For examples of this see H. Weber.

4 In *Intertextuality: Debates and Contexts*, Mary Orr usefully identifies how the term intertextuality has come to obscure the myriad of techniques which produce it (14).

5 Hilary Mantel, 'Email Interview – Answers, Appendix 2', Arnold (254).

6 The significance of this historical and literary context for the exploration of textuality as unavoidably intertextual is underlined by Mary Orr's assessment that 'commentary, translation, exegesis, all return pre-modern views on interpretation and interpreting reference texts, including the bible, to the post-modern world of texts and intertextuality' (17).

7 This passage resonates with Mantel's own description of her approach to her writing process of which she says 'the remnants linger … bob back into another story, or intrude themselves into another medium […] Nothing's wasted. Nothing's gone. Nothing's lost'. Hilary Mantel, 'Email Interview – Answers', Arnold (259).

Bibliography

Arnold, L. (2016), 'Where the Ghosts of Meaning Are: Spectrality and Haunting in the Work of Hilary Mantel', Unpublished PhD Thesis: University of Leeds.

Barthes, R. (1975), *The Pleasure of the Text*, translated by Richard Millar, New York: Hill and Wang.

Biller, P. (1994), *Heresy and Literacy, 1000–1530*, Cambridge: Cambridge University Press.

Byatt, A. S. (2000a), 'Fathers', in *On Histories and Stories: Selected Essays*, 9–35, London: Chatto and Windus.

Byatt, A. S. (2000b), '*Forefathers*', in *On Histories and Stories: Selected Essays*, 36–64, London: Chatto and Windus.

Derrida, J. (2001), 'Sarah Koffman (1934–94)', in P. Brault and M. Naas (eds), *The Work of Mourning*, 165–188, London: University of Chicago Press.

Derrida, J. and Stiegler, B. (2002), *Echographies of Television: Filmed Interviews*, translated by J. Bajorek, Cambridge: Polity Press.

Eisenstein, E. (2011), *Divine Art, Infernal Machine: The Reception of Printing in the West from First Impressions to the Sense of an Ending*, Oxford; Philadelphia, PA: University of Pennsylvania Press.

Eliot, T. S. (1963), 'The Lovesong of J. Alfred Prufrock', in *Collected Poems, 1909–1962*, London: Faber and Faber.

Greenblatt, S. (2001), *Hamlet in Purgatory*, Princeton; Oxford: Princeton University Press.

Holland, T. (2009), 'Books of the Year', *Daily Telegraph*, 6 December. Available online: http://www.telegraph.co.uk/culture/books/6710158/Books-of-the-Year.html (accessed 24 June 2015).

Lander, J. M. (2006), *Inventing Polemic: Religion, Print and Literary Culture in Early Modern England*, Cambridge: Cambridge University Press.

Low, A. (1999), '*Hamlet* and the Ghost of Purgatory: Intimations of Killing the Father', *English Literary Renaissance*, 29: 443–467.

Loewenstein, D. (2006), 'Writing and the Persecution of Heretics in Henry VIII's England: *The Examination of Anne Askew*', in *Heresy, Literature and Politics in Early Modern English Culture*, 11–39, Cambridge, Cambridge University Press.
Mantel, H. (2003), *Giving Up the Ghost: A Memoir*, London: Fourth Estate.
Mantel, H. (2010a), *Wolf Hall*, London: Fourth Estate.
Mantel, H. ([1989] 2010b), *Fludd*, London: Fourth Estate.
Martz L. L. and Sylvester, R. S. (1969), *Thomas More's Prayerbook: A Facsimile Reproduction of the Annotated Pages*, New Haven, CT: Yale University Press.
McMurtrie, D. (1934), *Concerning Quotation Marks*, New York: Privately Published.
O'Reilly, S. (2010), Interview with Hilary Mantel, 'Making It New', in *Wolf Hall* London: Fourth Estate.
Orr, M. (2003), *Intertextuality: Debates and Contexts*, Cambridge: Polity Press.
Raymond, J. (2003), *Pamphlets and Pamphleteering in Early Modern Britain*, Cambridge: Cambridge University Press.
Rex, R. (2006), *Henry VIII and the English Reformation*, Basingstoke: Palgrave Macmillan.
Scribner, B. (1994), 'Heterodoxy, Literacy and Print in the Early German Reformation', in *Heresy and Literacy, 1000–1530*, Cambridge: Cambridge University Press.
Stoker, B. D. (2012), 'Bygonese: Is This Really the Authentic Language of Historical Fiction?' *New Writing* 9: 308–318.
Taylor, C. (2009), '*Wolf Hall* by Hilary Mantel – Review', *The Guardian*, 2 May. Available online: http://www.theguardian.com/books/2009/may/02/wolf-hall-hilary-mantel (accessed 13 April 2015).
Weber, H. (1996), *Paper Bullets: Print and Kingship under Charles II*, Lexington, KY: University of Kentucky.

9

'I Am a Settlement, a Place of Safety, a Bombproof Shelter': Hauntings, Hospitality and Homeland Insecurity in Hilary Mantel's *Beyond Black*

Kathryn Bird

This chapter reads Hilary Mantel's *Beyond Black* in relation to recent scholarship on biopolitics and on the female Gothic in order to examine the novel's depiction of strategies for managing bodily vulnerability, with a particular focus on Mantel's use of the Gothic trope of being locked inside or out of the home. It argues that *Beyond Black* locates the home, a place which ideally promises security, as a space of unseen and often unacknowledged physical and psychological violence. The chapter considers how the novel's Gothic aesthetics open out onto contemporary preoccupations with and responses to the dichotomy of security and hospitality, and explores what the novel might suggest about the possibilities and limits of negotiating precarious lives in the contemporary era.

*****

In an interview with *The Guardian* on the publication of *Beyond Black* in 2005, Hilary Mantel remarks on her frustration concerning how some of her earlier novels have been 'gendered' by reviewers. For example, she notes that her 1986 novel *Vacant Possession* is 'very obviously [...] a state of the nation novel'; however, she goes on to point out that 'because it was by a woman, it was reviewed as domestic black comedy' (Cooke 2005). *Beyond Black*, which covers some similar terrain to the earlier pair of novels *Every Day Is Mother's Day* (1985) and *Vacant Possession* (1986), might easily be described as a 'domestic black comedy', particularly because of its scrutiny of suburban domestic settings. However, in this chapter I argue that *Beyond Black*, like these earlier novels, illustrates Mantel's predilection for exploring the 'state of the nation' in and through precisely such domestic settings and through women's experiences in these locations, and, by extension, her insistence on the impossibility of separating the private from the public, the domestic and local from the national and global.

Beyond Black charts the journeys of the medium Alison Hart and her manager Colette as they endlessly circle London's orbital road attending psychic fayres in the surrounding commuter towns, during the period from the late 1990s to the first years after the millennium. The latter half of the novel focuses on Alison and Colette's move to a new-build suburban house in Surrey in a bid to outrun the abusive men from Alison's childhood home in Aldershot, who now continue to haunt the medium from beyond the grave, and who eventually begin to invade her suburban idyll. As well as resuming this focus on suburban England evident in *Every Day Is Mother's Day* and *Vacant Possession, Beyond Black* also resumes the 'state of the nation' emphasis on the failures of state care which these earlier novels foreground. In *Beyond Black*, for example, the spirits of the elderly often do not realize that they have died. Instead, they believe that 'they're in a corridor, lying on a trolley, and nobody comes [...] they've actually gone over, but they think it's just the NHS' (2005: 150). However, *Beyond Black* also focuses extensively on the psychic life of the nation – and especially on the 'common repression and anxieties' of Home Counties England (Cooke 2005) – in the millennial period, with a notable emphasis on the death of Princess Diana in 1997, an event described elsewhere by Mantel as 'that dislocating time, when the skin came off the surface of the world', unleashing 'a pagan outpouring, a lawless fiesta of grief' (Mantel 2013). Yet in the same breath in which Colette recalls that 'she got to know Alison properly' in 'the week after Diana's death', she also describes this period as 'another era now, another world: before the millennium, before the Queen's Jubilee, before the Twin Towers burned' (Mantel 2005: 140). And it is the ramifications of this latter event which I suggest play a significant role in Mantel's exploration of the 'state of the nation' in *Beyond Black*.

Published only four years after the events of 9/11, and only a few months before the 7/7 bombings in London, *Beyond Black* emerges from a period in which the 'language of security' was busy 'colonizing every arena and idiom of daily life and political culture' (Kaplan 2008: 16). In particular, the novel's emphasis on the psychic's purported ability not only to speak with the dead but also to predict the future – Colette, for example, is 'afraid to act at all' without the intervention of fortune tellers (Mantel 2005: 70–71) – resonates with what Didier Bigo describes as the 'anticipation or "astrological" dimension' of contemporary security practices in Europe (2005: 89). The objective now, Bigo argues, is always 'to monitor the future', to be able 'to designate in advance who and what are the dangers [...] to "ban" some people', to consistently focus on staging 'a preemptive defense' (2005: 89). My focus below will be on Mantel's depiction of haunted suburban houses as the terrain on which to explore contemporary anxieties about 'homeland security' and the defensive attitudes and measures which are established in response to this persistent fear of attack.

Mantel's exploration of global security issues in domestic spaces resonates with Amy Kaplan's argument that the concept of security 'does the seductive work of creating a framework for seeing and experiencing the world in a way that fuses the macro level of global and national politics with the intimate world of home and psyche' (Kaplan 2008: 16). Moreover, this emphasis on security in the context of 'the intimate world of home and psyche' also enables Mantel to explore the related issue of hospitality, which, like security, is concerned with 'questions of territory and border, of private and public spaces, [...] of belonging, membership, citizenship, and exclusion' (Friese 2004: 74). In *Beyond Black*, Mantel examines the central dilemma – which has become increasingly urgent in the context of global terror threats – of how to balance the obligation to offer hospitality with the defensive apparatus necessary to offer security and protection from violent attack, which she focuses through women's historical and contemporary experiences of bodily vulnerability in the home. The first section of this chapter will outline contemporary approaches to the idea of security and their relationship with the concept of the home and 'homeland', with a focus on Mantel's depiction of suburbia. Following this, the second section will explore Mantel's depiction of suburban homes in more detail, emphasizing the function of hauntings in the novel as troubling the division between the public and private realms, especially where domestic violence is concerned. Finally, the third section will examine how Mantel draws on women's experiences of bodily vulnerability in the home to explore the relationship between hospitality and security, and will consider how contemporary national and global security anxieties concerning immigration and terrorism are played out in local suburban communities in *Beyond Black*.

Homeland insecurity

According to Amy Kaplan, although the practice of 'referring to the nation as a home, as a domestic space through familial metaphors' is 'probably as old as the nation form itself', the use of the term 'homeland' to refer to the United States after the 9/11 attacks – particularly in the collocation 'homeland security' – signalled a significant shift in contemporary political and cultural attitudes to national security (2003: 84–85). The term homeland, she argues, draws on and amplifies the fact that 'the notion of the nation as a home, as a domestic space, relies structurally on its intimate opposition to the notion of the foreign', such that the term 'domestic' can be understood to have 'a double meaning that links the space of the familial household to that of the nation, by imagining both in opposition to everything outside the geographic and conceptual border of the home' (86). The term 'homeland' therefore has the capacity to provoke 'a profound sense of insecurity', not only concerning the immediate and contemporary 'threat of terrorism' carried out by 'foreign' agents, but also because the home or 'homeland' is always already 'a fundamentally uncanny place [...] haunted by all the unfamiliar yet strangely familiar foreign specters that threaten to turn it into its opposite' (89). Home, Kaplan concludes, proves itself to be a particularly apt conceptual 'battleground' for the so-called War on Terror (90).

This conception of the home as the fundamentally unstable terrain on which contemporary security anxieties are played out forms the background for Mantel's exploration of what we might call 'homeland *in*security' in *Beyond Black*. Of course, unlike the United States, the United Kingdom has no department of 'homeland security', and this is not a phrase which has gained the same purchase in the British political imagination. However, as Kaplan points out, the concept of home does play a significant role in British political discourse, not least in such terms as the 'Home Office' and 'Home Secretary', which derive their meaning 'in the context of the British Empire that demarcated the space of England as home as distinct from its colonial possessions' (Kaplan 2003: 89). Indeed, there is a similar precedent for the use of the noun phrase 'the homeland' in a British context, which the *OED* states is used to designate 'Britain, as opposed to (former) British colonies and territories'. In this sense, then, the term 'homeland' in a British context also carries intimations of the authentically national as opposed to the foreign, that which by definition comes from outside the home.

This is also what makes Mantel's focus on suburban homes in *Beyond Black* so striking, in that suburbia embodies and even amplifies anxieties about the security of both home and nation, and indeed of the home-as-nation. As Ged Pope points out, since the 1930s in particular, suburbia has been strongly related 'to national identity, to notions of Englishness', not least because 'suburbia is often seen as incorporating key national stereotypes (the predilection for the pastoral, for privacy, for the house and domesticity)' (2015: 209). Similarly, Dominic Head suggests that in 'the popular imagination [...] suburbia is Middle England' (2002: 213). Yet Middle England's residence in such territories might nevertheless be understood as an uneasy experience, in terms of ideas of both Englishness and social class: according to Todd Kutcha, suburbia 'is both the epitome and the antithesis of the nation's home – on the one hand quintessentially English, on the other hand bristling anxiously over its perceived inferiority' (2010: 5). For Kutcha, part of this 'ambivalence' towards suburbs stems from their ability – particularly in the post-war period – to 'represent a national reversal of fortune, their reputation for petty lives and mortgaged futures belying an era when Britannia ruled the waves' (5).

Moreover, as Pope observes, suburbia was not always a haven for the middle classes. Instead the 'proto-suburban sites' of the sixteenth century contained all the 'unwanted and inassimilable elements' that had been 'banished' from the city. It was only later in the eighteenth century that a different kind of suburban space began to develop, and suburbia became not 'a negative, debased space containing deviant elements unhappily expelled from a broadly assimilative core', but instead a 'potential welcome space for expansive elements actively escaping a threatening core urban milieu' (2015: 23). However, these affluent suburban spaces are never quite secure. Indeed Pope paints a rather Gothic portrait of affluent suburban spaces, arguing that they are troubled by a 'permeable' temporal boundary between slum and suburb, through which 'a horrible slum past of indiscriminate co-mingling threatens to return to the desired suburban present' (25, 22).

Similarly, for Lara Baker Whelan, it is this essential 'mutability' of suburban territory which underpins the sub-genre of suburban ghost stories (2010: 76, 78) – into which we might place *Beyond Black*. Whelan argues that over the course of its development, suburbia formed 'a constantly shifting, socially heterogeneous space where once respectable middle-class neighbourhoods could become working-class refuges within ten years, and full-blown slums within forty' (2010: 2). Hence, instead of finding 'a green suburban idyll', people who moved in search of a pleasant middle-class enclave found 'a repetition of the evils of urban living they had been trying to escape', including 'poorly constructed houses' and 'bad drains' (24). This disturbing mutability of suburban territories manifests itself in the figure of the ghost, which was often depicted (especially in Victorian suburban ghost stories) as 'a member of the "wrong crowd"' who would inevitably bring 'other unsavoury elements' to threaten the sanctity of this middle-class space (82).

This certainly seems to be the case with suburban hauntings in *Beyond Black*, especially when it comes to the construction of houses on the new-build estate Admiral Drive. Although Alison and Colette seek a blank spot 'nowhere near a racecourse, a dog track, an army camp, a dockyard, a lorry park nor a clinic for special diseases', their peaceful idyll is quickly disrupted by poor building work on the new estate, such that they observe other 'householders running out into the streets [...] fleeing from gas leaks, floods and falling masonry' (Mantel 2005: 221, 235). Moreover, the 'hastily built and shoddily finished architecture' of Alison and Colette's new house 'readily offers itself up for possession by malevolent spirits', particularly by Alison's 'belching, farting spirit guide' Morris, whose attempts to haunt her new-build suburban home can be interpreted as the return of Alison's own 'ignominious background', and, by extension, as 'the haunting of the recently middle class by their lower-class upbringing'. (Spooner 2010: 87, 84). Indeed, Alison's immediate reaction to the news that the estate's drains have 'filled up with black sludge' is to hope that it is not her 'fault', and to wonder whether Morris has 'pissed on the plot' (Mantel 2005: 251–252).

'Homes are very unsafe places to linger'

Suburbia can therefore be understood as a highly defensive territory, whose homeliness turns on its uneasy relationship with the foreign, and whose affluence depends on a careful maintenance of temporal and spatial boundaries which simultaneously recall and deny suburbia's past as a subordinate site. But there is yet another form of border security at work in suburbia which makes this territory an ideal location for Mantel's exploration of contemporary security anxieties: the separation of the public world of politics and commerce from the ostensibly private world of the home. Scott MacKenzie draws attention to the ideal of the home as that which is situated 'beyond the threshold of the world as the definitive interior that orients all exteriority'; as its most basic condition, the home is supposed to be 'untroubled by commerce, history, politics', and is emphatically 'where the state is not' (2013: 215–216). In its affluent form, suburbia is modelled on precisely this idealized separation of the 'the public world of work and politics' and 'the private world of the home', something Janet Wolff argues was 'marked, as well as constructed, by both geography and architecture' in the affluent suburban spaces which developed over the course of the eighteenth and nineteenth centuries (1988: 118–119).

In particular, this idealized separation of public and private has implications for Mantel's exploration of contemporary security anxieties through the lens of women's domestic experiences in suburbia. For example, Alison Blunt and Robyn Dowling argue that suburbia's 'socio-spatial separation of spheres of home and work' enables the production and maintenance of boundaries between 'public and private, masculine and feminine spaces' (2006: 101). Pope also identifies suburban development with a 'reorganisation and compartmentalising of spatial function' around the association of men with 'public roles and the spaces of work' and women with 'domestic ideology' (2015: 25). Even now, the repeated failure to recognize the problematic nature of this gendered separation of public and private spheres remains a source of deep frustration for feminist scholars – despite the fact that, as Geraldine Pratt notes, a wealth of feminist theory has long drawn attention to the ways in which 'women's issues are often depoliticized by being enclaved within the private sphere', something which is evidently still the case, given that the act of 'recasting private domestic issues such as childcare and domestic assault as public ones remains an area of intense political contest' (2005: 1056–1057).

As I noted in the introduction to this chapter, Mantel is similarly frustrated by such attempts to relegate 'domestic' concerns to the margins of the political sphere, not least in reviews of contemporary literature. She states that one still hears

> from female critics as well as male, a regular complaint, a bleat [...] that even today women writers play safe with small, domestic novels. They have forgotten that grand truth we learned, or relearned, at the close of the 20th century: the personal is political. The domestic novel need not be small, or tame. (Mantel 2008)

Indeed, Mantel insists that 'homes are very unsafe places to linger. The crime statistics will tell you the streets are safer. Everything, even warfare, happens first in the kitchen, in the nursery, in the cradle' (2008). These ideas are certainly foregrounded in *Beyond Black*, a 'domestic novel' which is neither 'small' nor 'tame': in fact, Mantel's novel places military violence and aggression directly inside the home. Alison grows up in the 'British Army town' of Aldershot, in which her prostitute mother's main customers are soldiers, including many of the 'fiends' who torment Alison when they are alive and who return to haunt her after their deaths, 'reassembling themselves' with a 'military rattle, as bone clicked into joint' (2005: 207). They perform 'some sort of military exercise' in her garden in the affluent suburb of Admiral Drive (406) whose name again hints at this military connection. But Mantel also suggests that this sort of violence is always already at work in domestic spaces through figuring young children playing in a suburban garden as 'scavenging and savaging, leaving scorched earth behind them, like child soldiers in an African war', while their mother is inside the house 'training up another one' (274).

Moreover, Mantel's depiction of Admiral Drive as haunted also emphasizes the porousness of the boundaries between the public and private realms. For MacKenzie, the 'domestic uncanny' is always symptomatic of the failure of attempts to separate the home from the public realm. Because such boundaries 'are never other than provisional or contingent structures of fantasy and effects of ideology', no real home can ever 'genuinely embody the immaculate, unpresentable asylum that the full conditions of home's hegemony dictate' (2013: 217). Hence, instances of hauntings and the 'domestic uncanny' are 'not the symptom of an intrusion into the home by some external power or agency but rather a fissure [...] through which home's hidden apparatus of coercion, historical determination, and power distribution casts its tenebrous glow'. Again, like Kaplan in her study of 'homeland security', MacKenzie turns to Freud's uncanny, stating that homes are represented in literature as 'endlessly hospitable to the intrusion of the monstrous, unnatural, and incommensurable', such that we constantly anticipate the 'perversion or disruption' of the home wherever it is represented (2013: 217). This is true not only of the ghost story but also of the Gothic genre more broadly, in which supernatural events emphasize the insecurity of the boundary between the home and the world outside. This is certainly the case where domestic violence is concerned. In her influential study of the relationship between the Gothic genre and 'domestic ideology', Kate Ferguson Ellis draws attention to the rise of the ideology of separate spheres – which rests on an image of the home as 'a refuge from violence' – and the simultaneous emergence of the Gothic as a 'popular genre [...] that assumes some violation of this cultural ideal' (1989: 3). It is therefore the 'failed home' which takes centre stage in Gothic novels as a site of potential and actual violence, manifesting itself in supernatural events largely directed at women (Ellis 1989: 3).

Security and hospitality

This Gothic emphasis on 'the troubled politics of domestic ideology' and its often 'nightmarish figuration' of women's experiences in the home (Heller 1992: 14) is certainly prominent in *Beyond Black*. In particular, Mantel draws on such imagery in order to explore the key contemporary dilemma of balancing security and hospitality, which she examines through women's experiences of violence in domestic spaces. This decision would come as no surprise to Judith Butler, who argues that women's experiences of such violence might enable them to offer a unique perspective on how to negotiate the dilemma of balancing hospitality against the desire for security in an increasingly unstable world. In her post-9/11 reflections on biopolitics and 'precarious life', Butler points out that women have been negotiating their 'bodily vulnerability' and 'exposure to violence' in 'nearly all times', and have thus always been familiar with the urgent dilemma of 'at what price, and at whose expense' one can 'gain a purchase on "security"', of how to 'negotiate a sudden and unprecedented vulnerability' without becoming 'mimetically violent' (2004: 42).

In *Beyond Black*, this dilemma centres on Alison, whose livelihood as a medium depends on her being hospitable, on her making room for 'a crowd of dead strangers whose intentions towards us we cannot know' (Mantel

2005: 9). These 'dead strangers' take up room both in Alison's house and in her body, which become interchangeable: hence she concludes 'I have to house so many people. My flesh is so capacious; I am a settlement, a place of safety, a bombproof shelter' (347). As Alison points out in the novel's opening pages, she has never 'had a choice' over whether she allows the dead to seek refuge in her body (2), but she does have some agency when it comes to the question of whether she allows them to remain with her. For example, she considers sending the elderly female spirits who cluster in her new-build house 'zinging to the next stage', but baulks at the idea of 'her strong psychic grip [...] snapping their feeble bones under her hand' (289). Although 'she knows psychics who will call in a clergyman at the least excuse', the violence of such exorcisms disturbs Alison: indeed, she likens it to 'sending the bailiffs in' (89).

However, Alison is also highly aware of the risks such hospitality poses, which is a common theme in the Gothic genre. In fact, hospitality itself, as Joanne Watkiss has recently argued, is a central but relatively underexplored theme in Gothic texts, in which the 'parasitical' or 'hostile guest' constitutes 'the persistent Gothic threat' (2012: 523). For Watkiss, it is not the stranger but the invited guest who most often constitutes the real threat, and she thus argues that 'the Gothic persistently advises us to *Let the Right One In*' (2012: 533). This advice is evident in Alison's warning to one of her audiences concerning the dangers of 'dabbling' in the psychic trade; as with her comments on exorcisms and bailiffs, she uses images related to housing to illustrate her point. Some spirits, she tells her audience, are 'like those kids you see on sink estates hanging about parked cars [...] those sort of kids, you wouldn't ask them into your house, would you?' She concludes that 'people are right to be afraid of ghosts' (Mantel 2005: 193).

Indeed, this fear is something Alison knows first-hand through her own experience of being haunted by Morris, who describes her as 'his hostess, his missus' (164), and whose physical and sexual abuse of Alison during her childhood continues to haunt her adulthood. One of the main narrative threads of *Beyond Black* concerns Alison's attempts to make sense of what happened to her as a child, for which her only clues (besides a highly unreliable memory) are the scars from wounds she received in an outbuilding of her childhood home at the hands of Morris and his cohort. These scars suggest she has 'been whipped with wire' (149). Women's experiences of bodily vulnerability in the home are also emphasized by Alison's garbled recollections of the fate of Gloria, a prostitute who haunted Alison's house during her childhood. Given that a woman's body parts keep appearing and disappearing before Alison's eyes, she believes that Gloria may have been murdered and dismembered by Morris and his cohort. This imagery resonates with the frequent depiction of women who have been trapped, murdered, dismembered or buried alive in houses in Gothic novels (Wallace 2009: 27).

Moreover, Alison's experience of abuse from these men continues during her adult life. She and her fellow psychic Mandy discuss what the 'guides' do 'while you're asleep' – a 'creak at the door, then a hand on the duvet, a hairy paw tugging at the sheet', followed by a 'violation' (Mantel 2005: 157). Morris's attempts at such violations are especially focused on Mandy, the 'unknowing hostess' in whom he hopes to be 'carried' and born again (205). Mantel's depiction of Alison's and Mandy's experiences of 'hosting' spirits resonates with the prevalence of women's bodily vulnerability, which Judith Still and Rosalyn Diprose identify in narratives of hospitality. Diprose, for example, focuses on 'the sacrifice of women's bodies' in the biblical examples of hospitality used by Jacques Derrida in his own study of the concept (2009: 145) while Still highlights the prevalence of rape, 'the most invasive of crimes', in these same narratives (2003: 2).

However, despite knowing through such first-hand experience that 'people are right to be afraid of ghosts' (Mantel 2005: 193), Alison nevertheless continues to act as 'a settlement, a place of safety, a bombproof shelter' (347) not only for the dead, but also for those living beings who have been excluded from the community. Chiefly she acts as sanctuary for a homeless man, Mart, whom Alison allows to live in her garden shed at Admiral Drive in the hope of doing 'a good action' (410). Like the malevolent spirits from Alison's past who haunt the suburban estate, Mart serves as another reminder of suburbia's slum past disturbing the security of its affluent present. Indeed, Mart seems at times to literally haunt the estate – for example, when Alison first encounters him, she is uncertain whether he is alive or already 'in spectral form' (293). And when Mart has committed suicide, he continues to trouble the estate's future as an affluent suburb: as one of Alison's irate neighbours exclaims, 'we'll be in the local paper as that place where the tramp topped himself, and that won't be very nice for our resale values' (409).

Yet Mart presents more than just a threat to the neighbourhood's house prices. Instead, he becomes a repository for the residents' anxieties about a broad range of security threats which necessitate a defensive management of the suburban estate, especially through the activities of the local neighbourhood watch. Most obviously, Mart's homelessness provokes intense anxiety. His presence in Alison and Colette's garden prompts their neighbours to remind Colette of the risks of having 'no lock on their side gate'. In response, she jokes that she and Alison should 'get some barbed wire on top', a strategy to which her neighbours object only because it would be 'unsightly'. They advise her instead to attend the neighbourhood watch's 'next meeting with community policing' to hear a talk on 'shed crime' (287–288). The fact that the neighbourhood watch in *Beyond Black* works in tandem with the police resonates with Jef Huysmans's argument that such 'local initiatives' are not examples of 'autonomous practice', but instead of 'a conduct that is to a certain extent governed by security apparatuses operating in the name of the state' (2006: 33). Indeed, Colette informs Alison of broader council initiatives to eliminate the presence of undesirable populations in their local area, including 'taking the benches out of the park, so that no one can sleep on them' (Mantel 2005: 318) – an initiative which has echoes of the so-called hostile or defensive architecture used in the contemporary management of homelessness in urban spaces.

The neighbourhood watch in *Beyond Black* also conducts a 'regular evening search among the cow-parsley meadows [...] for any poor wastrels or refugees who had grubbed in for the night' (374). This is not the only moment when localized issues with homeless populations and broader questions about national and international security provoked by larger unsettled populations are yoked together in *Beyond Black*. Indeed, I have examined elsewhere Mantel's emphasis in this novel on the extent to which mobile populations are imagined as a threat to the security of 'ordinary' citizens (Bird 2016: 124–125). *Beyond Black* was certainly written and published at a time of heightened anxiety about immigration in the UK, as is evident in the February 2005 publication of the Home Office's Command Paper on its immigration strategy, in which the government warned that Britain's 'traditional tolerance' for migrants was 'under threat from those who come and live here illegally by breaking our rules and abusing our hospitality' (Mantel 2005: 5). In *Beyond Black*, Mart comes to embody all such figures for the residents of Admiral Drive: as well as being described as a 'vagrant' (315), Mart is also described as an 'asylum seeker' and an 'illegal immigrant' (318). Alison's offer of hospitality to Mart is therefore interpreted as a 'crime of hospitality', an instance of 'harbouring' and 'failing to denounce' the illegal, the unwanted, an act through which she herself risks becoming a criminal (Still 2005: 92). Indeed, the other residents of Admiral Drive intend to 'call the police' and 'get up a petition' against Alison if she continues 'aiding and abetting' Mart's presence (Mantel 2005: 406).

However, the security anxieties stirred up by Mart's presence in Admiral Drive reach their apogee when Colette describes Mart as a terrorist (317). Nor are Colette's concerns an aberration among her neighbours: alongside their fears about homeless people, paedophiles, asylum seekers, Japanese Knotweed and illegal immigrants, the residents of Admiral Drive receive lectures from the local police at their neighbourhood watch meetings on what to do 'in case of terrorist outrage or nuclear explosion' (44–45). Interestingly, Mantel's emphasis on the fear of terrorism in suburban locations like Admiral Drive seems strangely prescient in light of newspaper headlines published after the London bombings in July 2005, which emphasized the attackers' mundane suburban upbringings. Chris Rumford suggests that this figure of the 'homegrown terrorist' is beginning to replace 'the "foreigner" and the "migrant" as a particularly threatening stranger figure', not least because this figure 'emerges from hiding within society' (2013: 83). Moreover, such figures are not only expected to emerge from outcast territories – in *Beyond Black*, Alison imagines 'terrorists in the ditches [...] fundis hoarding fertiliser [...] fanatics brewing bombs on brownfield sites' (Mantel 2005: 450) – but from affluent suburbs. Before committing an act of terrorism, the homegrown terrorist is 'an apparently ordinary and unremarkable citizen, a regular member of the community', and therefore 'represents a double threat: terrorism, coupled with the realization that this threat comes not from without but from within' (Rumford 2013: 83–84).

In having the residents of Admiral Drive label Mart a terrorist, Mantel therefore foregrounds on a microcosmic scale the broader security anxieties about violence emerging from inside rather than outside the nation-as-home which preoccupied Britain after 'the Twin Towers burned' (Mantel 2005: 140). Through her depiction of Alison's experience of suburban hauntings, Mantel suggests that there is no obvious solution to the problem of balancing an obligation to provide hospitality with the need for security measures against the threat of violent attack. In offering hospitality both to the dead and to the living, Alison avoids being 'mimetically violent' (Butler 2004: 42) but is exposed to further violence in her turn, and she seems to end the novel having given up on the idea of a secure home altogether. Yet the behaviour of the residents of Admiral Drive and the fate of Mart show the dangerous consequences of increased security measures for already-vulnerable populations who are thereby excluded further still from the rights of citizenship and the benefits of a secure home.

However, by exploring these 'state of the nation' questions in the context of suburban homes, Mantel usefully draws attention to the foundational terrain on which violence and vulnerability are experienced. Indeed, Mantel's emphasis in *Beyond Black* that 'everything, even warfare, happens first in the kitchen, in the nursery, in the cradle' (Mantel 2008) continues to resonate with more recent studies and analyses of contemporary terrorism, which have begun to explore the frequency with which the perpetrators of terrorist attacks have previously committed domestic violence offences (Berman 2017; Smith 2017). Hence, the ostensibly mundane territory of the suburban home is crucial to *Beyond Black*'s exploration of responses to vulnerability, violence and security in twentieth and twenty-first-century Britain. Not merely because this space stands in for more important stages on which momentous global issues are played out, but because *Beyond Black* insists on the difficulties of separating the large from the small, the public from the private, the global from the local, and foregrounds the structural relationships between experiences of vulnerability and of abandonment to violence – ranging from domestic violence to being stateless – which are evident in these spaces.

Bibliography

Berman, M. (2017), 'One Crime Connects Mass Shooters and Terror Suspects: Domestic Violence', *The Independent*, 19 August. Available online: http://www.independent.co.uk/news/link-between-domestic-violence-terror-mass-shootings-crime-a7901971.html (accessed 19 August 2017).

Bigo, D. (2005), 'Frontier Controls in the European Union: Who Is in Control?', in D. Bigoand E. Guild (eds), *Controlling Frontiers: Free Movement into and within Europe*, 49–99, Aldershot: Ashgate.

Bird, K. (2016), '"Weren't All True Nomads at Their Happiest in Limbo?": Hauntings in Non-Places in Hilary Mantel's *Beyond Black* and Nicola Barker's *Darkmans*', in D. Downey, I. Kinane and E. Parker (eds), *Landscapes of Liminality: Between Space and Place*, 111–133, London and New York: Rowman and Littlefield.

Blunt, A. and R. Dowling (2006), *Home*, Abingdon and New York: Routledge.

Butler, J. (2004), *Precarious Life: The Powers of Mourning and Violence*, London: Verso.

Cooke, R. (2005), 'Other Voices', *The Guardian*, 24 April. Available online: https://www.theguardian.com/books/2005/apr/24/fiction.features1 (accessed 9 August 2017).

Diprose, R. (2009), 'Women's Bodies Giving Time for Hospitality', *Hypatia* 24: 142–163.

Ellis, K. F. (1989), *The Contested Castle: Gothic Novels and the Subversion of Domestic Ideology*, Urbana, IL: University of Illinois Press.

Friese, H. (2004), 'Spaces of Hospitality', translated by J. Keye, *Angelaki* 9: 67–79.

Head, D. (2002), *The Cambridge Introduction to Modern British Fiction, 1950–2000*, Cambridge: Cambridge University Press.

Heller, T. (1992), *Dead Secrets: Wilkie Collins and the Female Gothic*, New Haven, CT: Yale University Press.

Home Office (2005), 'Controlling Our Borders: Making Migration Work for Britain – Five Year Strategy for Asylum and Immigration', 07 February. Available online: https://www.gov.uk/government/publications/five-year-strategy-for-asylum-and-immigration (accessed 9 August 2017).

Huysmans, J. (2006), *The Politics of Insecurity: Fear, Migration and Asylum in the EU*, Abingdon and New York: Routledge.

Kaplan, A. (2003), 'Homeland Insecurities: Some Reflections on Language and Space', *Radical History Review* 85: 82–93.

Kaplan, A. (2008), 'In the Name of Security', *Review of International American Studies*, 3.3–4.1: 15–25.

Kutcha, T. (2010), *Semi-Detached Empire: Suburbia and the Colonization of Britain, 1880 to the Present*, Charlottesville, VA and London: University of Virginia Press.

MacKenzie, S. (2013), *Be It Ever so Humble: Poverty, Fiction, and the Invention of the Middle-Class Home*, Charlottesville, VA: University of Virginia Press.

Mantel, H. (1985), *Every Day Is Mother's Day*, London: Fourth Estate.

Mantel, H. (1986), *Vacant Possession*, London: Fourth Estate.

Mantel, H. (2005), *Beyond Black*, London: Harper Perennial.

Mantel, H. (2008), 'Author, Author', *The Guardian*, 24 May. Available online: http://www.theguardian.com/books/2008/may/24/1 (accessed 9 August 2017).

Mantel, H. (2013), 'Royal Bodies', *London Review of Books* 35 (4): 3–7. Available online: https://www.lrb.co.uk/v35/n04/hilary-mantel/royal-bodies (accessed 9 August 2017).

Pope, G. (2015), *Reading London's Suburbs: From Charles Dickens to Zadie Smith*, Basingstoke and New York: Palgrave Macmillan.

Pratt, G. (2005), 'Abandoned Women and Spaces of the Exception', *Antipode: Journal of Radical Geography*, 37: 1052–1078.

Rumford, C. (2013), *The Globalization of Strangeness*, Basingstoke and New York: Palgrave Macmillan.

Smith, J. (2017), 'The Seeds of Terrorism Are Often Sown in the Home – with Domestic Violence', *The Guardian*, 10 July. Available online: https://www.theguardian.com/commentisfree/2017/jul/10/seeds-terrorism-sown-home-domestic-violence-islamic-state (accessed 19 August 2017).

Spooner, C. (2010), '"[T]hat Eventless Realm": Hilary Mantel's *Beyond Black* and the Ghosts of the M25', in L. Philips and A. Witchard (eds), *London Gothic: Place, Space and the Gothic Imagination*, 80–90, London and New York: Continuum.

Still, J. (2003), 'Acceptable Hospitality: From Rousseau's Levite to the Strangers in Our Midst Today', *Journal of Romance Studies* 3: 1–14.

Still, J. (2005), 'Derrida: Guest and Host', *Paragraph* 28: 85–101.

Wallace, D. (2009), '"The Haunting Idea": Female Gothic Metaphors and Feminist Theory', in D. Wallace and A. Smith (eds), *The Female Gothic: New Directions*, 26–41, Basingstoke and New York: Palgrave Macmillan.

Watkiss, J. (2012), 'Welcome the Coming, Speed the Parting Guest: Hospitality and the Gothic', in D. Punter (ed.), *A New Companion to the Gothic*, 523–534, Oxford: Blackwell.

Whelan, L. B. (2010), *Class, Culture and Suburban Anxieties in the Victorian Era*, Abingdon and New York: Routledge.

Wolff, J. (1988), 'The Culture of Separate Spheres: The Role of Culture in Nineteenth-Century Public and Private Life', in J. Wolff and J. Seed (eds), *The Culture of Capital: Art, Power and the Nineteenth-Century Middle Class*, 117–134, Manchester: Manchester University Press.

'Between the Real and the Imagined': Hilary Mantel's Craft

Eileen Pollard

An interview with Hilary Mantel

EP: Following on from your sell-out reading at Manchester Metropolitan University in September 2015, I have been reading the short story 'How Shall I Know You' again, as you read from it hilariously at that event! I understand there was an odd real life sequel to that story, after it was published?

HM: Let me explain a little about how I came to write it. One day about 30 years ago I was reading the Bible, as you do, and I came across the strange phrase, 'a spoiler at noonday'. At once I thought – book title. Fifteen years passed, and the novel attached to the title had yet to show up. But meanwhile, I had invented other titles to go with it – so it had become a trilogy, as my novels tend to do.

Along with 'A Spoiler at Noonday' went 'Teatime in Bedlam' and 'The Right Side of Midnight'. The latter intrigued me particularly: because which is the right side of midnight, and who decides?

When a few more years had gone by, and there was no sign of the books, I took the next step: I invented a fictitious author to write them. And wrote a story about her, called 'How Shall I Know You?' If you are going to invent an alter ego, it would be a bad idea to invent one who was doing better than you, professionally: you might develop envy towards your own creation, and try to kill her. So I invented someone who was doing rather worse. In mid-career, for most of us, comes a wobble. We think, how good am I, really? Something inside you is saying, how am I classified? Premier League? Championship? Evo-Stik League? Northern Premier Division? Or am I on my way to becoming someone who (figuratively speaking) kicks a ball around the local park then flops on a bench, saying, 'I used to be a proper writer, I published a novel once'. Even the least competitive writer sometimes wants to know, 'Am I going up, or down? In my own estimation? In the view of my publisher? In the view of my readers – if I have them? Do I know who they are and what they want? And if I do, can I give it to them? Will I?' Occasionally, if you are foundering, like the invented author of this story, you stop and ask yourself, 'Who is the work for?' It's easy to feel becalmed, or that you are slipping backwards, and easy to get lost in the middle of a big project.

I've always had problems writing short stories, and one of the possible techniques I've learned to try is this: just write it as if it's true. First person; don't worry about the structure; just write down the events as they occur to you. For one reader, this was too convincing, because she took the story to be true. It appeared, and I had an indignant letter: this reader had enjoyed the account of the writing life, so been to the library, and tried to take out 'A Spoiler at Noonday', 'Teatime in Bedlam', and 'The Right Side of Midnight'. And the librarian told her they did not exist: and she was writing to me to complain.

I found this made my head spin. I didn't really know what to write back to her. I suppose the only thing more disconcerting would have been if the librarian had said, yes, there they are, third shelf on the left.

Of course the connection, the cross-over, between art and life: this is the place where I work. In historical fiction I cross and re-cross the border between fact and fiction, every time I sit down to write.

EP: Do you think that that space between what is real and what is imagined is where the reader can 'pour themselves in', so to speak, very, *very* literally in some cases?

HM: The reader wouldn't necessarily know what is real and what is imagined. Unless they had tracked all my research, they wouldn't know. Only a few historians would. This makes some people uneasy. You can only ask them to trust that you will deploy imagination on the basis of good evidence. You won't make wild guesses. You won't fill gaps unless you feel you must, and unless to the best of your knowledge they really are gaps, and they must trust that your infilling process will be scrupulous. Your conjecture should be plausible and should not be unhistorical – that is to say, you shouldn't build it on wishful thinking about how the world ought to be.

I prefer working with the best facts I can get, imagining as a last resort – even if the facts are an inconvenient shape and sound unlikely. That's the challenge and the art. It don't see why otherwise you would be attracted to historical fiction. You must be aware that readers come to you for facts plus enlightenment – they do need to know that you are upholding your part of the bargain. But the wise reader will know where the limits are. Every time I say, 'He thought that ...'. – well, I'm making it up. We don't know what he thought, or she thought. It is irretrievable. You can't rely on the written record. People lie even to their own diaries.

EP: I want to ask you about the intertextual relationship between the Tudor books and the Tudor plays. You have said that when the plays were performed in Stratford, you were watching *Wolf Hall and Bring Up the Bodies* – as plays – during the day and then writing *The Mirror and the Light,* the novel, in the evening. Can you tell us more about that fascinating writing experience?

HM: I was in a unique position. Usually when there is an adaptation for theatre or film, the primary work is finished. In this case the adaptation is of work in progress, because I am still writing the third novel, The Mirror & The Light. You can't even say the first two novels are finished, because the writing and reading of the third makes them 'live' again. Flashbacks and reruns will make the reader question what she thought she understood, first time round. As we move on, our own construction of our past changes. Our memories rewrite themselves. We may come to think of our younger self as 'a character' rather than as aspect of our present being. If you lead the examined life, you will be witness to your own shifts in consciousness. Your position relative to your younger selves is changing all the time. I want to capture this process. Thomas Cromwell is a person of historical importance, but he is also just a man. One who has a longish run, for the era – he's about 55 at his death – and one who sees immense change not only in his outer world but in himself. He loses his country and becomes an Italian. His construction of himself as a young man is as an Italian. Then he comes back and reclaims England, and changes it.

He is not basically introspective – and this adds to the challenge. He is the sum of his actions. So he is a natural character to put on stage. But of course, as the action of the books are seen from a very close viewpoint – not through his eyes, but through the camera on his shoulder –there is a challenge as to how to mediate that consciousness to the audience. Thomas Cromwell is on stage almost the whole time through the 2 plays. In Wolf Hall he has half a scene off, in Bring Up the Bodies it's a matter of seconds. The plays move very fast. Mostly he just turns on his heel and we're into a new locale. He's not necessarily talking the whole time. Sometimes, particularly at the beginning, he's just watching, and he's learning, and he's doing it on our behalf. Like the book, Wolf Hall begins with Cromwell's patron, Cardinal Wolsey, dominating the action. Cromwell just feeds him his lines. Then we see Wolsey destroyed, and the long slow process of Cromwell's revenge for him. The patterning of that revenge is far more obvious and prominent in the plays than in the novels. It has to be. We have to simplify and condense, and we have far fewer characters to play with.

I worked from the beginning with Mike Poulton, a very experienced adaptor. His name was on the plays, he took the lead, and I learned from him and helped where I could. The plays went through a lot of changes as they moved from Stratford-on-Avon to the West End and from there to Broadway. By the time we went to New York Mike was needed by his other projects and I was doing the rewrites; our producers there wanted the plays to be significantly shorter, though that was less an artistic imperative than a function of audience habits and the public transport system. One thing you must take to heart, if you're going to be involved in adaptation, is that you have many more interests to serve than when you're in a room by yourself working on a novel. Your artistic needs must be respected but you must acknowledge the commercial demands, otherwise there will be no play. That sounds so obvious that it's hardly worth stating, but I imagine that many people would find it hard to make the change – and I'm still trying to sort out in my mind whether this new world is for me – whether I am suited to it – whether I am a team player and whether I have the temperament for the instant demands that can arise.

Of course, the usual course of a play would be more peaceful. The writer would do her part, then hand over to the director. The Wolf Hall plays weren't like that. The sense of the new book going on in the background made for a project that never came to rest. It was a tumult, a ferment. Or so I felt. I sat in the audience so many times and learned and understood what live theatre can be. It wasn't a vanity project. I was learning all the time about audience comprehension and reaction and if something wasn't working I would coming back with ideas of how to make it work, or what to do instead.

I was also building my characters through working with the actors. That doesn't necessarily mean I will write them differently in the third book, but I may write things I wouldn't have if it weren't for the insights I gained from the process and the actors. In a sense the characters were beyond reach. They had a core, a way I saw them, that was not going to be redefined because I watched a different body perform the actions. Katherine of Aragon was very small and round – a bit like Queen Victoria in shape, I imagine, after many pregnancies – and red-haired. She was played by Lucy Briers, who was the tallest woman in the cast by far, has well-defined features rather than Katherine's pudding face, and was the essence of stately dignity. But when I see Katherine, I see the one who was there in my mind before. She is not made of portraits, incidentally, nor re any of the other characters whose faces Holbein left us. They are made of portraits plus a long consideration of what it might be like to live in that body.

The influence of the plays is more subtle than people imagine, more hard to define. I would write a scene from the third book and sometimes show it, or tell about it. That would change what the actor knew about him or herself. The lines would be the same, the actions would be the same, yet the performance would have something else going on, below the surface.

EP: You have spoken about your conversations with Ben Miles, who plays Thomas Cromwell on stage. In particular, how Miles commented upon Henry's desire that he and Cromwell visit his foundries together – as a kind of day-trip – and, although this visit never occurs, Miles felt that later Henry would imagine it had. You have explained how the result of this conversation is reflected in *The Mirror and the Light*. Could you tell us more about that reflective process?

HM: I think in this case it was I who decided that Henry would be subject to a sort of time-slip – and I was encouraged because when I told Ben about it he immediately saw the point. Henry becomes more self-deluding as time passes, and a nightmare for his ministers because you don't know what version of the past he's entertaining that day – and actually, in that particular scene, as I've now written it, it appears that Henry may be testing Cromwell out – will he go along with the story? Henry was distrustful – as I suppose a ruler must be – and though he wanted to be flattered and cushioned from the impact of his choices, he also needed people who would talk straight to him. Ben has done a good deal to 'recover' Cromwell's own memories of childhood and youth, which feed into the third book.

This is material outside history. We have no access to it. It was never on the record. So where is it going to come from? There is one scene towards the end of Bring Up the Bodies *where Henry, in silence, signs a sheaf of death warrants. Cromwell simply watches him. It is a very long and tense pause, and during that time, Cromwell's attention is riveted on the hand moving across the paper, and the hypnotic motion as the clerk sands the documents and whisks each one away: but his mind is free to range. And it did. Ben brought back all sorts of treasures. I think that though the whole process he never said a word I couldn't work with. There was a point where I felt he knew the novels better than I did. He found out the resonances in the text, whether play or novel, and would pick them up throughout. Everything was congruent with the man he was representing. Nothing was alien – though it might be surprising. I didn't know if in the third book I would go back beyond the point where the first novel begins, to find out what happened the night before. But I do. Again, it was triggered by an image that came to Ben, of being under a bridge. I said, it's not a bridge … and so this segment of story began.*

All the actors were flexible and generous and risk-taking, and they deployed their intuition to help me. One of the reasons the scripts changed so much was that I kept getting more insight into how to bring each character through an arc, within the constraints of the two plays we were performing. The storytelling got stronger. But while it is simple when you are writing a novel to keep every character in play, and think of all their needs at once, I found that in a play the characters have to queue up a bit. After a certain point you can't stop the whole mechanism and strip it down. You can improve it a piece at a time. But half a line can alter a character. And the results are instant – you test it that night.

EP: When we have spoken previously you have said that this final instalment of the trilogy will 'reflect' and also *refract* all that has gone before. How does this process work?

HM: The title is taken from a line in one of Cromwell's letters. The primary narrative covers the next four years of his rise and rise, beginning with the moment when Anne Boleyn dies, and ending 4 years later with his own execution. It tells a new story, but it mirrors what has gone before and it sheds new light upon it. I would like each book to work separately, in terms of structure, but also to work in an over-arching way, as if it were one super-novel. The amount of information the reader can carry and retain is limited and so I aim to give the reader enough continuity, without ever repeating – no simple recapitulation. The information comes at you from a different angle, so it looks different. There'll be, I hope, images that carry the reader from book to book, but they work almost subliminally. The glimpse is quick. Maybe it was an illusion?

EP: As I have said, Ben Miles has played Cromwell very successfully in the RSC productions of the Tudor plays. Now Mark Rylance has interpreted the part differently, yet no less successfully, for the BBC version. Would you like to comment on these two interpretations, and how the ambiguity of the 'real' Cromwell makes this breadth possible?

HM: It is a question of the actors playing to the strengths of the different media. Ben had to power a huge theatre. Mark only had to blink. It's a position of great power: millions of viewers wondering, is that a smile?

The amount we don't know about Thomas Cromwell is immense. He kept no diaries, few of his letters are self-revealing, and his early life is off the map. As a public servant, as a minister, he is extremely well-documented. But though we know what he did, we often don't know why. Historians have interpreted him very differently. In academic history he looks very different from in popular history, but then the notion of 'character' is not of great concern to academic historians. The study of his career has been bedevilled by an ultimately sterile debate called for shorthand purposes 'Minister or King?' Who is it who leads, and who follows? Is Cromwell the brains of the outfit, and the dominating character, or does he just do as he's told?

I don't believe you can sort this out. It's a bad question. Henry was a very clever and subtle man, and we shouldn't detract from that. Cromwell, I suspect, was cleverer than anybody. Sometimes they're a team. Sometimes they're pulling against each other. Henry's intentions are veiled behind a discourse about honour and virtue, suitable for princes. Cromwell's intentions are just veiled; he's cautious, because Henry is changeable. The relationship between them has to be negotiated within every encounter. Cromwell has no power of his own. It's all borrowed. And a great deal of his power comes not by virtue of an office or title, but by the king's temporary permission. He has to bid for it every day.

There is a dispute among historians as to how 'creative' Cromwell was: how far he did new things in the structure of government, and how far he built on existing institutions. Again, it can be a sterile debates that introduces false polarities. He did new things, and old things, and he did new things then pretended they were old, to stop them being so alarming. A more interesting question is his attitude to religion. Some of his biographers have seen him as a cynic who simply manipulates the faith of others. To me, their position does not make sense. But I have spent a great deal of time, and will spend more, trying to work out exactly what he thought about God and man. And I know he's not going to tell me. If you didn't agree 100% with the king, it was as well to keep your disagreement to yourself. But Henry could be nudged, he could be influenced. He could be changed. So there was no firm ground for Thomas Cromwell. Everything is in hazard, day by day. Mark Rylance brought out his vigilance, the tension of someone who must always be ready to turn on a sixpence. And in the theatre, we almost literally demonstrated how he did that: as I say, a spin on the heel, and on to the next thing.

EP: I reread an earlier short story of yours recently called 'The Clean Slate' where the narrator is a writer who hails from a 'drowned' village; she recognizes that this makes her uncertain origins all the more murky. I wonder if you might say more about the significance of these obscured, evaded and elided origins that haunt your work? Cromwell's, of course, being no exception.

HM: Water seems to be important. It reflects, it dissolves, it washes away. Identity vanishes. A drowned corpse is not easy to identify. In The Mirror & the Light *there is a repeated phrase, 'the river will bring you home'. That is both a consolation, and a threat. It will wash up a corpse, restoring it to its relatives: vaguely comforting, if that body is yours. But if you are the murderer, the water will bear witness to your crimes and bring them to your door. I remember the emotion I felt when I at the age of twelve when I made my first visit to the south of England and first saw the Thames. t was like putting your finger on a pulse. This was the great artery that fed the history you found in books, as opposed to family history, which came from muddier springs – it was oral and ambiguous, highly variable depending on who told it, and driven by occult, adult purposes a child can't divine. People want to sell you a view of the family past, and it's not always clear why, or how you can sort it out with only the information available to you. The narrator of 'The Clean Slate' is desperately trying to sort fact from fiction, but realizes at the end of the story that a family's version of itself reposes in myth and image, not documented facts. She's not comfortable with that, but she is beginning to know it. That reflects my own process. You go through a stage of asking 'Can we have this straight, please?' Then a stage of realizing, 'No, in fact, we can't'.*

EP: In your *Woman's Hour* interview of some years ago, Jenni Murray quoted you as saying that feminism has not failed, it has simply not been tried. I wonder what your thoughts are on feminism today, and what 'trying feminism' might look like?

HM: Jenni was quoting Carmel, the heroine of my novel An Experiment in Love, which is set in 1970. She makes that comment in later life – she is perhaps 40 – and she in her turn is half-quoting the billboards you used to see outside churches that read, 'Christianity hasn't failed, it's just never been tried'.

In one sense, it is disappointing that the word 'feminist', in the west, is not of purely historical interest, like 'suffragette'. The battles should have been won, in terms of equality of opportunity. I think, though, that in the later part of the last century there was a misperception about what feminism meant and what it was, and the error still has some purchase. Feminism isn't a complete philosophy – it only makes sense in the context of a wider struggle for social justice. It requires the dismantling of hierarchies, and washing your eyes clean to re-evaluate the world. It is not a self-serving philosophy that justifies individual women achieving their personal ambitions by grinding their high heels into other people's feet. Women like Mrs Thatcher thought feminism was about permission to imitate men – 'beat them at their own game'. Such women are not good role models and their success masks a general failure. I think that in the arena of private life, we have made huge progress. Women have changed and so have men. Sexuality and self-definition is more flexible and less prescriptive. But in public life the rules are still those of the tournament and the bullfight – a lot of shouting, boasting and unnecessary ritual blood-letting. We may need to rethink the nature of work and ambition, and ask ourselves what success looks like, at a personal and political level. That's why Carmel says feminism hasn't been tried – because it is a radicalising movement, and can't be tried alone – it's only possible to be a feminist when you are aware of other forms of oppression and commit to fighting them.

But to be honest, I don't like debates conducted in such general and abstract terms. I'd rather say, 'Let's look at an example' or 'Let me give you a for instance'. That's what a novelist does – work from the particular to the general and back again. The product engages people first of all, it entertains them – and then perhaps it makes them think and question.

EP: You have now gained the recognition and fame that your writing so richly deserves; do you ever feel, like Alison Hart in *Beyond Black*, that you are always on the road between venues and performances? How has fame affected your writing life?

HM: *Hardly at all, in the sense that when I sit down to write, it feels exactly like the first day I ever wrote. The uncertainty is the same. The solitude – tricky word, because it sounds faintly pathetic – but at the desk, I am putting on a one-woman show. The pressure for me has always been internal. Every writer must count on her own judgment first and last. And only she can define her scope. If other people are defining it, your career has gone wrong.*

People assume I am much busier these days. The truth is I am just more visibly busy. It is hardly possible to put in more hours than I put in when I made most of my living by reviewing. In those days I fought for writing time and I fight now. But I always have many, many projects on hand. I find it hard to leave one of them aside for the sake of another. I am mystified by the people who write a novel and then have a nice rest and think what they would like to do next. I think that the prizes and all that has come with them have been wholly positive for me – it's powered me up. For a long time my faith in myself felt like lonely defiance. It's good to be affirmed, as they say. Because lonely defiance and giving yourself encouraging talks and trying to keep up your morale – all that uses a lot of energy that you could spend on the content of your work. So it's good to outsource all that.

To be serious, what I think of myself as a writer is still more important to me than what the outside world thinks, because only I know the gap between what I intend and what I achieve. And my opinion of myself as a writer depends on how good my last paragraph was.

Further Reading

Hilary Mantel: In order of publication

Every Day Is Mother's Day, London: Harper Perennial, 2006
Vacant Possession, London: Harper Perennial, 2006.
Eight Months on Ghazzah Street, London: Harper Perennial, 2004.
Fludd, London: Fourth Estate, 2010.
A Place of Greater Safety, London: Fourth Estate, 2010.
A Change of Climate, London: Fourth Estate, 2010.
An Experiment in Love, London: Fourth Estate, 2010.
The Giant, O'Brien, London: Fourth Estate, 2010.
Learning to Talk, London: Fourth Estate, 2003.
Giving Up the Ghost, London: Fourth Estate, 2010.
Beyond Black, London: Fourth Estate, 2010.
Wolf Hall, London: Fourth Estate, 2010.
Bring Up the Bodies, London: Fourth Estate, 2012.
Ink in the Blood: A Hospital Diary, London: Harper Collins e-books, 2010.
The Assassination of Margaret Thatcher and Other Stories, London: Fourth Estate, 2013.
The Mirror and the Light (forthcoming).

Critical sources on Mantel to date

Arias, R., 'Exoticising the Tudors: Hilary Mantel's Re-Appropriation of the Past in *Wolf Hall* and *Bring Up the Bodies*', in E. Rousselot (ed.), *Exoticising the Past in Contemporary Neo-Historical Fiction*, 19–36, Houndmills: Palgrave, 2014.

Arias, R. and H. Mantel, 'An Interview with Hilary Mantel', *Atlantis*, 20.2 (1998): 277–289.

Arnold, L., 'Spooks and Holy Ghosts: Spectral Politics and the Politics of Spectrality in Hilary Mantel's *Eight Months on Ghazzah Street*', *Critique: Studies in Contemporary Fiction*, 57.3 (2016): 294–309.

Bird, K., '"Weren't All True Nomads at Their Happiest in Limbo?": Hauntings in Non-Places in Hilary Mantel's *Beyond Black* and Nicola Barker's *Darkmans*', in D. Downey, I. Kinane and E. Parker, *Landscapes of Liminality: Between Space and Place*, 111–133, London and New York: Rowman and Littlefield, 2016.

Eagleton, M., 'The Anxious Lives of Clever Girls: The University Novels of Margaret Drabble, A. S. Byatt, and Hilary Mantel', *Tulsa Studies in Women's Literature*, 33.2 (2014): 103–121.

Funk, W., 'Ghosts of Postmodernity: Spectral Epistemology and Haunting in Hilary Mantel's Fludd and Beyond Black', in Siân Adiseshiah and Rupert

Hildyard (eds), *Twenty-First Century Fiction: What Happens Now*', 147–161, Houndmills: Palgrave, 2013.
Garcia-Hernandez, S., 'A Sense of Loss in Hilary Mantel's *A Change of Climate*', *Revista Canaria de Estudios Ingleses* 74 (2017): 109–124.
Hidalgo, P., 'Of Tides and Men: History and Agency in Hilary Mantel's *A Place of Greater Safety*', *Estudios Ingleses de la Universidad Complutense* 10 (2002): 201–216.
Horner, A. and S. Zlosnik, '"Releasing Spirit from Matter": Comic Alchemy in Spark's *The Ballad of Pekham Rye*, Updike's *The Witches of Eastwick* and Mantel's *Fludd*', *Gothic Studies* 2.1 (2000): 136–147.
Knox, S. L., 'Giving Flesh to the "Wraiths of Violence": Super-Realism in the Fiction of Hilary Mantel', *Australian Feminist Studies* 25 (2010): 313–323.
LaCroix, A. L., 'A Man for All Treasons: Crimes by and against the Tudor State in the Novels of Hilary Mantel', in M. C. Nussbaum, R. H. McAdams and A. L. LaCroix (eds), *Fatal Fictions: Crime in Law and Literature*, Chicago: University of Chicago Press, forthcoming. Public Law Working Paper No. 511. Available online at: SSRN: https://ssrn.com/abstract=2571355 (accessed 25 August 2017).
Lehtimäki, M., 'Anamorphic Narrativity: Hilary Mantel's *Wolf Hall* in the Renaissance Perspective', in M. Salmela and J. Toikkanen (eds), *The Grotesque and the Unnatural*, 43–66, Amherst, NY: Cambria Press, 2011.
Pollard, E. J., '"Mind What Gap?": An Interview with Hilary Mantel', *Textual Practice* 29.6 (2015): 1035–1044.
Prodromou, A., 'Writing the Self into Being: Illness and Identity in Inga Clendinnen's *Tiger's Eye* and Hilary Mantel's *Giving Up the Ghost*', in A. M Sánchez-Are (ed.), *Identity and Form in Contemporary Literature*, 195–209, Abingdon: Routledge: 2014.
Spooner, C., 'That Eventless Realm: Hilary Mantel's *Beyond Black* and the Ghosts of the M25', in L. Phillips and A. Witchard (eds), *London Gothic: Place, Space and the Gothic Imagination*, 80–90, London: Continuum, 2010.
Stewart, V., 'A Word in Your Ear: Mediumship and Subjectivity in Hilary Mantel's *Beyond Black*', *Critique: Studies in Contemporary Fiction* 50 (2009): 293–307.

Works that include some detailed reference to Mantel's texts

De Groot, J., 'Reading and Ethics', in *Remaking History: The Past in Contemporary Historical Fictions*, 13–14, Abingdon: Routledge, 2016.
Gilmore, L., 'Agency without Mastery: Chronic Pain and Posthuman Life Writing', *Biography* 35 (2012): 83–98.
Keen, S., 'The Historical Turn in British Fiction', in J. F. English (ed.), *A Concise Companion to Contemporary British Fiction*, 167–187, Oxford: Blackwell, 2006.
Lembert, A.'Hilary Mantel – Fludd', in '*The Heritage of Hermes: Alchemy in Contemporary British Literature*', 190–193, Berlin: Galda and Wilch Verlag, 2004.

Prodromou, A. '"That Weeping Constellation": Navigating Loss in "Memoirs of Textured Recovery"', *Life Writing* 9.1 (2012): 57–75.

Wilson, L. 'The Historical Novel and the Crisis of Fictionality in the First Decade of the Twenty-First Century', in N. Bentley, N. Hubble and L. Wilson (eds), *The 2000s: A Decade of Contemporary British Fiction*, 145–172, London: Bloomsbury, 2015.

Index

Note: The letter 'n' following locators refers to notes

www.ingramcontent.com/pod-product-compliance
Lightning Source LLC
Chambersburg PA
CBHW071518100726
47908CB00004B/1216